SUPERVISOR'S
STANDARD REFERENCE HANDBOOK
Second Edition

SUPERVISOR'S
STANDARD REFERENCE HANDBOOK
Second Edition

W.H. Weiss

PRENTICE HALL
Englewood Cliffs, New Jersey 07632

Prentice-Hall International (UK) Limited, *London*
Prentice-Hall of Australia Pty. Limited, *Sydney*
Prentice-Hall Canada, Inc., *Toronto*
Prentice-Hall Hispanoamericana, S.A., *Mexico*
Prentice-Hall of India Private Limited, *New Delhi*
Prentice-Hall of Japan, Inc., *Tokyo*
Simon & Schuster Asia Pte. Ltd., *Singapore*
Editora Prentice-Hall do Brasil, Ltda., *Rio de Janeiro*

10 9 8 7 6 5 4 3 2 1

Library of Congress Cataloging-in-Publication Data

Weiss, W. H.
  Supervisor's standard reference handbook.

  Includes bibliographical references and index.
  1. Supervision of employees—Handbooks, manuals, etc.
2. Personnel management—Handbooks, manuals, etc.
I. Title.
HF5549.W4313   1988   658.3'02   88-5815
ISBN 0-13-877168-5

ISBN 0-13-877168-5

PRENTICE HALL
BUSINESS & PROFESSIONAL DIVISION
A division of Simon & Schuster
Englewood Cliffs, New Jersey 07632

Printed in the United States of America

How This Book Can Help You with Your Supervisory Problems

This second edition of the *Supervisor's Standard Reference Handbook* is an updated compilation of tested solutions to supervisor's problems. The techniques that this book reveals can be relied upon absolutely because they have been used by many supervisors and proven on the job. Much of what I've put into this book comes from the experiences of supervisors I've known and worked with the past 38 years.

Supervisor's Standard Reference Handbook is written to fill all your needs for a standard reference work on the subject of supervising. Since it covers the full range of supervisor's responsibilities and duties, in just about every type of business—in the office or the plant—all supervisors can benefit from using it regularly.

Some things have changed since I wrote the original version thus justifying this second edition. Change is constantly taking place in how people on the job think and act, and what it takes to motivate them. This edition of the book brings you the latest answers to the problems of the ever-advancing technology. You will find new material on subjects such as: use of the computer, participative management, ergonomics, positive discipline, advancements in ways of communicating, being aggressive, making better use of your time, career planning, social responsibilities, and many others.

You'll see that Chapter 8—How to Handle Problems of Communication—has been greatly expanded to reflect and inform you of the new technology. You'll be pleased with Chapter 20—Guaranteed Ways to Move Up the Management Ladder. This is a new chapter which contains much valuable information.

All the chapters in the book are organized around the types of problems supervisors face in their day-to-day work. I show how supervisors have effectively dealt with them in managing people and getting jobs done. The information and advice is presented in as concise a manner as possible. There's minimal "background" discussion of a topic, just the key points and how-to-do-it. In addition, you'll find a number of "cases-in-point" which illustrate the solutions to supervisors' problems. In covering practically all supervisory problems, the material presented confirms the basic premise that skill in handling people is a *must* if you want to be an effective supervisor and also move up in management.

Supervisor's Standard Reference Handbook is intended to be kept on your desk, ready for use. The contents are therefore arranged so that you can locate information quickly. Thus, the material is given not only in the usual manner by chapter and subject, but also by section number. For instance, if you want to know how to become skilled in persuading, and the table of contents, the index, or a cross-reference in the text refers you to Section 5.4, you simply turn to the fourth section of Chapter 5. The numbered paragraphs will make it easy for you to spot items in an instant.

To present know-how and information in the clearest, most concise way, *Supervisor's Standard Reference Handbook* offers you over 300 fact-filled sections arranged among 20 chapters:

1. How to Get Action: Proven Methods That Get Results
2. Tested Supervisory Techniques That Keep You in Control
3. Training and Development Know-Hows That Assure Results
4. Getting to Know People and Motivating Them
5. How Successful Supervisors Use Persuasion
6. How Effective Supervisors Handle People
7. Supervisory Decisionmaking: How the "Pros" Do It
8. How to Handle Problems of Communication
9. Proven Techniques That Make Giving Orders Easy
10. Guaranteed Methods for Getting Cooperation
11. Positive Techniques for Maintaining Control of Quality
12. Sure-Fire Ways to Control Costs
13. Tested Ways for Evaluating Performance: Handling Appraisals Effectively
14. Proven Methods for Getting Along with the Union
15. Productivity and What to Do About It
16. Successful Ways for Getting the Most from Skilled and "Special" People
17. Working Out Answers to Your Problem People
18. Tried-and-Proven Ways to Handle Safety and Health

19. How to Promote Creativity and Sell Change
20. Guaranteed Ways to Move Up the Management Ladder

Every effort has been made to fill this book with the latest successful supervisory procedures covering nearly every conceivable situation or problem you might encounter. Here are just a few of the wide range of subjects included:

1.12 Techniques That Work on Raising Enthusiasm
2.7   Tips on Making the Most of Meetings
3.3   Successful Ways of Getting New Employees Started
4.11 How You Can Be the Boss Without Being Obvious About It
5.2   How to Avoid Putting Others on the Defensive
6.5   How to Be a Good Coach
7.16 What to Do When Your Decision Is Challenged
8.21 Positive Ways to Fight Computer Fears
9.3   Tips on How to Give Orders
10.17 Participative Management: What It's All About
11.4 Quality and Productivity: They Go Together
12.12 How Just-in-Time Operations Reduce Costs
13.16 Five Pitfalls to Avoid in an Appraisal Interview
14.6 How to Get the Cooperation of the Union Steward
15.16 How to Cope with a Shortage of Space
16.10 Tips on Supervising Today's Young Employees
17.21 Positive Discipline: Why It Pays Off
18.13 Right-to-Know Laws: What They're All About
19.10 How to Protect Your Idea
20.17 Guidelines to Working with a Mentor

With coverage like this, *Supervisor's Standard Reference Handbook* will prove to be a big help to you in carrying out your supervisory responsibilities and enabling you to get ahead in your organization.

W.H. Weiss

CONTENTS

SUPERVISOR'S
STANDARD REFERENCE HANDBOOK
Second Edition

1

HOW TO GET ACTION:
PROVEN METHODS THAT
GET RESULTS

AMONG the many responsibilities that supervisors have, one of the most important is to get the work done. Companies look to their supervisors to get action from employees in order that the company can be profitable and grow.

You can be an effective supervisor by motivating and organizing your people to do their work efficiently and productively. But you need to do more than this. You need to know how to deal with people, and be able to contend with pressure and stress. You must recognize the value of time and take advantage of it; you must know how to combat excuses. Most of all, you must follow up to see that the action you start with your people gets the job done.

1.1 Sure-Fire Methods for Organizing People to Action

Psychologists and personnel experts say that the key to motivating and organizing people to action is to understand their needs on the job and to provide a work environment which goes along with those needs.

One of the most basic of all job needs is the satisfaction of knowing one's job well. People need to master their jobs before they can perform them safely and efficiently. You should see that they do this if you want to organize them to action.

People who are going to put a lot of effort into their work also want and need appreciation from their supervisors. They like to feel that their leaders will react the same today to their good work as they did yesterday. Manual workers, in particular, dislike vacillation. They want a predictability about their leaders and their job environment. They want to be sure that if they do a specific thing, the act will likely lead to a certain consequence.

You must be consistent in the day-to-day performance of your job. A wishy-washy attitude one day, followed by being stubborn on doing things your way the next, destroys people's confidence in you and turns off their enthusiasm for the work.

If the people on the job know they are going to get credit and recognition for doing a good job, the work is more interesting and less tedious. The feeling of being valued personally is a strong motivator to action. When a man knows his work is appreciated, it is natural for him to reciprocate by doing his best.

The Dartnell Institute of Business Research has stated that management people should stop stripping jobs of creativeness. The statement includes advice for supervisors, saying, "A supervisor should guard against fragmenting tasks into meaningless chores, robbing workers of all opportunity for inventiveness. Instead of fitting a worker into a rigid job, the supervisor should try fitting the job to the individual's aptitudes."

Case-in-Point: Ralph Jenkins, supervisor in the Job Shop of the Acme Co., a firm specializing in the manufacture of unusual tools, says, "A supervisor in my department is a psychologist in some ways because you have to continually bring out the creativity of a designer and also learn his or her inherent skills. When you accomplish these things, you can give the individual assignments that will not only interest him or her, but also help the company."

1.2 Tips on Dealing with People

Leadership is a mysterious quality of human endeavor which many people aspire to but only a few attain. With leadership, your supervisory skills come to life; without it, your abilities and talents lay dormant and you have little influence on others.

Your company expects you to use your leadership skills, and your people look to you for guidance and direction. But to be a successful leader, you must be able to also deal with people. This includes being a comfortable person for others to be around by having a pleasing personality. Here are some tips on dealing with people that will enable you to maintain your leadership while at the same time run an efficient and productive department:

1. Learn and remember people's names. People's names are very important to them. Be sure to use their names when greeting them, assigning them work, and asking for their help.

2. Take an interest in people and get to like them. Notice and play up people's good points. Overlook their faults.

3. Develop a positive and optimistic attitude. Be easy-going so things don't bother you.

4. Avoid know-it-all and egotistical remarks. Most people who know you are aware of your knowledge, skills, and accomplishments.

5. Talk about the other fellow's interests and deeds. Forget about your own.

6. Remember to always set a good example in what you do and say.

1.3 Seven Ways to Contend with Pressure

According to psychologists, a substantial amount of pressure that a supervisor feels is job tension. You can take a big step toward contending with it if you define and pin it down. Attack the problem by making a list of the things that are probably causing the pressure. Put down what you must do, when you must get it done, and how much time you think it's going to take. You'll find that by listing what's causing the pressure, you'll reduce its impact—you'll see the problem as simply another job which you have analyzed and now have under control.

Here are seven other ways you can hold down pressure on the job:

1. Get help in handling your problems. Share them with other supervisors and your boss. The advice and help you'll get will make a big difference. Even simply talking about problems without solving them helps.

Case-in-Point: Tom Jackson, supervisor in the production department at one of Goodyear's synthetic rubber plants, found himself continually under pressure at the end of his shift because of the paperwork he had to complete before he left the plant. He mentioned this one day to another supervisor in his department. The other supervisor told Tom that he simply did most of the paperwork and recordkeeping during the shift. Attendance records, time sheets, and reports of jobs completed are examples of the type of paperwork which can be handled at free times. Tom immediately adopted this idea and found that he no longer was under pressure at the end of his shift.

2. Handle a problem that arises as quickly as possible. Postponing or delaying taking care of a problem simply results in stacking it up with others and increases the pressure on you. Learn to handle problems automatically instead of setting them aside and you'll wipe them out without as much stress.

3. Develop a system for handling problems and putting them in proper perspective. Know beforehand which tasks you can delegate so that you can immediately pass them off when they come up, and set up a standard procedure for handling others. By filing written procedures where you can easily refer to them, you will be able to make such work almost routine.

4. Establish a work place which suits your temperament and is below the level which causes you to be under pressure. The working level which is comfortable varies from person to person, so don't try to set it in comparison with another person's. Watch that you do not start your day too fast. You'll do better at a steady, level pace.

Case-in-Point: Perhaps you've noticed that some company employees who perform a service for people do not change their work pace to match the number of people waiting in line. Most store clerks, airport agents, ticket sellers, and others on similar jobs have learned to work at a steady pace because they have learned that a speedup invariably results in stress and mistakes.

5. Maintain yourself physically and mentally. The better condition you are in, the more capable you are of handling problems with a minimum of pressure. Try to avoid fear and worry; both build pressure, sometimes without you being aware of it. Believe in yourself; believe that you'll be able to contend with future problems when they arise. Keeping your emotions under control will also help you to prevent buildup of pressure.

6. Include some form of relaxation in your day. Get some exercise frequently, even if it's only a short walk. Periodic breaks in your routine are good for relieving pressure. Take a few minutes now and then to think about your family, your friends, and your outside interests. Getting your mind off the job can refresh you and enable you to resume your work, feeling less pressure.

7. As a last resort, concede a point or let something happen that you were trying to prevent. You might feel that this is "giving up," and in a way it is—but what you give up isn't as important as your health and well-being.

1.4 What to Do When Your Idea Isn't Accepted

It happens to every supervisor at one time or another, so you may as well be prepared to handle the problem. Your request to one of your people to do something on the job meets with an objection. What should you do?

The first and most important thing to do is to be calm and not lose your temper while you try to learn why you or your idea is opposed. Ask yourself several questions in your search for an explanation.

Was your request fair? Were you understood? Did you ask the right individual? If you've not been out of line with any of these, you'll have to ask why the individual is objecting.

You may hear that a change has taken place that you didn't know about, one that would make carrying out your request unwise or impossible. Or, the individual objecting may have a logical excuse which hasn't been expressed. Then again, he or she may simply be irritated. After you allow some time for complaining and blowing off steam, you'll get compliance. You may need only to be patient and not be insistent for a few minutes.

However, if the individual is stubborn and simply refuses to do what you've asked without explaining, you have a disciplinary problem on your hands. If you are unable to get your way through persuasion, see if you can get a partial agreement and then work on getting a complete one. If this fails, you have no choice but to consider disciplinary action appropriate to the circumstances.

An easy way to get ready acceptance of your idea is to let one of your people "originate" it. Pick the individual you want to handle the project, explain the problem, and subtly indicate the line of reasoning you want followed. Once the individual presents an idea as his or hers, make him or her defend it—and allow yourself to be won over. This approach will likely result in the action being carried out quickly and enthusiastically.

1.5 Getting People to Follow Your Orders and Instructions

Occasionally you are going to run into a situation where your instructions have not been followed as you requested. Although you'll find that the reason is simply a misunderstanding rather than disobedience, you'll want to take steps to prevent this from happening again. Most often, you must make certain your people really understand what you want. This is not as obvious and easy to handle as it may seem.

If you spell out the details of assignments, you must leave nothing to the imagination since any step you omit could cause trouble. It's up to you to anticipate every contingency. But you can ease unexpected problems which accompany step-by-step instructions if you give assignments in terms of results you want.

Speak the other fellow's language to get understanding, and don't assume that people always understand what you say. If there is any doubt in your mind, ask them to repeat back to you in their own words what they are being asked to do. This gives you a chance to discover any misunderstanding and correct it.

1.6 Excuses Have Never Helped Anybody

Too many people on the job today feel they're justified in making excuses for not carrying out their responsibilities. It's nothing new to some of them—they've been doing it for a long time. But they overlook the fact that they're in the same position now that they were in years ago. They don't realize that you just can't get ahead with making excuses.

We are often too quick to make an excuse for a mistake when we should look at it as a learning experience. After making the mistake, we are smarter in that we now know the right way to do something.

An individual who really wants to do something finds a way to do it. The individual who doesn't care finds an excuse. Very few jobs in today's workplaces are really tough. Something unusual comes up now and then, but this is to be expected. We should look at problems as challenges and say to ourselves, "We can do it!"

Management knows that employees will talk about subjects other than the job, that workers need rest breaks, and that people can't be productive every minute on the job. But there's a limit to everything. People are hired to do certain jobs, and management expects them to be at work every day.

Stop to think a bit before you tell your boss you could have done something if you'd had the time. Recognize that such words are just an excuse for lack of motivation or interest. Excuses never helped anybody.

1.7 Combating Excuses Painlessly

Supervisors hear all kinds of excuses from people on the job when work is not done on time or at all. One man may say that he didn't have the right tools, another may complain that the job was too tough or he didn't have enough time, and a third may blame it on the material he had to work with. Some workers won't do their best because they think they'll be taken advantage of and end up doing more than their share. Others are afraid someone else might get credit for their efforts. A few don't cooperate because of lack of interest. Whatever, all are excuses and there are few you should accept.

How do you combat excuses on the job? Losing your temper, threatening, and raising a big fuss will usually not change matters—and worse, may cause hard feelings. What you must do is work on the attitude of the people who make excuses. You do this most painlessly through good communication.

How to Do It: The individual who makes the excuses that the work is too hard should be asked to take a little time to study the job. What part is difficult? How much of the whole job is the tough part? Is it lack of proper tools or knowledge that makes the job hard? Is it inexperience?

Get across to the man who makes excuses that life would be very humdrum if he were never challenged, if he didn't run into an occasional problem, if he didn't have to do a little more now and then. He would never get the satisfaction of cracking a tough nut, helping somebody out of a mess, and getting things in better shape.

Along with discussing an excuse, you should, of course, take steps to provide what is needed to make the job easier. You will thus eliminate that as an excuse next time as well as show that you are interested in your worker's welfare, safety, and ease of getting the job done.

To relieve their supervisors from having to continually contend with repetitive excuses, many companies have disciplinary programs which impose increasingly severe discipline, ending with discharge for various types of offenses. Business and industry need such programs to deal with misfits (see Chapter 17), but combating periodic nonserious excuses is better handled through persuasion and reasoning.

1.8 Proven Ways of Making Good Use of Time

Wasting time is one of our most costly activities despite the fact that each of us can do something about it if we try. There is no such thing as "not enough time." The same amount of time is available to all of us—some people just use their time better.

Since time is valuable, you should figure out how to get the most from it. A few minutes each morning spent planning your day can make you more efficient as well as increase the amount of work you can get done. The executive who accomplishes much usually has his or her time planned days ahead. You don't need to go to that extent, but you can decide daily how you will use your time and also you can adopt timesaving habits.

When you have several jobs to do, start with the one that is most on your mind. The reasoning behind this is logical—your effectiveness and efficiency are not the best when you are concerned or worried, so you should try to relieve such feelings as soon as you can; you will be able to do a better job on your other tasks. If you have a disciplinary step to take with one of your people, do it as soon as possible. If some dirty or unpleasant work faces you, handle it early to get it out of the way.

Always give a high priority to a job which someone has requested of you. Doing work that your boss has requested usually should be put ahead of all jobs that you need to do. After satisfying the boss, give attention to jobs that your people have asked for. Work which needs to be done to satisfy only yourself should be your last choice.

Being punctual is an excellent way to get in the habit of using time effectively. Another is to avoid dawdling at tasks which can be done quickly and without much effort. Take advantage of the time during the day when you are waiting for someone. Use this time to read and think out a problem. Carry a notebook or pad with you so that you can write down a thought or idea that you want to remember.

3. It prepares you for what to do in case certain things happen, what to do under particular circumstances, and how you should react to future events.

4. It provides the steps for you to follow to improve yourself and get ahead.

When you plan, you keep in control of people and events because planning involves getting information, facts, and data which enable you to make good decisions. The more knowledge and know-how you have, the better equipped you are to handle your job.

How do you go about planning? To illustrate what planning is all about, let's assume you are a production supervisor. You are expected to get out the product, and you have people, material, and equipment to work with.

When you plan, you decide which people you are going to assign to which jobs. You determine the material that will be needed and you make arrangements to have it available. You think about the machines and equipment which will be operated and the tools which will be used. You consider the time factor such as when the work will start, how long it will take, and when it will be finished. You think about quality and quantity in regard to the product and how you will assure them. And throughout all this thinking and deciding, you keep in mind safety, good housekeeping, costs, and human relations.

Successful supervisors are effective planners. They achieve optimum performance and results from people, material, and equipment through use of that skill.

2.3 Five Requirements of Good Plans

To get the most from your planning, you must be careful how you do it. Experienced supervisors say that to make good plans you need to:

1. Be specific rather than general. The more explicit and clear your plan is, the less chance there is for it to be misunderstood or misapplied. Define your goals and objectives and indicate the means for attaining them.

2. Distinguish between the known and the unknown. Estimate the probable effects of the unknown. Make your planning more than just anticipation and reaction.

3. Make your plan as logical and practical as possible. The more facts it is based on, the better it is. Make reasonable judgments if facts are not available. Intelligent thinking should serve as the foundation for a plan.

4. Introduce flexibility and looseness so that the plan may readily be modified if circumstances require it. Recognize that no plan is infallible nor can it cover all possible contingencies. Conditions under which a plan will be most effective change as do the variables and factors on which the plan is based.

5. Be sure the plan is consistent with the aims and goals of the company and the way the company conducts its business. Formulate the plan to be acceptable to the people who will implement it and those who will be affected. Acceptable plans are more willingly adopted and carried out than ones which are objectionable in one or more respects.

2.4 How to Get the Best from Your People

You should always try to get the best from your people. By doing so, you carry out the responsibilities of your job which includes holding down costs, maintaining quality, and meeting production goals. When you accomplish these things, you also prove your worth as a supervisor as well as enjoy and get satisfaction from your work.

People on the job tend to live up to what is expected of them. If you treat them like mature, responsible individuals, most of them will act the part.

Having confidence in the abilities of your people to do their jobs will help you in motivating and persuading them to do their best. You will not be inclined to tell them exactly what to do nor to insist that things be done your way. You will discover sooner or later that some of your people will do a job better than you can. Knowing that your people will do good work will also deter you from watching them closely, something that most workers dislike.

Many workers will do their best when you give them the responsibility for getting the job done and don't interfere when they are doing it. They will also do their best if you show that you appreciate their efforts. Praise for a job well done is welcomed by everyone provided it is sincere and deserved.

The supervisor who shows an interest in people and their welfare is usually liked and respected. When people think well of their supervisor they are more likely to do their best on the job.

2.5 How to Avoid Oversupervising

By planning the work to be done, supervisors can increase the productivity of their people. Knowing their people's likes, dislikes, and skills, and what they expect from their work enables supervisors to fit jobs to their people whenever possible. More cooperation and higher job satisfaction will result. However, you must be careful how you fit jobs and how you supervise those jobs.

Studies have shown that oversimplifying the job and oversupervising the worker can cause problems. Limiting someone to a single task leads to boredom and frustration, both of which may result in low productivity. Oversupervising suggests to the worker that the supervisor questions or has doubts whether the worker can and will do the job satisfactorily. Too much supervision destroys

Here are some suggestions on the arrangements you make:

- If you have a choice of two or more meeting places, pick a room that is appropriate to the size of the group.
- Pull the blinds or shades on the windows and face chairs away from them to prevent distractions.
- Make sure the chairs are not crowded together.
- Limit access to the room from the rear to minimize disturbances from people who arrive late and leave early.
- See that there is a sufficient supply of fresh air and there is adequate ventilation.
- Check on the location of electrical outlets for supplying power to audio/ visual equipment.
- Make certain you can control lighting at each door and from the front of the room.

2.9 Special Assignments: Why They Are Important

Although some supervisors dislike special assignments, a study of people who have reached upper management in their company usually reveals that they handled quite a few special assignments on their way up. There is proof that a good record in handling them helps in moving up the management ladder.

Special assignments vary widely in size and scope. Many times they may start out small, but frequently they are loaded with growth and opportunity, particularly if they deal with new technology. Typical ones include; implementing a new procedure, investigating an idea, clarifying a complex system, and handling an emergency situation brought about by an unexpected turn of events.

Since making a good showing on a special assignment could add to your job description, your stature with management, and the size of your paycheck, why not volunteer for the next one that comes up?

2.10 Tips on Being an Efficient Coordinator

The supervisor who is an efficient coordinator keeps in control of people and events, and this invariably results in getting more done for both himself or herself and the company. To be an efficient coordinator, you must emphasize getting the work done through others and through the cooperation and teamwork of the group. Here are some tips on how to do it:

- Have a friendly disposition and smile frequently.
- Tell people the reason behind every job that they do.
- Give people a voice in how the work should be done.

- Organize activities confidently and competently into order of priority.
- Break down complicated jobs and projects into step-by-step procedures.
- Encourage the sharing of ideas and opinions of the group to promote teamwork.
- Try to have people who get along well work together.
- Be sensitive to friction among people so that you can do something to prevent trouble from developing.
- Make yourself available to members of the group when they are in need of advice or guidance.
- Be a model in getting along well with others.

2.11 Authority: Misused and Misunderstood

Few things in business and industry today are more misused and misunderstood than authority. Some supervisors fail to use it when it should be used. Others try to show it when it doesn't belong to them, and some even use it to flagrantly dominate other people.

Many people do not understand that authority carries with it obligations of respect in two ways: the individuals with authority must respect the problems and needs of their subordinates, and subordinates should respect the authority of the leaders who are responsible for providing guidance and supervision.

Authority is often overused; new supervisors and experienced ones who are assigned special projects are especially vulnerable. If you are unaccustomed to directing or coordinating the efforts of others, be careful. Don't let your newly acquired authority affect how you handle people. When authority is overused, cooperation is hard to come by.

2.12 Techniques for Exercising Authority

Every supervisor wants to feel comfortable with authority and exercise it like a pro. However, it isn't easy for those who just acquire it and are accustomed to following orders. Those supervisors experienced with the ins and outs of authority say you should adopt the following techniques with it:

1. Be aware that authority can go to your head if you are not careful in exercising it.
2. Realize that the best supervisors are those who don't flaunt their positions.
3. Clarify in advance to exercising authority what you do and don't have.
4. Recognize that the purpose of delegating authority is to get a job done, not to show that you are the boss.

5. Be polite and considerate when exercising it.

6. Try to promote team spirit when exercising authority.

7. Avoid using authority when you sense that simple persuasion will do the job.

2.13 Five Ways to Sell Good Housekeeping

Failure to practice good housekeeping is a major reason why accidents continue to happen in offices and plants. But, safety isn't the only reason for a company wanting and needing to keep working areas picked up, neat, and orderly. Many companies have demonstrated that employee attitude and productivity are much better in a clean working place than in a dirty one.

However, you occasionally are going to meet with opposition when you tell someone to spend more of their time housekeeping. For example, you might hear, "Housekeeping? You must be kidding. I've got a job to do," or "That's not my job. We've got janitors for that type of work." How do you answer such remarks? How do you sell people on the importance and necessity of good housekeeping? Here are five ways to do it:

1. Point out that good housekeeping makes a job safer because it eliminates most of the causes of accidents and fires. Safety is everybody's business and certainly everybody wants to be safe on the job.

2. Prove that good housekeeping has a positive effect on people in that work areas are more cheerful and pleasant when they are neat and clean. Work is more fun. People feel better and get along better with each other.

3. Demonstrate that good housekeeping makes work less tiring. When you have all your work tools right at hand and don't need to search for materials and instructions, you don't suffer frustration or aggravation. Poor housekeeping brings on mental fatigue in that depressing surroundings can make the work seem more difficult and boring than it really is.

4. Show that good housekeeping helps in maintaining health and well-being. Dust and dirt never did anybody any good. Scrap and waste in the work area limit work space, lead to poor quality workmanship, and result in low or no satisfaction with job accomplishment.

5. Convince a person that good housekeeping is a personal thing—that nobody can expect someone else to do it all—that a person on the job knows his or her work area better than anybody else—and that a person develops pride from being a good housekeeper.

2.14 Recordkeeping: A Vital Means of Control

Keeping records is one of the responsibilities of people who make decisions and give orders. Supervisors must not only document much of their work but also see that the data gets into the files. Maintaining an up-to-date set of records is the only way to keep track of production operations, maintenance jobs, service, and procedural changes of a business.

Most supervisors dislike paperwork, preferring instead to spend their time with their people to see that problems are solved and work accomplished. Yet records must be made and kept if costs are to be controlled, operations conducted at optimum efficiency, and the business properly managed.

Although some supervisors may have relatively few duties involving records, the ones they do have are vital. Unless the department has a clerk, they are responsible for the time spent by their people on the job and records of absenteeism. In the office, a supervisor may be expected to see that accounting records of various types are kept including purchase orders, invoices, insurance and tax documents, wages and salaries, and the many fringe benefits which companies give their employees. In the plant, a supervisor may need to keep records of machines, parts, equipment capacity and rating, preventive maintenance, raw materials, finished stock, inspections, accidents, and the various process data relating to the products manufactured or the service the company performs.

Accurate data and records are a "must" in today's business and industrial operations for several reasons. Data is needed for making management decisions and to measure operating efficiency. Good records are needed to support proposals for capital expenditures or for improvements in existing systems. Records are also needed to supply the various local, state, and federal governments the many types of information and data they want.

The best way to handle records on the job is to keep up with them as you create the information and data. Postponing the making of a record can lead to stress to do it later when you may be busy with other matters. There is always the risk, too, that you will forget to make the record. This can lead to criticism as well as frustration when the information is needed later.

2.15 How to Handle Employee Complaints

A complaint is always justified from the viewpoint of the individual making it. Prompt handling of a complaint is always desirable. If you remember these two points about complaints, you will do a better job of handling them.

One of the poorest ways a supervisor can go about handling a complaint is to put the blame on someone such as upper management. Passing the buck only raises suspicions—it's like the supervisor saying, "It's not my fault, but I'll help you anyway." Instead of looking for excuses, ask the complainer, "What's wrong?" or "What happened?" That way, you attack the problem by concentrating on *what* went wrong rather than *who* is to blame. The two of you can then work together to get the complaint handled.

Many complaints that people have fit certain categories. For example, a lot of complaints can be classed under lack of information or misunderstanding of the facts. Complaints about the amount of employees' benefits, deductions from pay, or company procedures can usually be handled with a few questions answered by you. If you don't have an answer at your fingertips, tell the individual you will get it, and be sure to do so.

Poor communications are behind many complaints. You may have thought your instructions were very clear but they were not. If a job is done poorly or wrongly, the person responsible may gripe in anticipation of being criticized. The answer to this problem is to make sure you're understood. Get feedback from questions you ask the person or the person asks you before the job is started.

Some complaints are a transfer-of-anger type. The man who comes to work after a quarrel with his wife or has trouble with his car on the way may be in a poor frame of mind and looking for something to complain about. A few tactful questions put to him about how things are going in general will reveal the situation. Sympathy and empathy on your part often may be enough to handle the complaint; if not, look into the matter as soon as you can.

Handling a complaint is probably one of the toughest parts of a supervisor's job. You've got to put yourself in the complainer's position and realize how the person feels. Once you do that, it'll be much easier for you to offer your help. You and the complainer will both feel better besides.

2.16 Seven Rules for Handling Complaints

You can handle a complaint easily and effectively if you go about it in a definite manner. Also, the individual complaining will feel much better about the complaint if you follow some rules in discussing it with him or her. Try the following the next time you must handle a complaint:

1. Agree that the individual has a valid complaint, that you'd feel the same way if you were in such a situation. Say you're sorry that it has caused the individual inconvenience or trouble.

2. Investigate by using questions to bring out details. Get the facts. Listen carefully.

3. Sympathize and commiserate with the individual to further reduce negative emotions. Show your concern.

4. Take at least part of the blame for the mistake or error which led to the complaint.

5. Make the complainer feel important. Recognize position, responsibility, and involvement.

6. Save the complainer's face when explaining a situation or why circumstances are as they are.

7. Try to help solve the complaint. Tell the person promptly when you have done so.

2.17 Ways to Discipline Which Get Results

Discipline is effective when its application eliminates the need for it in the future. This is simply another way of saying that effective discipline gets results. You should never apply discipline without also giving an explanation and providing instruction or correct behavior.

For discipline to have a long-lasting effect, it must be acceptable to the employee receiving it. Unacceptable discipline causes resentment and hostility, either of which may bring on feelings of wanting to get revenge. Poor discipline also results in creating a "don't care" attitude. Supervisors who have been successful at disciplining get results without making people angry. Here are the ways you can do the same:

● Get all the facts before you say or do anything. Disciplining someone is a serious matter—you don't want to make the mistake of disciplining the wrong employee or of taking unwarranted action.

● Consider each incident separately. Circumstances vary and people are different in their thoughts, motives, and deeds. You may not be able to apply a standard type of discipline for the specific incident.

● Maintain control. Don't lose your temper. Never attempt to discipline when there is a possibility that emotion rather than reason is controlling your thinking. You will be less likely to make the mistake of being unfair to both the employee and the company.

● Be consistent. Enforce the rules of behavior and conduct with the same degree of strictness in every case. Being rough with one employee and gentle with another for the same infraction leads to nothing but displeasure and unrest. You may be accused of being unfair and prejudiced besides.

● Have set rules concerning discipline for common incidents. When penalties for failure to comply with rules are made known to everyone, people know what to expect in the way of discipline. The employee who is disciplined knows also that no personal factor of the supervisor was involved in his or her discipline.

2.18 Three Key Features of an Effective Discipline Program

A discipline program can be effective only if it is uniform, corrective, and progressive. Each feature is of equal importance in getting results.

A uniform program prevents the imposition of different discipline for the same offense. Without a guideline, one supervisor might issue a written warning for fighting in the plant while another might suspend the guilty individual for two or three days. A spelled-out, understood penalty for fighting prevents such inequities.

Corrective discipline defines what proper conduct is, thus giving an individual the opportunity to correct his or her improper conduct. This discipline also warns other employees that improper conduct or the breaking of company rules will not be tolerated and will subject guilty individuals to disciplinary action.

The progressive feature of a discipline procedure provides for increasing the severity of the discipline with repeated offenses. Typical procedure might be oral warning for the first offense, written warning for the second, a one-day suspension for the third, a five-day suspension for the fourth, and discharge for the fifth.

2.19 How to Choose the Most Appropriate Discipline

Deciding what disciplinary action you should impose for breaking a rule may be difficult if your company has not established penalties for specific rule infractions. You must decide between discipline that is too severe to be fair and discipline that is too mild to be corrective. Here are six questions which when answered will help you choose the most appropriate action:

1. How serious was the rule infraction?
2. What were the circumstances?
3. How long has the employee been with the company?
4. What is the employee's past conduct record?
5. When was the last time the employee required discipline?
6. What is the discipline usually administered for this rule infraction?

Making judgments: A common procedure today in companies which have severe personnel behavioral problems is to take a "cooling off" period after a serious rule infraction before imposing discipline. Better decisions have resulted when time is taken for more investigation, reasoning, and thought before deciding the proper discipline.

Case-in-Point: Late one afternoon, two employees of the Wilson Co. in Detroit, Michigan began fighting in the plant, disrupting production operations. Although company rules state that *all* employees who engage in fighting in the plant should be suspended without pay for a minimum of one week, their supervisor decided that the incident should be thoroughly investigated before imposing any discipline. He therefore told both employees to leave the plant immediately and return for a meeting at 1:00 pm the next day. He also notified the personnel department and the union of the incident so that representatives of both groups could be present for the meeting.

2.20 How to Be Noted as a Top-Notch Disciplinarian

Most supervisors dislike disciplining their people. But supervisors who have been successful at disciplining report that the job is easier and the discipline is better accepted if they are noted for handling it expertly and fairly. Here are the ways you can attain that reputation yourself:

- Make sure there's a good reason for every rule you enforce.
- If the reason for a rule isn't obvious, be sure to explain it to everyone who might be involved.
- Eliminate or avoid unnecessary rules wherever you can.
- Review departmental policy from time to time to see if all of the rules are still needed.
- Ask for the help of your people when formulating new rules.
- Never adopt a rule simply to show your rank or authority.
- Before disciplining, always give an individual an opportunity to tell you his or her side of the story.
- Consider and study your company's labor agreement before taking disciplinary action with a member of the union.
- When imposing discipline, be careful to give fair and equal treatment to all.
- View discipline primarily as a training function.

3

TRAINING AND
DEVELOPMENT KNOW-HOWS
THAT ASSURE RESULTS

PEOPLE make a company. Their skills and abilities, their performance on the job, and their productivity determine the company's profitability and its growth. The better the people are at doing their work, the more successful the company is likely to be in selling its products or performing services.

Almost everyone hired by an organization must be *trained* to do their work. Although they may be experienced to a degree from previous jobs they've held, they still must learn the company's policies, methods, and procedures and abide by its rules and regulations. To get satisfaction from their work, they must know how to do it efficiently. Moreover, these needs and requirements of employees are continuing matters because of the constant change which goes on and our rapid advance in technology.

Supervisors play key roles in training and developing employees from the day they are hired until they become skilled and productive on the job. How quickly they do and how adept they become depends on the abilities and know-hows of their supervisors and trainers. You as a supervisor are a greater asset to your company if you are a good teacher and trainer.

3.1 Handling the Job of Inducting and Orienting New Employees

The supervisor handles the job of inducting and orienting new employees best by communicating personally with them. Effective communicating paves the road for understanding and provides the basis for good relations between the employee and the company in the future. The time and personal attention that's given a new-hire during the first few days on the job is invaluable in making the employee feel wanted and important. Such contact gives the person a sense of security as well as demonstrates that the company is interested in the employee's future.

Introductions and a tour of the department and work area should be one of the first steps to make the employee familiar with people he or she will work with. Show the individual what each employee does and how people work together in putting out the product or performing a service. Point out the company's facilities such as the restrooms, canteen or cafeteria, supply sources and how the employee can find and talk to you.

Inducting and orienting a new employee includes discussing company rules, procedures, and policy, and also handing out manuals on safety and the various fringe benefits the company provides. A supervisor should distribute the manuals in person to call attention to the employee that the supervisor is the one to go to for information and advice. You should tell the individual also how the job will be learned and who will provide the training.

Motivation, attitude, and morale are greatly influenced with events which occur the first few days the new employee is on the job. You can help promote these by giving him or her considerable attention. Certainly, the employee will appreciate it. Regardless, your objective should not be forgotten—to have the company acquire a satisfied and productive employee.

3.2 Eight Principles of Effective Orientation of Employees

Getting a new employee off to a good start on the job is a responsibility of the supervisor. How you handle this responsibility may decide what the employee thinks of the company and the job.

You can do an effective job of orientation if you apply the following principles and act accordingly:

1. Make new employees feel welcome. Try to allay any fears and anxiety they may have.

2. Recognize that most of them have big adjustments to make. Adjustments are not always easy or quickly made.

3. Give them reasons for wanting to work for you and the company. First impressions are important.

4. Be friendly and helpful. Work at having new employees like you.

5. Promote new employees with other people and make friendly introductions. Do what you can to make it easy for them to get along with other employees.

6. Point out the good features of the work; play down the poor ones. Sell the job, the department, and the company.

7. Enlist the help of one or more other employees to see that they learn their way around. Be sure they are not ignored.

8. Follow up frequently to answer questions which they may have. Show interest and appreciation for the abilities and skills which they develop.

3.3 Successful Ways of Getting New Employees Started

The first two to three weeks on the job are usually the most critical for a new employee; if you are the supervisor of the individual, this period is just as critical for you. How you treat the new employee will in large part determine his or her subsequent performance and attitude. Also, your boss will judge *your* success based on the achievement of the new employee. How effective are you in getting new employees started on the right foot? The following ways have proven to be successful with supervisors who have become pros at handling new employees:

- Make plans for the new employee's arrival so that you are ready the day he or she starts.

- Take care that the individual's personal needs—locker, desk, desk items, personal information, etc.—are attended to on the first day.

- Encourage the new employee right from the start to ask questions and make suggestions regarding the job.

- Try to give him or her the feeling that the job is important in the department.

- Give the individual a good general breakdown of the job he or she will be expected to handle.

- Make an effort early to determine what his or her job preferences are.

Remember that the small things you take for granted because you've been on your job so long are comforting to someone trying to get used to a new place.

3.4 How to Know When Training Is Needed

Supervisors are responsible for the development, progress, and perform-ance of their people; seeing that their people are trained is one of the first steps in carrying out this responsibility. But, how do supervisors know when training is needed? What are the signs that tell them people need training on the job?

The need for training should be considered when:

1. New methods or work procedures are being started.
2. Production goals are not being met.
3. Employees lack a sense of purpose.
4. Costs of operation are increasing without apparent reason.
5. Quality of the product or service is declining.
6. Accidents are increasing.
7. Pride in the job is missing.
8. Complaints and grievances are excessive.
9. Workers are asking numerous questions about the job.
10. High turnover and absenteeism are prevalent.

This list is not complete since training needs and type vary with companies. However, it serves as a guide for supervisors to determine when training is needed and where training efforts may need to be directed.

Case-in-Point: Tim Blackwell, a supervisor in a large South Carolina company, told me why he likes to see his company push training of the men who work for him. "Sure, training costs money," he said, "but it costs a lot more to slow down work or shut down an operation because someone's absent and you have no replacement person to step in."

3.5 Training: Make It Your Responsibility

As a supervisor, you should consider training and developing people who work for you as one of your prime responsibilities. Granted, some supervisors don't agree with this thinking. They feel that training should be the sole province of the training department of the company, thus giving them more time to manage. Others may concede that training is their responsibility, yet they may try to avoid it or spend a minimum of their time on it.

There are several reasons why some supervisors prefer not to become involved. One is that they actually don't know how to go about training, and they are not eager to have that made known. A second is they believe that to train and develop subordinates properly, they would need to know all the details of each of the jobs the subordinates perform. A third is they simply don't know the difference between managing and developing people. They are unaware of what constitutes training as distinguished from communicating, directing, controlling, and disciplining.

Nevertheless, many companies, particularly the smaller ones, operate with the principle that supervisors should be responsible for the training and developing of subordinates. Management's thinking in those companies is that you, the supervisor, usually know the qualifications of the employees who report to you better than anyone else.

Even when you are not sure what steps to take with certain employees, you are still in the best position to appraise their current performance because you can spot both good and poor work. Although the problem may be compounded by the fact that each employee is different in his or her abilities, in the need to know, and the need to develop new skills, you are in the best position to deal with these problems.

Standards of performance are specified for most jobs, requiring in some cases that employees fully apply themselves. Supervisors are most qualified to know both job requirements and employee's capabilities.

3.6 Successful Ways of Selling People on Training

Although you are aware of the value of training and how it helps people with their work, you may need to convince some of your people of this. They may feel that training is a waste of time. You must show them how training pays off.

You can sell training most successfully by pointing out how it helped others to get ahead, how it brought them job security, and how it raised their income.

You can increase a person's interest in training by mentioning the advantage of being able to handle a job well. Training enables a person to learn the what, the how, and the why of a job. When a person knows these, the job becomes interesting and provides more satisfaction, with accomplishment besides.

3.7 Five Easy Steps to Conducting a Training Program

Supervisors may train employees or may assist in setting up the company's training program. In either case, they should be aware of the steps involved. They are: defining the area where the training is needed, planning the presentation, obtaining the training resources and media, recruiting the training personnel, and implementing the program.

Defining the area: Do the office workers need training in operating the machines or in office procedures? Do the men in the maintenance department need instruction on reading blueprints or understanding hydraulics? The specific need of the employees should dictate the scope and range of the training program.

Planning the presentation: How will the instruction and training be provided? Who will conduct it? On the job or in a classroom? How will it be administered? How complete will it be? Factors such as these must be considered and decided.

Training resources and media: Many resources are available for training programs. The training departments of companies have learned that the best programs they can present include several training tools. Resources they use include: programmed instruction manuals, high school and college courses, vendor and manufacturer training sessions, on-the-job training, in-house training classes, seminars, and current literature.

Recruiting the trainer: Even though many of the resources and media include material and tools, individual personal attention is important to any training program. Some person or persons must be recruited to see that classes are conducted, to answer questions and provide assistance, to act as monitors, and to see that the training accomplishes its objectives.

Implementing the program: Dedication and hard work are behind successful training. If the preliminary steps have been carried out industriously and sincerely, this last step will go well and trainees will benefit. Training should not be delayed or postponed once a decision is made to do it. The sooner the program can be implemented, the sooner trainees will begin to improve their skills.

3.8 The Technique of On-the Job Training

Supervisors usually are responsible for giving instruction when the performance of an employee falls below an acceptable standard. Such instruction is generally called on-the-job training.

With today's demand for greater productivity in business and industry, pressure is on management to improve the performance of both new and long-time employees. Whether it is called training, educating, or coaching, it basically consists of the supervisor helping the employee to be more productive. The ultimate goal of on-the-job training is to develop self-reliant employees.

On-the-job training is successful only when the supervisor/employee relationship has a foundation of mutual acceptance and trust. Employees who feel they are being judged rather than helped will not talk freely and when asked questions may defend their actions rather than change or agree to cooperate. Supervisors must recognize that employees are individuals with human emotions, and that they cannot be treated as machines. Employees often decide *what* they will hear and *how* they will respond.

Effective on-the-job training puts three requirements on the supervisor:

1. The supervisor must see the training as a joint effort. Both the supervisor and the employee must be willing to view their attitudes, feelings, and work problems constructively.

2. The supervisor must develop a trust relationship with the employee. Information is not shared in a threatening situation.

3. The supervisor must listen and accept what is said in a nonjudgmental manner. Listening with attention encourages employees to fully communicate and accept suggestions for improving their work.

3.9 Tips on Teaching and Training: Making Sure You're Understood

Successful teachers and trainers possess a skill which serves them well—their technique in communicating makes them easily understood. They are effective trainers because they constantly work at being simple, concise, and clear. Here are some tips for you on the technique:

- Use an easygoing approach. This puts trainees more at ease and in a mood to learn.
- Speak the language of your listeners. By using words they know and understand, you leave no doubt in their minds.
- Prefer short words to long ones, simple words to complex ones, and short sentences to long ones. Being brief and concise helps you to be clear.
- Keep emotion out of your style. Facts may be ignored when emotion is present. Emotional ideas may cloud the issue for some listeners.
- Connect new ideas with old ones and modern procedures with outmoded ones. Learning is easier when the relationship to something familiar is pointed out.
- Explain simple things first. Save the difficult ones for later when trainee's minds are better adjusted to learning.
- Pause between steps of procedures and change of subjects to give trainees time to absorb the instructions. Let them think a bit—it helps learning.
- Encourage feedback. Promote questions to determine if you are getting through and to find out what you should repeat and where you may need to place emphasis.
- Avoid negative approaches to subjects. Attempt to put the record straight on negative comments from trainees. Your effectiveness as a trainer is always better when you stress the positive.
- Limit the number of ideas or points covered at a single session. It's better to do a thorough job with a few ideas than an incomplete job with many. When time is short, be satisfied to get across one idea clearly and completely.

3.10 How to Train by the Four-Step Method of Instruction

A four-step method of instruction of new employees is a proven method of training today, particularly in the operation of machinery or equipment. To be effective at training your people on how to do a job, you should know and practice this method. Here's how to do it:

Step 1: *Get the person ready to learn.* Describe the job and find out what the person knows about it. Familiarize the person with the work area and the surroundings. Encourage and enthuse the trainee in doing good work.

Step 2: *Show how to do the job.* Give tools, material, and equipment their proper names. Demonstrate each step, describing it as you go. Emphasize the key points. Go slowly so that the trainee will not miss anything and gets the whole picture. Teach and instruct only as fast as you think you are being understood.

Step 3: *Let the person do the job.* Watch carefully and correct any mistakes, noting where the person needs more instruction. Ask the trainee to explain the key points of the job and where mistakes, if any, were made. Have the person do the job several times until you are sure he or she can handle it without help.

Step 4: *Turn the job over to the person.* Follow up frequently to see if the person has a problem or question. Give praise for a job well-done to encourage future good performance.

3.11 Use of Training Corporation Programs Pays Off

Several corporations are in the business of selling training material in the form of programs and/or providing training services. Operations, safety, maintenance, and instrumentation and control are among the most popular subjects covered in these programs. Many industrial companies are using them with great success.

The objectives of these training programs are to train new personnel in the skills they will need to become accomplished operators and maintenance personnel and to improve the skills of personnel already assigned to such work. Training programs generally consist of as many as 50 individual instruction units covering several subjects. Each instruction unit is a complete training package—videotape, student text, and instructor's guide. Although designed for the classroom, units can also be used for self-instruction.

It usually takes 3 to 4 hours of learning to complete a unit. By presenting the material in 8- to 12-minute segments, an instructor is easily able to keep the attention of trainees at a high level while also pausing for questions or testing for comprehension.

Some training corporations help their clients with consulting services by offering assistance with testing on a time-and-material basis. For those that request it, most corporations can implement their programs with qualified instructors at the company's site. In addition, the corporation can train instructors at either the company's or the corporation's facility.

3.12 Answering How Much You Should Teach at One Time

The amount you should try to teach people at one time depends on how difficult the job is and how fast the trainee can learn. Each trainee on the job is different just like each student in school is different. Some learn fast while others learn slow. Set the amount you teach at one time to the learning rate of the slowest individual being trained.

New employees usually are nervous and eager to do well, adding to the difficulty of their learning a job. You need to be understanding and patient. Try to put them at ease. Compliment them when they make progress and do well. They will learn faster if you are not demanding or critical.

Always start teaching and training slowly to allow trainees to get accustomed to the job and their surroundings. Recognize that trainees may be under tension. They also don't want to look bad in the presence of others.

Make teaching the basics and the fundamentals your main objective. When people know the rudiments of a job, it is easier for them to learn the refinements of it.

Avoid comparing the progress of one individual with that of another, remembering that each person is different in how fast a job is learned and how much is remembered. Give the slow learner more of your attention than the fast one.

3.13 Delegating: When and Why to Do It

Most successful supervisors are skilled in the art of delegating. In case you're undecided about your need to do it, be convinced if you frequently find yourself in one or more of the following situations:

- Taking work home at night or working a lot of overtime.
- Failing to give important jobs the amount of attention they deserve.
- Getting important jobs done just on time or a day or two late.
- Spending too much time on relatively unimportant jobs.
- Finding that much of the work you're doing is very routine in nature.

You must certainly practice delegation if you have hopes of moving up in your company. Your skill in delegating could be the deciding factor in whether you can handle greater responsibilities and a bigger job since a successful manager gets things done through others.

If you are hesitating to delegate because you are afraid of a subordinate moving up too fast or because you feel you must do a job yourself to have it done right, such arguments are false. A subordinate moving up fast shows your boss and others that you are ready for advancement—you've got a person ready to take your place. If you feel that your subordinate can't do a job as well as you can, consider whether it's really necessary that the job be done that well.

Unwillingness to delegate may be a psychological problem with some supervisors. They may fear that credit for the job being done will go to someone else, that it will become known that others know more about a particular job than they, or that someone may do the job better than they've been doing it. After they begin to delegate, these fears become inconsequential or disappear entirely. All supervisors have much more to gain than to lose by delegating.

3.14 Five Tested and Proven Steps to Successful Delegating

Nearly all supervisors today must delegate some duties and tasks at one time or another. You, therefore, should know how to delegate. Here are the steps you should follow to be successful at it:

1. Decide what part of your work you can delegate. One obvious choice is a job which another individual can do as well or better than you can. Reserve for yourself those tasks which require the experience, skill, and training which only you possess.

2. Delegate to more than one person, if possible. Carefully select the person to whom you're going to delegate a specific task by suiting the task to the person. By spreading assignments among all your people, and especially among those who have the ability and desire to get ahead, you enable each to demonstrate their potential as well as gain recognition for getting a job done.

3. Be clear and concise when delegating. Right from the beginning you must clarify what decisions you are delegating and what you are reserving for yourself. Delegating fails when the person to whom you have delegated a task fails to perform it or makes a decision beyond the scope of authority granted.

4. Tell other people in the department or company about your delegation. If you fail to let people know what and to whom you have delegated, you make it difficult for your helpers to get cooperation and to avoid resentment when making decisions.

5. Follow up on people and tasks. Even though you may have delegated some decision-making responsibility, you still have the total responsibility. You must keep up-to-date too, on what you have delegated. Stay on top of these things by asking that your people report to you from time to time.

Caution: When you delegate your work you must be careful not to go overboard. Some of your duties and responsibilities should *not* be delegated. Management expects you to handle such matters as planning, scheduling, policy formation, coordinating, control, and supervision. If you give those away, you might just as well start looking for another job—your company won't need you.

3.15 Tips on Delegating

Delegating is not easy for many supervisors. Since most of them feel a bit uneasy when they do it, tips on how to delegate are always welcome. Here's what the experts say in this respect:

- Be sure the lines of communication are open. Encourage employees to offer their opinions and ask questions. Listen to what they say.
- Do a thorough job of planning what you have to say beforehand. Present the entire assignment at one session.
- Watch for stumbling blocks in the procedure. Agree on objectives. Try to speak the same language.
- Be specific and precise. Avoid generalizations.
- Differentiate between fact and opinion. Facts are evidence and history, while opinions are thoughts, feelings, and conjecture.
- Provide all pertinent data and information. If you omit something, you risk having the employee not do exactly what you want.

3.16 How to Recruit a Temporary Supervisor

You can't be on the job every day. Everybody takes a vacation now and then, and few people are not ill once in a while. Somebody is needed to handle your job in your absence. Since you know your people better than anyone else, it is logical that you be asked to recommend someone. Talk to your boss about this to get agreement on arranging for someone to replace you.

Although you would be pleased if all of your people would like to have your job, face the fact that not everyone wants the responsibility which goes with being a supervisor. Since you want the best qualified individual for the job, look for qualities of leadership among your people. Note if the individual who qualifies gets along well with other employees. Is he or she concerned with efficiency and cost? Quality and quantity of product or service? A desire to get the job done? When you find such an individual among your people, talk to him or her saying that you think the individual would make a good supervisor. Then ask if he or she would be interested in taking your place the next time you are absent.

If you meet with reluctance or refusal, point out that the experience would be good and that acting as a temporary supervisor is a step to a better job with the company. Also, suggest that the person try the job for only one or two days to start.

When you gain acceptance, be considerate and understanding as you show the person how to do your work. How you help the person to handle the job as well as how you show confidence in his or her ability to do it may be a factor in how effective the person turns out to be.

Caution: When offering one of your people the opportunity to act as a temporary supervisor, you may be tempted to pick the individual with the most education. You could make a mistake in doing so. The three vital attributes a first-line supervisor must have are leadership, sensitivity, and initiative. Astute and knowledgeable managers know that the presence or absence of these attributes has nothing to do with a candidate's educational level. College graduates may lack them while up-from-the-ranks, practical-experienced individuals may have them in abundance.

4

GETTING TO
KNOW PEOPLE AND
MOTIVATING THEM

YOU are a leader of people, and you get things done through knowing and motivating them. To be a successful leader you've got to make decisions, direct people and follow through on tasks which take skill, energy, drive, and enthusiasm. Along the way you will run into obstacles and problems, both with people and things. Often, in working with people and to overcome these obstacles and problems you will need to level with people.

In this chapter you'll find ways to be firm and forceful when you ask your people for something or give instructions on the job. People look to their supervisor for guidance. You provide that guidance when you're the boss without being obvious about it. You have to know, of course, what your people want and how to earn their respect.

4.1 How to Know What Your People Want

The supervisor who knows what his or her people want has a big jump on having good relations with them because he or she recognizes their needs and can do something about them. Making your point and making it stick are a lot simpler when you understand your people. Logically, people are more willing to cooperate when they know that their boss is looking out for them and is interested in their welfare.

There is no single answer to good supervisor-worker relations. However, aside from decent treatment and fair pay, all people want and need certain things from their job. Most employees, for example, need a sense of security. They want to know that they will still have their job tomorrow, next month, and next year. They want to feel secure within their group, to accept the people they work with, and to be fully accepted by them.

Employees like to feel that they belong, that they are part of a team. They want a sense of participation, a feeling of being "in" on things. When you tell your people, for example, that a new product is coming through that will require a change in procedure, make sure *all* are informed, not just the few that may be directly involved. When you announce the new hours for the cafeteria, tell *everyone* including those who usually don't eat their lunch there. If you start the use of a new tool, give *all* your people a chance to use it.

People on the job usually have a desire for challenging work. They look for opportunities to use all of their talents; therefore, they welcome assignments which require they do their best and, at the same time, enable them to discover abilities they didn't realize they possessed.

Case-in-Point: "Casey" Jones, supervisor of the pipefitters at an Ohio oil refinery, recognized the value of letting his craftsmen show their job skills. "Although most of our work is of a repair nature," he said, "we occasionally make some new installations such as putting in a heating system, an eye wash, or a safety shower. When I assign the fellows such a job, I don't give them all the details of how to do the job. Letting them figure out elevations, source of supply, and locations of valves, among other things, gives them some responsibility and makes their work more satisfying."

A number of surveys have been conducted in recent years among employees in which they were asked what they want and expect from their jobs, and the degree of importance of those things. The supervisors of these employees were also asked what they thought were important to the people they supervised.

Employees generally rated the human aspect of their jobs as being far more important than the tangible monetary factors. For example, people wanted "full appreciation of work done" and "help on personal problems." Linda Combs wanted to be told that the department management appreciated the time and effort she put into tracing and expediting the shipment of forms the department needed. Bob Smith expected his supervisor to "hear him out" and express sympathy on his problems with his new car.

Before the survey, many supervisors thought that "good wages" and "job security" were most important to their people. They also minimized the human aspect of earning a living. Have you ever thought about how boring the job that Charley White does must be and how you might make it more interesting for him?

The surveys show that often we are incorrect in our assumptions of what we think is important to another person. They also show us that a problem exists when employees who think "full appreciation of work done" is important are being led by a supervisor who thinks this is relatively unimportant.

Get to know what your people want and you'll find that your job is more challenging, yet easier.

4.2 Proven Ways of Getting to Know People's Skills

People are like fingerprints in that no two are exactly alike. So the better you know them as individuals, the better job you can do of leading and supervising them. Your task of placing them on jobs suited to their abilities becomes much easier when you know more about them.

How can you determine when you really know your people? Because people change in how they think and feel from day to day, this can be difficult. But you can test yourself by seeing if you can answer these questions about any one of your men:

1. How skilled is he on his job? Does he need training?
2. How is the quality and quantity of his work? Is he accurate? Does he make errors?
3. Does he show initiative? Is his judgment good?
4. Does he accept responsibility? Can he proceed on his own or does he continually need guidance?
5. Is he impulsive? Can he think out a problem?
6. Does he work well with others? Is he a loner or a team member?

If you can answer most of these questions about each of your men, you probably know them well.

4.3 Nine Principles of Effective Motivation

Of the many ways that workers may be motivated, a few stand out as basic in that they motivate while also satisfying the needs of individuals. The more these principles and conditions can be provided in the working atmosphere, the more people will respond productively:

- Being a member of a "good bunch of fellows" is important for job satisfaction and good productivity.

- Socialization on the job without influencing output negatively is desirable.
- Working conditions which make communication easy satisfy the worker's need for socialization.
- Good compatibility of persons working together promotes good performance.
- If a worker does not get satisfaction from the job, it is only an unpleasant interlude to the hours after work.
- Supervisors should be viewed by workers as friendly helpers rather than drivers or dictators to be resisted as much as possible.
- Supervisors should speak and act with authority. Appearing unsure causes anxiety and worry in the minds of their people.
- Motivation of workers is at its best when supervisors are accepted, respected, and liked.
- Supervisors should be as informal and down-to-earth in their relations with workers as management will permit.

4.4 Leveling: What It Can Do for You

Leveling is being honest with employees about their performance, goals, good and bad points, where they are going, what they can expect, and what they should do to improve their capabilities. Supervisors use leveling because they are afraid of alienating employees and undermining morale. Employees use it because they are worried about ruining their chances for promotion. Leveling allows both supervisors and employees to understand all the factors involved in any situation and to honestly explore the alternatives.

Although leveling involves openness and honesty with an individual, it does not entitle you to say just anything you feel like—to let someone have it with both barrels. This approach unquestionably breeds resentment and hostility.

Many supervisors are afraid to speak up for fear of alienating an employee. But failing to do so does both the supervisor and the employee a disservice. Employees will not usually try to improve their performance if they are unaware that it is unsatisfactory. By avoiding the issue, the supervisor is arbitrarily depriving the employee of the chance to improve. The supervisor is also adding to his or her own responsibility because he or she must somehow fill the gap between the employee's actual and expected performance.

4.5 Five Proven Methods for Leveling Effectively

You should recognize that there are risks involved in leveling with people. Genuine honesty carries the potential of hurting egos or forcing the acknowledgment of unpleasant truths. There are, however, responsible ways to level. Here are five proven methods for leveling effectively:

1. Carefully control the content of any leveling session you embark on. Concentrate on the sharing of ideas and feelings rather than on giving advice. It's possible to change a habit such as the number of coffee breaks taken during the day. But it's almost impossible to change a personality trait such as procrastination.

2. Focus a leveling session on the needs of the employee, not on your needs. Provide an amount of information that the employee can use rather than everything you have and might like to unload. Explore alternatives. The more attention that is given to the alternatives for reaching a goal, the more likely the best solution to any problem will be found.

3. Level without damaging the employee's ego and self-esteem. Always conduct leveling sessions in private, and begin with praise and appreciation, if warranted. It's always easier to listen to unpleasant things after hearing some praise.

4. Make the employee responsible for his or her own behavior. Hold him or her strictly accountable for results. Describe behavior in terms of "more-or-less" rather than "either-or." The more-or-less approach stresses quantity which is measurable, rather than quality, which is judgmental.

5. Stick to your points of contention and have the courage of your convictions. Stand firm on your position, even if the employee raises objections. Once you've made a particular point and it's understood, move on to other subjects.

4.6 Positive Result-Getters: Making People Feel Important

If you can make people feel important, they will be more willing to cooperate, do good work, and be pleased with their job. The psychology behind this is simple—feeling important makes you look at your work as worthwhile, necessary to the company, and something not everyone can do. When you don't feel important, it's natural not to be enthusiastic about your work or eager to get it done.

How to Do It: A good way to make a man feel important is to thank him for something he has accomplished, adding that not everybody could have done what he did. Pointing out that his skill, knowledge, and experience enabled him to do a good job is another way of telling him of his importance.

The most pleasant word to a man's ears is his own name. It makes him an individual distinct and unique from others. It adds identity. So, to make a man feel important, use his name when talking to him and when talking to others about him in his presence.

Alternate Action: You can motivate someone and also make the person feel important by giving him or her responsibility. But you must do this carefully— it's not sufficient for you to simply ask a person to do a certain job for you. You have to point out the importance of the job.

Case-in-Point: Jack Cramer, supervisor in a chemical manufacturing plant, received an order for some special chemicals. The order came from a company that the plant had been trying to sell for more than a year. Jack could have routinely turned over the job of filling the order to his clerk without mentioning its importance, but he saw an opportunity to motivate as well as raise the ego of Bill Willis, one of the order clerks. He approached him saying, "Bill, there's a special order coming through that I'd like you to personally handle. It could be a big factor in the plant's future business. I want to be sure the order is filled properly and also that it gets out on time, so I'm asking you to do this."

Jack accomplished his objective of making Bill feel important as evidenced by Bill's enthusiastic and careful handling of the job. And, of course, the order was given the special attention and consideration it deserved.

4.7 Tips on Handling People Responsibilities

Some supervisors are truly concerned about their "people" responsibilities. They wonder if they are giving adequate attention to *all* the areas involving people that are included in the supervisory function, and whether or not they are handling them properly. Here are some tips on what you should know about your people and what you should be doing on their behalf:

Qualifications: Do you know the present qualifications of all of your people? You should at least know whether or not their qualifications match their present jobs. Sharp supervisors are aware of the qualifications of their people that are presently unused.

Goals: Have you discussed your people's goals with them? You should have pointed out at some time the benefits and advantages of setting goals; encouraging them to set goals for themselves should be an ongoing matter.

Performance: Do you talk periodically to each individual about his or her performance on the job? People want to know how they are doing. They want to know if their performance is satisfactory or if it is lacking in some respect.

Opportunities: Have you told each individual in your department of the opportunities in the company which are available to him or her? Another responsibility involving opportunities is to see if there are additional opportunities for your people which you can arrange.

Progress: Do you know who is and who isn't making progress with their work? Those people who are moving ahead should be commended for their advancement and encouraged to continue. Those who are failing to progress should be made aware of the problem and plans made to enable them to change for the better.

4.8 Six Ways to Inflate the Ego of People

Would you like to puff up your people and satisfy their need to feel appreciated? If you succeed at this they'll like their work more and do a better job besides.

How to Do It

1. Give them your full attention and show interest when they communicate with you. They especially appreciate this when they know you are busy.

2. Keep them completely informed on all matters which concern them. You show that you're interested in them and their work.

3. Treat them with courtesy, dignity, and respect. Put them on your level or higher, if possible.

4. Provide them opportunities to do things they usually aren't privileged to do. Let them represent the department at a function, for example, or excuse them from work when they have a personal problem to handle.

5. Give them a chance to perform unusually well so they will look good in the eyes of others. Compliment them in the presence of their peers.

6. See that they get rewards for job accomplishment. A personal letter from management, recognition on the company bulletin board or in the company newspaper, or a personal gift are a few of the ways this can be done.

4.9 How to Develop Followership

To be an effective supervisor, you must be an effective leader. A successful supervisor/leader is someone who has followers to carry out his or her orders and directions.

To develop followership, you must demonstrate that you conform to recognized principles or accept rules and standards in giving directions. Two issues are pertinent: one, your people are the ones who determine if you conform; and two, your people also decide what constitutes conformity, what qualities in a super-visor create conformity, and what qualities either are irrelevant to such conform-ity or serve to thwart it.

In order for you to develop followership, you must show that you are knowledgeable in the technical aspects of the work and the jobs you are supervising. In addition, you must also know your company's goals and objec-tives, and be able to impart that information to employees.

You will have more followers and they will be more loyal to you if you show interest in them as individuals. The specific way in which you show this interest will vary from person to person, but some actions expected from supervisors include:

- Conducting appraisal interviews periodically.
- Listening to personal concerns.
- Giving credit when credit is due.
- Providing support at times of need.

If you treat your people fairly, never play favorites, and are generally consistent, it should not be difficult for you to develop an enthusiastic fol-lowership. In almost every case, your followers will respect your role and willingly play their roles as loyal, productive employees.

4.10 Solving the Problem of Placing Blame

It's natural when something goes wrong to look for someone to blame because everyone has a self-preservation instinct. Yet, more often than we care to admit, we, ourselves, are guilty. However, whether we are at fault or someone else is, how we undo a wrong or correct a mistake should be of more concern to us than placing blame.

How to Do It: When reprimanding an employee becomes necessary, be careful to avoid finding fault with the person's abilities. Although you may accuse an individual of almost anything such as laziness, carelessness, forget-fulness, or negligence, and not damage the person's ego, if you call the individ-ual "stupid," even indirectly, you hit that which the person values most highly, his or her opinion of himself or herself as a competent, above-average person.

Case-in-Point: Jack Martin, an impulsive, aggressive supervisor in a ma-chine shop in Chicago, Illinois, learned one day that a machinist working for him had made a serious error in the cutting of a shaft. Angrily, he approached the man at his machine, blurting out, "How could you have made such a stupid mistake? My eight-year-old son could have done this job and he doesn't know the first thing about machining."

When the man's face reddened, Jack realized he had said the wrong thing, but it was too late. Making matters worse, bystanders at other machines had heard him. Jack lost the respect of some of his people that day, and they didn't let him forget the incident quickly either. Weeks later, some of the men occasionally used the words "stupid mistake" when they sensed he could hear their conversation.

4.11 How You Can Be the Boss Without Being Obvious About It

With a few exceptions, successful supervisors do not carry out their responsibilities by telling the world, "I am the boss. You do as I say." It takes an egotistical and commanding personality to behave in such manner. Few supervisors are built that way. Most effective supervisors have learned that they get along better and get more accomplished if they play down their position as "giver of orders."

Yet, there are times when you've got to make your point and make it stick. Being decisive will minimize the difficulty of getting through when there is no question of what should be done. A vigorous and confident approach to solving a problem also commands respect. The supervisor who is steady and consistent has no trouble in making his point and making it stick.

Your people, the ones who work for you, are well aware that you are their boss. Some people dislike taking orders from anyone. Then, too, consider the general feeling of many workers who want to have a voice in what they do and how they handle their job. The aware and perceptive supervisor realizes that his personnel relations stand to be better if he can be the boss without being obvious about it. Successful supervisors can be in the background yet make their point and make it stick.

Case-in-Point: "I like to keep out of the limelight when my department receives recognition for being safe on the job or keeping work areas neat and clean," reports Stan Weber, supervisor in the Acme Steel Products Company in Los Angeles. "After all, my people's efforts more than mine achieved these things—they should get the credit. And I sense that some of them feel that way, too. I'd be out of line in their eyes to act otherwise."

A few supervisors today believe that being inaccessible is the sign of a true leader, some even think it is a status symbol of their authority. They couldn't be more wrong. When someone who works for you wants to talk to you, it's only right that you be available. After all, you should know what the problem is and it shouldn't have to get worse before you hear about it. Being around and knowing what's going on makes you more a part of the team, as well as being an inconspicuous boss.

How to Do It: Your best way of knowing what's going on is to keep a close, friendly relationship with your people. If they see you are interested in what they are doing, they'll gladly talk. But if you are impatient, disinterested, or suggest you are not concerned, people are not going to consult you about anything until they absolutely have to.

Sharp supervisors make it easy for workers to get through to them because they know that being reachable enables them to stay on top of the job. Good supervisors also don't become angry or irritated when they get bad news. They know that if people find that their bosses become upset when things aren't going right, there's a reluctance to let them know when there's trouble.

If keeping you informed is not difficult for your people, they are more likely to do so. You won't need to continually ask or give the impression you are in charge and must make decisions. Follow up on job assignments after a reasonable length of time. You will get the reputation of being efficient as well as in control, both of which will enable you to make your orders stick. Keeping in touch makes it possible for you to be the boss without being obvious about it.

4.12 Pressuring Doesn't Pay Off

Do you pressure or coerce your people into doing what you want done? Some supervisors do this without realizing it; perhaps because they are more drivers than leaders.

A driver demands that jobs be done rather than requesting the action in a normal tone of voice. Thus, a driver doesn't seek respect or cooperation but relies mostly on authority to get his or her way. However, pressure tactics simply don't pay off in dealing with subordinates.

What are the ways of treating your people that amounts to pressuring? Here are some of the common ones along with the reasons why they are considered poor supervisory tactics:

Setting impossible goals. If you encourage people to plan their own work and set their own goals, you will avoid setting impossible goals for them. When you demand increased productivity, you are likely to have stressed and frustrated people on your hands.

Finding fault. Since everyone needs to feel that they're doing a good job, effective supervisors avoid finding fault with the work or performance of their people. Besides, most jobs are done well rather than poorly anyway. Show that you are as skilled at recognizing good work as you are at recognizing bad.

Introducing fear. You can't get more work or better performance out of people by threatening them. Similarly, punishment has little, if any, effect on productivity. Introducing fear into people's minds results in low morale, dissatisfaction and high absenteeism.

Oversupervising. After you assign people jobs, get out of their way and let them do the work. You show confidence in their abilities and skills by not watching them closely. If you give them too much attention and stay with them constantly, you deprive them of being creative and thinking out problems on their own.

Arguing and bickering. Your people know that you are the boss. If they do poor work, or are wrong in their thinking, tell them. But recognize that if you make an argumentative remark, you are in for trouble. Although you probably will win an argument, you will lose something more important—the cooperation and respect that you need to be effective as a supervisor.

Overruling. You must have a very good reason to reverse or cancel one of your people's decisions. Also, never criticize someone for a bad decision. Instead, take the opportunity to improve your communications with the individual and commend his or her initiative. If you must overrule someone, find a face-saving reason for your action. You want to avoid destroying the individual's ego and self-esteem.

4.13 The Art of Saying "No" Diplomatically

All leaders occasionally have to say "no" to their people much as they may dislike doing so. Whether it's a request for time off, additional pay, or a simple suggestion relating to how work should be done, it still is a negative response you're making. Recognize that it is inevitable that you must now and then say "no" because every suggestion, idea, or request cannot be granted.

How to Do It: If your answer to a request is "no" don't hesitate to say so. Also, don't delay your refusal because you only make it harder to say later. Be aware, however, that many times it would be more satisfying to your listener and more to the advantage of yourself and your company if you would explain your decision. Give the reason for the refusal first, and then add, "I know this probably isn't the answer you'd like to hear, but for this reason you can understand why I am unable to say yes."

Sometimes you may be able to offer an alternative after saying "no" when you are dealing, for example, with people other than those who work for you.

Case-in-Point: Dan Boyle, supervisor of a maintenance crew in a Dow chemical plant in Michigan, was approached one afternoon by a supervisor from another department with the request to show the fellow how a mechanical seal is replaced on one of the new pumps recently acquired by the company. Although Dan felt that the maintenance superintendent should handle such a request, he didn't refuse to do it. Instead he replied, "I don't have time today, but I could help you out first thing in the morning."

Although "no" is sometimes hard to take, you may be surprised how much your being frank and honest is appreciated. Also, your people will realize that your position requires you to sometimes make your point and make it stick.

Be careful, however, of the quick, emphatic "no" because it can cause trouble. Better that you discuss the reasons that will lead to your eventual negative answer. You will find that most people will convince themselves that they could not expect a positive answer and that they will reason "no" was a fair answer on your part.

4.14 Popular or Respected: Which is Better?

Every supervisor wants to be liked by his or her people—it's normal to feel that way. However, the difficulty of handling some of today's business operations along with solving human relations problems dictate that supervisors who have the respect of workers are much better off than those who are popular with them. Of course, you don't want the workers to dislike you or fear you. But you should want those you direct and lead to respect you.

The reasons why you should prefer respect to popularity are logical. Getting good workmanship and cooperation from workers in most cases is easier if individuals think of you first as their supervisor. The day you become a very good friend to them may be the day some of them decide to take it easy on the job and not do as much or as well as they could. They may reason that you won't mind if they coast now and then.

Think about your classroom experiences for an example of the relationship between popularity and respect. You may remember that when a teacher or instructor didn't have the respect of his or her class, the quality of the teaching and what was learned by the students was less. Some students may even have tried to be overly friendly with the result that the teacher found himself or herself involved in a popularity contest. When a teacher becomes too friendly with students, it usually leads to trouble because teachers need respect to maintain discipline and order in the classroom.

As to how to attain and maintain a happy medium between being friendly and holding your worker's respect, there are several things you can do and several you should not do. While you naturally want to be pleasant, you don't want to overdo it. A loss of respect may be the result if you allow yourself to get too informal with those you supervise. You must be both pleasant and businesslike.

Be careful, also, to not give the impression that you're hard to please, that a job wasn't done as well as it could have been, or that more work should have been done within a certain time period. Many workers find fault with their supervisors on such matters. This is not to say that you should never discuss such problems, however. A good time to do so is during a performance appraisal session.

It is probably true that you could be more popular with the workers you now direct and supervise if you decided you wanted to do so. But if you become too friendly, your job could become more involved and difficult. To what degree this could happen depends a great deal on the nature and personality of the people in your department. What you want is the smoothest-running operation that is possible.

4.15 How to Earn Respect Without Forcing It

Everyone needs to feel worthy and respected. Supervisors, especially, hope their people respect them because knowing this gives them confidence in carrying out their responsibilities. You should want to earn the respect of your people if you do not already have it. When you have respect, you have no problem in difficult situations with making your point and making it stick.

How to Do It: One way you can gain respect is by admitting when you're wrong. It isn't true that admitting when you're wrong weakens your image and effectiveness on the job. Job holders don't expect their supervisors to be right all the time. They do, however, respect a supervisor who admits an error.

Face-to-face personal contact is always preferable to written communications. Your expressions, voice inflection, comments, and manner of speaking all help to promote understanding and leave no doubt of your intentions.

The supervisor who lets his people know that he expects them to fulfill their job requirements will get respect and loyalty *provided* he also lets them know he is there to help them meet those requirements.

You can win respect of employees by being naturally friendly and by showing concern for human dignity. Avoid being biased or prejudiced. Give recognition to suggestions. People always respect honesty and sincerity. Moreover, they expect these qualities in their supervisors. They also look up to a leader who is strong, creative, and decisive.

Another way you can earn the respect of your people is to *not* prove to them that you can still do every job in your area as well or better than anyone else. You may not realize it, but your people know your capabilities and your skills—you don't have to remind anyone of them. Besides, it is wrong for you to do what is their work. Your job as supervisor is to help, advise, and suggest how work should be done. Your people will respect you more if you limit your activity to those things.

4.16 Five Ways to Avoid Discriminating

A tendency has been growing in personnel relations to put up with incompetence in order to avoid a charge of discrimination. For instance, you might approve the hiring of a worker that you would not have considered before, or you might put off the firing of a person who is performing unsatisfactorily and shows no inclination to change for the better.

Of course, you must never discriminate against people on the basis of color, race, sex, or creed, or for any reason that is immaterial or irrelevant to the job. Favoring a minority person over a more capable majority person—reverse discrimination—is just as bad. If business or industry discriminates at all with employees, it must be only on the basis of skill, ability, or performance.

How to Do It: As a supervisor, you don't need to put up with poor performance. In fact, you must do something about it. But how do you avoid charges of discrimination after you take action? Here are five ways to protect yourself:

1. Set standards and rules of conduct and performance for your people. Make sure everyone is aware of them. A proven way of assuring this is to give each person a letter listing the rules and what the company expects from its employees.

2. Let people know about unsatisfactory behavior and performance. Warn them that you will not tolerate such behavior. Although you may give an individual time to learn and change his or her ways, there is a limit to how far you can go with this.

3. Conduct performance appraisals periodically making a written record of each interview. A history of such personnel information in your files will enable you to determine if an individual's performance is changing for the worse or the better. The records will serve as justification if you must apply discipline or take other action.

4. Give people who perform unsatisfactorily a second and even a third chance if you see improvement. But treat people alike in this respect in that you are not more lenient with a minority than a majority person.

5. Discuss termination with the personnel department if this route appears to be the best course to follow. Make sure your reasons are justified and your records are complete.

5

HOW SUCCESSFUL
SUPERVISORS USE
PERSUASION

SUPERVISORS are managers—they get work done through other people. Their success at this depends on how effectively they communicate in suggesting, asking, and requesting. Problems sometimes arise since the communication between supervisors and their people is mostly in one direction. People have their own ideas about why a job is necessary and how and when it should be done. Their thinking on these matters may differ from that of their supervisors. They may see things differently and they may not want to go along with what they are asked to do. Yet supervisors should avoid putting people on the defensive—and when disagreements arise, it's often advisable to not have the last word.

Successful supervisors are skilled in the art of persuasion. They persuade in different ways depending on the circumstances and the people involved. It pays to learn and know how they do it.

5.1 How to Get People to Want to Do Something

Simply urging people to do something will often cause them to respond, but you shouldn't count on this to get results day after day. You've got to come up with more than this to realize continuous agreement with you and good performance. What you need to achieve is have *them* see for themselves what is needed, have *them* want to do something, and have *them* decide what they will do.

The trick behind successful persuasion is getting people to make decisions on their own. Most people prefer that *they* rather than *you* decide how to reach a goal. Doing and reaching it their way gives them some responsibility and makes them feel they are more than just order-takers.

Your ability to persuade is put to the test when you ask your people to make a change in their way of doing things or to stop doing one thing and begin doing another. Naturally, you would like to have them go along with you with a minimum of grumbling, complaining, and objecting. How do you do it? Here are the ways to effectively go about persuading them:

● When you explain something, do a complete job by including the bad with the good. Since the facts will eventually be known anyway, see that they come from you. But, play up the good—it makes acceptance easier.

● Avoid overselling. Although it's expected you will praise something you're in favor of, don't go too far. People have good memories when it comes to promises and predictions you make. You could be embarrassed later if things don't work out right.

● Be careful not to exaggerate. Don't lead people to think you're going all out when actually you plan to make only a small change, or that a complete new way of doing a job is coming up when you're changing only one step.

● Introduce change slowly. Don't spring a new way of doing things suddenly and without warning. Prepare people for change by talking about it beforehand, saying what you're thinking about doing, and why it's necessary that it should be done.

● Be timely. Clear the way for something new before announcing it to make sure you aren't faced with a postponement before you get started. Pick the opportune time for a change that greatly affects people. Be ready to follow through on a proposal once you make it.

● Ask for comments and suggestions when you are considering a change. Show that you want everyone to know what you are proposing, that you are concerned with their acceptance, and that you want their approval. People will go along with you more readily if they are permitted to have their way.

5.2 How to Avoid Putting Others on the Defensive

People on the defensive are inefficient and lack initiative. Defensiveness also affects people's reasoning and creativity. With such demerits chalked up to it, you should avoid the practice, especially with your people. Here are four ways you can avoid putting others on the defensive:

1. Concentrate on what the problem is and how it can be solved rather than who is at fault. Blame doesn't resolve a problem.

2. Respond instead of react to a communication problem or an emotional situation. Reaction focuses on the tone of voice or attitude of the speaker rather than the message. Response focuses only on the message.

3. State the benefits or advantages of an action. This is much preferable to telling an individual that he or she must do something because it's been ordered.

4. Deal with effects. Refrain from judging. Instead of telling someone he or she was wrong, concentrate on the problem that resulted.

5.3 The Advisability of Not Having the Last Word

Some supervisors like to feel they are better than others in knowledge and ability. One of the ways they try to affirm this belief is by having the last word when they exchange remarks with another person. The theory behind their reasoning is that the individual who has the last word knows more, is sharper, and is smarter. Thus, the speaker of the last word is the winner and the individual who doesn't have the final say is the loser.

The loser often wishes that he or she could have thought of a good comeback before the winner departed. He or she probably spends some time rehashing the whole affair, thinking of some appropriate remarks that could have been made, not to mention some words that can be said at the next encounter.

But have you thought about the advantages and disadvantages of having the last word? Will it save your face or damage your status if it goes one way or the other? What about the emotional stress it might cause? Can you quickly recover your composure after being tense and upset?

The advisability of *not* having the last word should be considered. A better approach to an emotional situation may be to counter with a surprised or bewildered look and a nonaggressive question such as, "What's up?" Another alternative is to simply keep your mouth shut, turn away, and leave.

The advantage of handling the situation in one of these ways is that you provide a cooling effect instead of heating up an already inflammatory situation. Your opponent will be left hanging in midair. He or she may have had a comeback ready for your comeback, and now can't use it! What can the individual do?

When you compare having the last word with these alternatives, you see that you increase your odds of "winning" with one of the controlled responses. Often the unspoken word keeps you out of an argument which could spoil the rest of your day. All considered, having the last word isn't that important.

5.4 Eight Tried-and-Tested Principles of the Art of Persuasion

If you can get people to willingly do something extra or go out of their way for you, you probably are good at persuading. Skill in persuading is invaluable when working with and leading people.

You can acquire the skill of getting people to agree with you, accept your thinking, and willingly cooperate. Here are eight principles of the art of persuasion you should practice to become adept at it:

How to Do It

1. Be honest and sincere. Say why you want something. Never conceal the fact when *you* have something to gain from what you're proposing. Practice "telling it like it is" to bolster and maintain your credibility.

2. Soft-pedal your approach. Recognize that you may be asking people to agree that you know more than they do, or that you are right and they are wrong. Expect to run into resistance occasionally and be prepared to counter it tactfully and discreetly.

3. Be logical and practical. State the facts that prompted your request rather than expect your listeners to be aware of these facts and reach the same conclusions from them. A methodical manner of attacking a problem shows that you are in command of the situation.

4. Stress the positive consequences of your requests. Point out how your listeners will benefit from what you propose. Call attention to the fact that good results will come from doing the right thing and bad results from doing the wrong thing.

5. Act as expected of a leader. People are more easily persuaded by an individual who has led and directed projects before, who knows the ropes, and who has a reputation for success as a leader.

6. Be patient. Give people time to think about what you are saying or suggesting, especially when you are selling a new idea or a different way of doing a job. Agreement or compliance that is reached slowly is better than none at all.

7. Avoid a demanding and assertive tone. It puts people on the defensive. You do not want people to feel that they are being forced into something or that they have little choice in the matter.

8. Recognize emotion and its importance. Concede before you contend. Listen before you talk. People are more easily persuaded after they have had a chance to have their say and get things off their chests. Allow time for emotion to drain away before you try to persuade with reason and logic.

5.5 Listen if You Want to Persuade

You will be much better at persuasion if you are a good listener. The supervisor who knows his or her people—their worries, ambitions, habits, and touchy points—comes to appreciate why they behave as they do and what motives stir them. The best and fastest way to know them is to encourage them to talk freely, without fear of ridicule or disapproval, and be a good listener. Listening to people enables you to understand how they feel on a subject, whether or not you feel the same way. Never dominate a conversation or meeting by doing all the talking yourself if you want to find out where your people stand. When you understand people, you know the best way to go about persuading them.

Listening is a key step when you have a problem to solve and need to sell people on its solution.

How-to-Do-It: Present and discuss the problem with the people who will be involved. *Listen* to the pros and cons until someone suggests the answer that you had reached when you first became aware of the problem. "That sounds good," you say, "but how do we go about it?" Lead them to the answer you've already reached, letting them think it's *their* idea. They'll make it work, and you will have done an excellent job of persuasion unbeknown to them.

5.6 How to Set an Example as a Means of Persuading

Your persuasion will carry more impact if you are already doing what you're asking of someone else. The following of company rules and procedures, for example, should always be your policy.

How-to-Do-It: If company rules limit coffee breaks to just two a day, be sure that you never exceed that. Wear your safety glasses in the work areas where you expect and ask your people to do so. Never run, even when you are being called for long distance phone calls. And don't smoke in the no-smoking areas.

You can set an example in many ways to help you persuade people to do or not do something. Having a good attitude undoubtedly has an effect on people and helps when the workload is heavy and pressure is on to get things done. Attitude, like enthusiasm, tends to rub off and influence how people think and act. If people know you are honest, sincere, and always try to do the right thing, they take this into consideration when you ask for something. If you are cooperative and friendly, people will find it difficult to treat you otherwise.

Optimists are usually winners, and this is generally recognized. People are more easily persuaded by someone who looks at things positively, sees opportunity, and isn't easily discouraged. If you set and live up to high standards for your organization, your people are more likely to follow your good example.

5.7 Making Your Presence Do Things for You

Despite your skill at motivation and your dedication to increasing the productivity of your people, you will now and then find that some of them are not doing their best work or the amount they are capable of. In addition, you will frequently be faced with the problem of how to get some people to reduce their idle time and work more efficiently.

Discussing their inadequate performance with them should be your first step to getting them to change for the better. In many cases you may be successful with this, but the better performance may last only a short time. You need to do something else to solve the problem.

Successful supervisors have learned that their presence is often all that is needed to keep people on the job and not abuse personal time allowances. The way to do this most effectively is to faithfully and frequently visit the work areas. You'll be showing an interest in your people, keeping up-to-date on job progress, and quickly getting a jump on problems which arise with the work. The supervisor who sits in the office much of the time can't stay on top of the job and know that his or her people are getting out the work.

5.8 How to Refuse Tactfully

Although you know you may be better accepted and that people will probably like you more if you always agree with them, you simply cannot do that. A supervisor often has to say no to a simple request, turn down a suggestion, or refuse an offer.

People do not like to be refused or told they cannot do something. Everyone believes they are right in their thinking and that what they ask for is not unreasonable. They expect a yes answer and are disappointed when they don't get it. They may be argumentative when you say no, so you must try to soften your refusal. You can refuse someone tactfully if you try.

How-to-Do-It: The best way to handle a refusal is to give it with honesty and understanding, using the kindest words you know. Never let someone leave you with your no answer without learning exactly why you felt you had to give it. Explain your feeling and your position.

Try to leave a way out for the person you're refusing. Acknowledge the good thinking behind it, and agree that it is reasonable to feel the way the person does. Offer to help by looking for a solution to the problem. Perhaps someone else can do what is being asked of you.

It never pays to trample a person with a flat no. Everyone has some dignity which should be considered. Be kind and wear a smile when you must say no.

5.9 Disagreeing Agreeably: How the "Pros" Do It

The ability to disagree agreeably—that is, without offending, irritating, or disturbing—is a valuable attribute to supervisors who have to periodically disagree with people yet retain their interest and cooperation. You can learn how to disagree pleasantly. Here's how the "pros" do it:

● Avoid words that show you are strongly of the opposite opinion or that the other person is wrong. Such words often cause people to defend themselves vehemently and become angry. Simply state the person's viewpoint accurately and fairly while you contrast it with your own.

● After careful listening, agree to the other person's logic. Point out the areas where you agree. You can probably accept at least part of a person's thinking—mention that. If you elaborate on areas of disagreement, you promote antagonism and appear to be argumentative.

● Appeal to the facts. Repeat those which led to your position and thinking. Bring to light as much evidence as possible to back you up.

● Stick with the issue at hand. Never bring up previous disagreements, past mistakes, or personalities.

● Maintain your composure and keep your cool. Smile when you discuss the issue. Avoid giving an impression of being demanding or stubborn.

● Admit you could be wrong but ask the other person to go along with you just this one time.

● Bring up indirection. Suggest another use for the person's idea or how the person's suggestion would be good for solving a different problem.

Case-in-Point: One of my supervisors early in my career was a whiz at turning down my suggestions without discouraging me. Harry Viergutz, Chief Chemist for The Milwaukee Road, would answer, for example, "That's good thinking. We can probably do that with the study we're going to make on that new steel we intend to use on axles. I don't think the idea will work on this study because . . ." Another comment I remember him making was, "I bet the boys in the research lab could use your idea."

5.10 Proven Ways of Developing Credibility

Supervisors who are effective at persuasion usually are reliable and dependable. They have also acquired a following of people who work with and for them. In a few words: they have credibility. Since they are respected and admired, they are easily able to persuade people to their way of thinking.

To be effective on the job, you must have credibility. Top-notch supervisors acquire it over a period of time on the job. You can do it too.

How-to-Do-It

1. Be consistent in how you treat people and predictable in what you do and say. People like to know that you will act and respond today the same as you did yesterday.

2. Show stability and a capability of controlling your emotions. Especially hold your temper in check. Be steady and constant in your efforts.

3. Be loyal to your people and your company. Carry out your promises by doing things when and how you said you would. Follow through on your plans and programs, particularly those that concern your people.

4. Recognize obstacles and work out ways to overcome them. Solve problems in a realistic and practical manner. Have convictions and face the truth. Don't hedge when you're on the spot.

5. Make yourself available for advice and help. Be aware of people and their feelings. Communicate this to them. Show empathy and sympathy. Be a friend.

6. Maintain your health and your appearance. Have clean thoughts and a high standard of decency and morale. Show faith and trust. Be a model of integrity.

Supervisors with credibility have an easy time on the job because they get along well with almost everyone. They seldom have a problem persuading others to agree with them or to do something.

5.11 Tested Answers to the Problems of Procrastinating

People procrastinate most often when they are faced with a difficult decision or have an unpleasant job to do. All of us are guilty of it to some degree at one time or another. Supervisors are no exception, nor are people on the job.

You can overcome the problem of procrastination by taking pride in your work and developing confidence in your abilities. Realizing that many situations are not as bad as they may seem also helps to beat procrastination. Decide early that you cannot continue to put off something indefinitely.

Although getting started on a distasteful job is not an easy matter, your best bet is to go after the job when you are fresh and in a good mood. Once you start, stay with it until you finish. This saves facing the unpleasantness a second time.

One approach to the problem is to apply self-psychology. Imagine yourself doing the job and succeeding without difficulty. Such thinking can inflate your ego so that your fear of failing or running into trouble is much less. You can literally talk yourself into starting the job.

What about solving the procrastination problem of other people? Effective supervisors have found three ways to go about this: minimize the distastefulness or difficulty of the job, calm their fear of failure, and bolster their confidence in themselves. Asking a person who is procrastinating if you can help will sometimes also get action.

6

HOW EFFECTIVE
SUPERVISORS HANDLE
PEOPLE

EXPERIENCED supervisors know that they need to be accepted by their people in order to be successful. They work with and treat their people accordingly, recognizing that each person they communicate with is different and responds differently to their direction.

You must know people and how they think if you expect to be able to handle them. A knowledge of emotion and morale, and what to do about them are requisites to getting along with others. Being patient and tactful pays off, and if you are also adept at gaining the confidence of people, you should be effective in handling them.

Everyone makes a mistake now and then. Supervisors who are skilled in remedying them as well as learning from them can reduce the number of mistakes that are made and their seriousness.

Criticism may be called for and should be given when an employee's work is not satisfactory or adequate. Effective supervisors are able to handle this unpleasant task without difficulty proving that adeptness in the art of criticizing is a valuable asset when handling people.

6.1 Understanding People: Why They Act as They Do

Your job is easier if you understand people because you know how they feel and what to expect of them. You can be prepared to handle most of the people problems that face you on the job. Thus, a supervisor who knows a bit about human relations and psychology usually gets along better with people than someone who hasn't had such education. Understanding what makes people tick can be learned outside the classroom. Here is some insight on why people act as they do.

If you wonder why a person sometimes acts strangely or doesn't do what you expect, look for the results of the person's action for the answer. People act the way they think they should act in a particular situation at that time. Their upbringing and their previous experiences account for much of what they say and do.

People usually will not try harder on a job unless they feel they are accomplishing something. If the job is difficult, they are more likely to become frustrated or discouraged than motivated to greater effort. Search for the incentive in what they are trying to do. If it is weak or nonexistent, you can expect the task will be difficult and not easily accomplished.

Praise for what has been accomplished helps to motivate people to further accomplishment. Criticism tends to demotivate, unless it is constructive and encouraging. Discipline is similar to criticism in that the way it is administered determines the effect it has. When people know they are appreciated they tend to justify that appreciation.

People are usually perceptive in knowing what you expect of them and how you think they will do on the job. If you expect them to do well they most likely will. If you don't have confidence in them, they will not try as hard.

Case-in-Point: Years ago a personnel manager told me about an incident involving two workers whom he transferred to a new department because they became surplus when a process was discontinued. The foreman losing the men praised them to their new foreman, saying "you're getting two good workers, Clark and Jackson. They have good attitudes and don't shirk on the job." As a result, their new foreman welcomed them and by his treatment of them the first few days in the department, led them to believe that he thought highly of them and expected them to be good workers. Confirming his expectation, they did very well on their new jobs.

When the two foremen met at a social function with the personnel manager a few months later, the subject of how Clark and Jackson were doing came up. The first foreman then admitted that he had sensed reluctance of the second foreman to accept Clark and Jackson so had made up the story of their good performance. The two men had been far from outstanding in the work they had done for him but he didn't want them to lose their jobs with the company.

6.2 Patience Usually Pays Off

Although you may find it difficult to do nothing when something is not happening as fast as you think it should, you'll find that being patient usually pays off. What you must be wary of is impulsive behavior; you must avoid feeling that you've waited long enough.

Mistakes are sometimes made when supervisors are in too much of a hurry. Unfortunately, the supervisor who acts too soon often doesn't learn that if he or she had been patient, the objective would have been reached. Consequently, many people don't feel that impatience is a fault. Even when they acknowledge it, impatient people find it difficult to change.

One way to develop the attribute of patience is to try to make decisions by logic rather than by emotions. The use of logic requires more thinking. Before you make a decision, stop for a moment to determine whether you reached it through reason or emotion. Better decisions result from reason.

When dealing with people, another way of thinking is to realize that each person has a different rate of learning, understanding, and taking action. Also, training takes time and habits are hard to break. People get nervous when they're pushed too much; they may also become antagonistic if they feel they are being asked to do what they feel is impossible.

You can be more patient with people by trying to see matters from their viewpoint. Learn to be tolerant with those who don't have your education and training. Confirm to yourself that impatience is a liability by noting that a person who is impatient with the rate of learning of another confuses the learner and may even drive that person to quit trying altogether. Recognize that a leader who pushes people to get work done faster may bring on resentment and even a slowdown.

6.3 Guidelines to How to Get People to Accept You

The most successful supervisors have the confidence of their people because people on the job generally do better when they respect and accept their leaders. When you are accepted, people go along and cooperate with you.

You cannot force people to accept you—you earn acceptance. The way you work with people, the things you say and do, determine how much you are accepted.

Here Are Some Guidelines on How to Get Acceptance

• Make people feel they are working *with* you rather than *for* you. You can do this by asking for help rather than by *demanding* it, by acting as a member of the team and contributing your share.

• Give people the best break you can on work assignments. If you have a choice of several ways to get a job done, pick the one which the people involved would prefer. Look for human rather than material answers to problems. Plan work projects to make them easy on people.

● Be fair and tolerant. Avoid favoritism when assigning work. Show that you are not biased or prejudiced by treating people equally.

● Have high morals and follow the rules. Know right from wrong and behave accordingly. Be loyal. Put the interest of your people and your company ahead of your own.

● Always keep your promises. Be reliable. People will learn that they can depend on you to correct a bad situation or solve a problem if it's possible for you to do so.

● Avoid being cold and aloof. Show that you like people. Become knowledgeable in their interests. Join in conversations. Don't be all business all of the time.

Caution: Telling people they are doing fine when they really are not doesn't help them or you. You mislead people if you don't express your true feelings. Worse, when people realize that you don't always mean what you say, they soon doubt everything you say no matter how you say it. You've got to be honest with people.

6.4 Sure-Fire Ways to Bring About Better Employee Performance

Supervisors play key roles in how employees work and the quantity of their output. This is to be expected since supervisors participate in training and instructing, assigning jobs, and guiding.

Successful supervisors get good performance from their people because they know the best ways to treat them, some of which are simply application of common sense. Good human relations and a cooperative approach to the work promote interest and reduce tension, both of which help people to do their work without taking shortcuts or being careless. Then, too, people are just naturally more conscientious and efficient if they feel their company represented by the supervisor is interested in their welfare and job satisfaction.

Case-in-Point: The Eastern Central Motor Carriers Association, with offices in Cuyahoga Falls, Ohio, does well in this respect. Don Leyland, office manager, says, "We don't have a set time for coffee breaks, so people can decide for themselves when they want to take a break. The company furnishes coffee-making facilities and a refrigerator for soft drinks. An office committee handles ordering supplies, paying for them, and preparing the coffee. Payments are made on the honor system, and the profits from the operation go toward an employee picnic in the summer."

Companies which try to have their employees get satisfaction from their work usually get better performance from them. For example, it pays for a company to renovate and remodel. Although industrial engineers knowledgeable in material handling and process flow can achieve higher production rates by making changes and modernizing the plant or office, much of the better performance of employees is psychologically rather than physically related to the change. Employees notice when management is concerned with their comfort and ease of performing the work. High lumen lighting helps avoid eyestrain, especially when the lights are placed so there are no shadows. The liberal use of colors, particularly the pastels, also contributes to efficiency. Color makes people more alert to their surroundings as well as less fatigued after several hours on the job.

Supervisors can promote efficiency and reduce frustration by pushing their people on housekeeping and cleaning of work areas, and the putting of tools and supplies in their places. A well-designed office has an adequate number of files and cabinets. Supervisors should see that their people use them rather than leave work material on desks and tables.

Case-in-Point: "Retrieval of records is faster and easier when they are properly filed," says Lynn Thompson, supervisor in an insurance office in Chicago. "We had one girl in the communications department who frequently left dockets on her desk at the end of the day. After the processing people had trouble finding specific dockets the next day, we talked to the girl about it. We seldom fail to be able to put our hands on a specific docket at any time now."

6.5 How to Be a Good Coach

The development of subordinates is a major supervisory responsibility, and coaching is a basic part of employee development. Just as in a sporting event, coaching is observing behavior and providing feedback which is both immediate and specific. If you are concerned with efficiency as well as with getting work done, you can easily help each of your people with their work problems. Here are ten ways by which you can be a good coach:

1. When one of your people undertakes a major project, track the individual's progress by first having him or her agree with you on the feedback system you will use.

2. When someone seems to be attacking a problem incorrectly, try to find out if he or she clearly understands the problem, and then help the individual to get back on the right track.

3. When you notice someone wasting time on unimportant details, explain to the individual what you have observed, and then suggest how to set priorities to make better use of time.

4. When a person is slowed on a job by a roadblock, discuss it with him or her and encourage the person to find a way to get around it.

5. When you see someone struggling with a particular job, let the person continue working at the job but stand by ready to give advice or help if requested.

6. When an individual proposes something that you know won't work, discuss the idea sincerely, point out the problem, and encourage the individual to modify his or her proposal.

7. When someone's attitude irritates the people he or she works with, discuss this with him or her, show what is happening and suggest ways for the individual to handle the problem.

8. When an individual's reports are not satisfactory, identify the failing or weakness in the reports and then suggest how they might be improved.

9. When a person needs to make considerable improvement, measure his or her performance on a graph and then use it as a training tool with the person.

10. When one of your people shows significantly improved performance, recognize this achievement immediately rather than waiting for the regularly scheduled appraisal meeting.

6.6 Tactfulness Pays off in Handling People

A successful supervisor understands people and knows how to get along with them. If you want to do the same, you must be perceptive to the feelings of people and be skillful in what you say to them. This specific skill is referred to as being tactful.

Being tactful enables you to talk and deal with people without offending them or turning them off. Although you may always try to be tactful, you may not always be completely successful. For example, highly educated and technically trained people may neglect this personal factor in their zeal and strive toward a group objective. Their failing to be tactful shows when they are abrupt or critical and when they have little if any patience with others who haven't their education or training. If you sense that you may have that problem, at least with some people, decide now on a self-improvement program.

How-to-Do-It: Ask your boss for help and advice. He or she will level with you and help you come across better with people. Your problem may be as simple as an annoying mannerism which you are not aware of.

You can practice tact on the job in many ways. Here are a few manners you can adopt to your advantage if you haven't already done so.

Put yourself in the other fellow's place when you ask for something. Will the fellow benefit from doing what you ask? Look for how and mention it. Is the fellow interested and concerned about the outcome? If you explain and give reasons for your request, you may create an interest.

Requests to do something are always better than orders to do so. Orders should be given only in emergencies or when immediate action is needed.

Asking for volunteers is even better and avoids putting a burden on someone who particularly dislikes what you're asking for.

Be slow to criticize or find fault—avoid doing it at all, if possible. If you must speak about an error or omission, find out what happened and how it can be prevented from happening again rather than placing blame on someone.

A positive and optimistic attitude helps in being tactful, especially when you talk with people about jobs and their work. Knowing people's likes and dislikes also makes it easier to be kind and considerate. Recognize that people think and act differently, one from another. Expect people to have different opinions than yours so that you are not surprised when you hear them and are at a loss as to what to say.

A tactful person makes good use of the words *please* and *thank you*. Add them to your vocabulary and watch for the effect they have on people.

6.7 Ten Ways to Promote Good Morale

Since the morale of people on the job affects their performance, supervisors must constantly try to maintain and improve it. Good morale means a healthy, optimistic, and positive attitude toward the job, the company, and life in general. When employees have good morale, the quality and quantity of their work meets or exceeds their supervisor's expectations.

"Good morale should begin with management, and one of the best ways to get it is to give every employee a feeling of participation in what's going on," says Earl G. Dobbins, Water and Sewer Administrator, city of Savannah, Georgia. Effective supervisors promote and sustain the morale of their people.

Here Are Ten Ways in Which They Do It

1. Treat each person as an individual distinct from others. Call each person by his or her name and provide each with the maximum rank and status possible.

2. Make it easy for people to communi ate. Have them feel they can talk to you about their problems and troubles at any time. Keep people informed. Speak to them as you would want them to speak to you.

3. Fight constantly against monotony. Boredom results from a dull routine. Vary people's assignments if you can, and show them something new occasionally.

4. Be sure people have all the information they need to do a good job. Let them know of changes that may affect them. Answer rumors quickly.

Case-in-Point: When the Pentagon announced an Air Force budget cut a few years ago, employees at one plant in the industry began to worry about their jobs. To handle the problem, the company president set up two bulletin boards in the work area. One board he labeled RUMOR, the other FACT. On the RUMOR board anyone could write down the current gossip and the president would promptly print the facts concerning it on the FACT board. Within two months, the president had answered about 100 questions; tension dropped and morale climbed.

5. Recognize good effort and achievement. Let people know how they are doing but avoid comparing their performance with others. Appraise frequently—being ignored is worse than being criticized.

6. Encourage talent and skill. Promote suggestions and creativity. Show an interest in people and their work. Compliment good performance and extra effort. Use words that show respect.

7. Be tactful and kind when correcting or criticizing. Be considerate. Work at having your words accepted. Avoid harsh, caustic remarks.

8. Provide good working conditions. Strive for efficient work methods. Try to eliminate unpleasant tasks and drudgery. Be concerned with the safety and health of people. Assume responsibility for what happens to them.

9. Give as much authority and responsibility as positions and skills permit. Pay fairly, consistent with output and accomplishment, and reward for extra contributions.

10. Promote enthusiasm. Maintain a cheerful, friendly atmosphere to make work less stressful.

6.8 High Morale: How It Pays Off

Your success as a supervisor will depend most of all on the cooperation and support you get from your people. If they are solidly behind you in working toward your department's goals, you will succeed. One of the requisites for cooperation and support is that your people have a high level of morale. Here's how that high morale pays off:

- You can depend and rely on them to do what is necessary when you're not on hand to advise and guide them.
- You will be in a better position to develop someone to take your place when you're ready to be promoted.
- They will display a lot of interest in and enthusiasm for their work. This will result in a high productivity and efficiency.
- They will feel obligated to see you through tough situations; they may even make personal sacrifices in your behalf.
- They will be proud to hold a job in your department; they will show it by being loyal to you.

If the people in your department who are important to you have feelings of good morale, they will respond in a way that will make your job much easier.

6.9 The Problem of Emotion: Proven Answers to It

In working with people, you will frequently find that emotion rather than reason is behind a person's action. If you hope to change a decision or get cooperation on a matter with an emotional person, you'll have to allow for the emotion in what you say and do.

Supervisors with many years of experience usually have learned how to work with emotional people. They know what words they should and shouldn't use when trying to persuade a person, and they know how to talk to someone without causing resentment or anger. In a nutshell, they know how to "handle" people.

You will find that most of the expressed emotions of people are minor in nature and easily dealt with. Once you are aware of them, you can act and talk accordingly. For example, some workers object to their supervisor *telling* them to do something rather than *asking* them to do it. Others don't want to hear, "*I* want it done this way." It the supervisors would say *we* rather than *I*, the workers would be more willing to cooperate.

You may irritate some individuals if you overgeneralize or exaggerate. Words like, "You *always* do things the hard way," or "You drinking coffee *again?*" tend to make people resentful. Being specific when referring to acts and deeds is a better way to get your point across.

It's also wise to avoid extremes in words. Seldom is something all bad or all good, all black or all white; people are not completely satisfied or completely dissatisfied. Between extremes lies a large area, one where most conditions are found. If you are moderate in the words you use, you are less likely to be challenged.

Try to separate facts from opinions when getting into discussions. Also, be slow to respond if you are not sure of what a person's words mean. Heated discussions usually develop when people are quick to contradict or disagree, when they don't take time to think and consider the other person's viewpoint.

Occasionally a supervisor is faced with working with a person who displays extreme emotions. How to get along with such a person is answered in Chapter 17.

6.10 The Importance of Controlling Your Temper

Anybody who works with people is going to get involved periodically in situations that put his or her temper to the test. You would not be normal if you didn't have this emotion. Yet if you can't control your temper, you don't have control of your other emotions. And, more importantly, you don't have complete control of your job. If holding your temper goes against your natural inclinations, you will have a problem sooner or later which will get you into real trouble.

There are several good reasons why you should avoid losing your temper:

● People judge your stability and maturity by how easily you become angry, what you become angry about, and how long your anger lasts.

● When you are angry, you lose control of yourself. You look and act foolish.

● What you say and do in anger you frequently regret later.

● Although some people take lightly what a person says in anger, many do not. Sensitive people are sometimes hurt and slow to recover.

The ability to control your temper is particularly necessary if you associate closely with people and depend on them for what you accomplish and how successful you are on the job. Anger destroys enthusiasm and weakens cooperation. Nobody likes to work with an angry person, much less help or do something extra for him or her. Even though some people may change what they say or do to appease you, they do this reluctantly, perhaps even with displeasure.

Anger is of little value except perhaps in prompting certain types of action. But there are better ways to accomplish this end.

6.11 How to Criticize Constructively

Criticizing is one of the most unenjoyable tasks a supervisor has to perform. Nobody likes to be criticized and few people like to criticize others. Supervisors should know how to criticize constructively to save hurting people and to have them benefit from it.

Getting all the facts is a prerequisite to criticizing. If you ask for facts and listen instead of talk, you are more likely to get the information you need to do the job right as well as avoid giving criticism which may not be justified.

To criticize constructively, direct the criticism at the task, not the person. Constructive criticism builds and instructs. It does not tear down. The trick to doing a good job of criticizing is not to belittle but to improve.

Criticism should be given without offending and in a manner which *you* would accept if *you* were being criticized; the person you criticize should feel that you are trying to help. If you do it properly, you will not cause hurt nor will the person feel you are overstepping your bounds. Criticizing a person for a failure is permissible, and even wise, *if equal consideration is given to the person's success*. This may be the only way the person knows he is being recognized.

Caution: Criticism should be directed at employees who have the ability and potential to do better. Don't waste your time criticizing a person whose performance is hopeless. Look for another job for that person.

6.12 Keep Your Criticism Positive and Productive

To most employees, criticizing implies finding fault, especially with work methods or intentions. Yet there are times when criticizing people is unavoidable. Supervisors must recognize that since it is one of their responsibilities, they must know how to do it effectively. Here are some suggestions on how to make your criticism sessions both positive and productive:

- *Watch the timing.* It can be the difference between success and failure. The best time to criticize seems to be in the morning. People may be touchy late in the day because of fatigue.
- *Get to the point quickly.* Avoid small talk and unnecessary preliminaries. While this approach may seem cold and unsympathetic, any other way only increases both your and the person's anxiety.
- *Make improvement your goal.* The objective of criticism is to change behavior through mutual agreement and complete understanding. Communication must be a two-way procedure with both parties discussing the problem and reaching agreement on how it can be solved.
- *Be accurate, yet tactful.* Avoid using words like *always, never,* and *completely.* Not only are you probably inaccurate when you use such words, but you also are likely to arouse justifiable resentment. Other taboos are phrases like *you don't understand, you don't think,* and *you're apparently unaware that . . .*
- *Don't evaluate.* Instead, describe what has happened. Evaluation tends to make a person hostile while a descriptive statement leads to a positive and factual assessment of the situation. The latter makes the person more willing to handle the problem.
- *Say that your criticism is meant to help.* Point out that everybody makes mistakes, but that a person is more likely to benefit from them if they are called to the person's attention.
- *Avoid overcriticizing.* The best way to do this is to keep your criticism simple and direct. Talk about only one serious behavioral problem at a session, and never criticize several weaknesses or indiscretions at the same time.

6.13 Expert Insight on the Art of Criticizing

Most people know when they deserve criticism. Often an individual expects to be criticized and is surprised if it doesn't happen. But whether or not an individual expects it, you must be the one to decide how and when to do it. Above all, you must be sure that it is necessary.

Successful supervisors are skilled in the art of criticizing. If you asked for their insight and advice on how to do it, here's what they would tell you:

1. Your effectiveness is determined by your manner. Losing your temper, being sarcastic, and acting disgusted are crude ways of criticizing. Never lower yourself to such levels. Criticize without being emotional. A calm, helping tone softens criticism and gets a better response besides.

2. Always criticize in private to avoid embarrassment. Everyone has some pride; you accomplish nothing by attacking it. The people you criticize will be thankful to you if you show respect and consideration for them and their feelings.

3. Give reasons why a person's actions or deeds are unacceptable. Suggest correct and better ways to do things and offer to help the person learn them. Say that you know the person can do better.

4. Be positive with your admonition and advice. Stress the value of the right way of doing things.

5. Say something friendly and in an uplifting manner after you have criticized. Leave the person feeling that he or she has been helped.

6.14 Effective Ways to Handle On-the-Job Mistakes

Anyone who has a job to do is going to occasionally make a mistake. Making errors and mistakes is a human trait and happens to everyone. Although you can expect the people who work for you to make mistakes, what you do about those mistakes should be your main concern. You have some control over the frequency and severity of mistakes if you deal properly with them.

Supervisors are effective in dealing with mistakes when they adopt techniques which enable themselves and their people to learn from such errors. As a result, fewer and less serious mistakes are made in the future. You should investigate a mistake as soon after it occurs as possible because you may still be able to limit the loss or damage by corrective action. Determine a mistake's importance and significance first. You will then see how much time and effort you should put into contending with it. Plan to investigate every mistake you learn about; this is the only way to assure that something is done toward preventing reoccurrence.

Don't jump to conclusions when investigating. You may not learn the cause if you do. It's difficult, if not impossible, to take corrective action if you don't know the cause.

Always maintain your composure by being careful to not show resentment against someone who made an error. Remember that everybody makes mistakes. If you discuss the mistake with the person at fault, be sure your comments are constructive and also given in private. Avoid belittling or ridiculing.

The most important step of handling on-the-job mistakes is what you do after investigating them. Take positive steps to prevent reoccurrences.

6.15 How to Investigate a Mistake

There's a right way and a wrong way to investigate a mistake. Doing it the right way gives you a far better chance of learning the reason why the mistake was made and also avoids hard feelings.

The right way is to forgo personal references to the incident. Simply ask, "What happened?" This approach takes attention away from the person involved and directs it to the mistake itself.

How-to-Do-It: In the plant you might say, "This is the first accident we've had in this area—what happened?" In the office you might ask when investigating a misrouted order, "Are the address files up-to-date?" and then, "What happened?"

Facts alone should tell you what the problem is. Since many of the facts you need can be supplied only by the person who made the mistake, try to get them from him or her with the least friction.

Case-in-Point: Linda Ellis, office supervisor for Superior Products in Camden, N.J., says, "I'm always very careful about my girls' feelings when I check out a mistake. I know that the person who made the mistake is embarrassed and nervous, so I try to be calm, sympathetic, and reassuring in what I say. The girls know this, so they seldom try to cover up an error and I can easily get the facts. As a result, we can usually do something to prevent the mistake being made again."

Caution: Mistakes are serious matters. Even though you may treat them as inevitable, never be flippant about them. If you let down on investigating mistakes you may give the impression that you are also willing to accept other breaches of performance of people on the job.

6.16 Making the Best Out of Mistakes

Everyone is embarrassed when a mistake is made. But that should not keep a person from doing something about it afterward. You may as well make the best out of a mistake.

It's wise to be quick to admit a mistake if you actually made it. People learn about a mistake sooner or later, and they don't readily accept evasion on such matters.

Try to remedy the mistake quickly, even if you have to put aside something else you're doing. Correct the mistake now, not tomorrow. You can show your concern by apologizing to the person who is affected, whether or not you are guilty. Trying to do something for the person to make up for the mistake is also a good gesture on your part.

A supervisor should maintain prestige and reputation by treating mistakes as rare occurrences when talking about them with other people. Putting up a good front can psychologically help to prevent mistakes by assuring people they are capable of performing error-free work.

7

SUPERVISORY DECISIONMAKING: HOW THE "PROS" DO IT

BEING decisive is a valuable attribute of a supervisor. When making decisions, he or she carries out the leadership responsibility of the job, while at the same time providing assurance and confidence to employees to go ahead with their work without fear. Motivation to action is behind any decision. The skill of making decisions under pressure must be developed if the supervisor is to be effective.

To be decisive you need insight and determination. You must want to solve problems and have the confidence to do so. Knowing how and when decisions should be made is basic to the art. Along with being familiar with the theory of making judgments, a decision-maker must be aware of the many factors which influence decisions and their relative importance. But, most of all, you need facts and information to work with.

What distinguishes a good decision from a bad one? What are the causes of poor decisions? How do you resolve a bad one? When supervisors know the answers to such questions they are better qualified to make good decisions.

7.1 Being Decisive: Tips on How to Go About It

Reluctance to make a decision can handicap a supervisor. People on the job expect their leaders to be decisive and in control. Workers become fearful, uneasy, and even unwilling to proceed when they sense that the supervisor is unsure of what direction to go and what move to make. A decisive supervisor commands respect and gets action.

You can learn to be decisive by being definite in how you handle your responsibilities. Once you get into the swing of it, you'll find it easy to hold to the pattern.

The Ways to Go About It Are as Follows

1. Make minor decisions promptly. Disposing of them quickly gives you more time to devote to matters that are really important.

2. Be solid and firm when you make a decision. Don't be half-sure or leave any doubt of your intentions.

3. Forget the alternatives once you make a decision. Don't waste time thinking about what you could or should have done.

4. Dispel any thoughts that you might make a mistake. Such thinking weakens your resolution to be decisive.

5. Carry out your decisions promptly. Until you take action, nothing happens and you aren't decisive.

7.2 The Need for Facts to Make Good Decisions

Successful decision-makers thrive on facts—they can't make decisions without them. This is a good point to remember the next time you are faced with an important decision. What do you need to know? What's been the practice with this type of problem? Who is involved? When must the decision be made? To make good decisions you must have the answers to questions such as these.

Case-in-Point: Rapidly increasing costs have caused managers' and supervisors' attention to be focused on maintenance activities in many of today's plants, particularly in the process industries where maintenance is a large variable in product cost. As a result, researchers at Louisiana State University decided to involve a management system for maintenance to assist all levels of management in decision-making. The initial objectives of this system, which were widely applicable to many types and sizes of process industries, included:

● Keeping historical records of all maintenance activities and accumulating labor and material costs for each facility.

● Providing schedules to initiate work orders for all requirements.

● Generating management reports describing costs, labor performance, resource utilization, and, in general, all other control reports which would aid in the management of a maintenance system.

The management system which resulted from the researchers' work helps managers and supervisors in maintenance departments to make good decisions. Supervisors often have trouble making decisions because their people throw problems at them without the facts. With little or no information to work with, a supervisor must dig and look into a problem at length before he or she can make a judgment. A Midwestern manufacturing manager wasn't pleased with the amount of time he had to spend this way and also felt he might overlook some facts relevant to a specific problem. His approach: he requires assistants to report *why* something is wrong in addition to *what*—and to suggest at least two possible solutions. With sufficient facts then available, he is able to initiate immediate and appropriate action or recognize the need for delay.

7.3 Insight to When and How Decisions Should Be Made

How can a supervisor decide when to act and when to leave a condition well enough alone? Even though a major responsibility of your job is to make decisions, sometimes the best decision you can make is to take no action.

Experienced supervisors have learned to distinguish between a real problem that requires action and a condition or situation that merely rubs them the wrong way. Before they act they consider a situation from several angles realizing that they can make better decisions through insight. You should follow such practices.

For example, make sure a problem is yours before you try to handle it—you might be assuming a responsibility that belongs to someone else. Approach a problem with the attitude of what you can do and how you can help, not how you're going to use your authority to get matters straightened out.

Resist being impulsive. Give your insight power a chance to work. Refrain from a startling or radical decision; save it for an emergency or crisis situation. If you feel you must act on a matter, direct your attention to prevention rather than cure. Work on the cause of a problem rather than the correction of it.

Insight will help you to avoid making important decisions when you're under pressure or stress; with insight, you'll be aware that you can make the best decision when you are calm and have time to think.

Supervisors who are adept at making decisions have certain attributes which help to make them successful. You can acquire those attributes through a program of self-discipline and using insight.

Here Is What You Should Do

1. Be active in seeking out problems rather than waiting for them to come to you. Develop an insight toward conditions and situations which should be changed.

2. Be knowledgeable and informed about your department, company, and industry. Know what the standard procedure is for handling certain problems.

3. Be quick at setting priorities. Understand the relationship between planning, scheduling, and implementing. Know your people and their capabilities.

4. Be creative and innovative. Find new and unique solutions to problems.

5. Be skilled at persuading and motivating people. See that your decisions are acted upon and carried out. Do a good job of following up.

7.4 Four Basic Steps to Making Decisions

You needn't have the experience of similar problems in order to make good decisions. You can make good decisions if you are not too hasty to act, get the facts, and take the time to think. Four basic steps are involved in making decisions.

First, be sure you understand the problem. Writing it down often helps to define it. The experts at problem-solving say you have gone most of the way to a decision if you have been able to clearly state the problem and what decision you have to make.

Second, look for all alternative answers. Get information and data. Talk to people to get their opinions and recommendations. Check the records. Examine the facts related to the problem and weigh them as to their importance.

Third, look at the good points and the bad points of each alternative. Will each alternative actually solve the problem? Are risks involved with some? What's wrong with what appears to be the best choice? An alternative which has a high degree of permanence as a characteristic may have the advantage of preventing a reoccurrence of the same or a similar problem.

Fourth, pick the best alternative as your decision. Take action and follow up to observe the results so that you have the experience to handle a similar problem in the future.

7.5 Decision Factors: Keys to Good Decisions

Experienced executives and managers know that many factors must be considered when making a decision. They have learned that the soundness of their decisions depends on whether they have given the proper weight to each of the factors they have considered.

What are the important factors when making decisions? You can be more sure of making a good decision if you go over the following checklist before you act.

- Is the decision clear and to the point? Does it leave any questions unanswered?

- Does the decision consider the risk involved and allow for it?
- If there are several steps to be taken, are they in the right order?
- Is the decision compatible with company rules and regulations?
- Has timing been considered? Is it optimum?
- Have authorized and interested personnel participated in the decision? Are they in agreement?
- Is the decision based on experience and history? Does it deviate from past practice?
- Will the expected results of the decision be acceptable to those who must carry it out?

If you find that your analysis of the problem doesn't include one or more of these factors, you should reconsider before you take action.

Case-in-Point: Bob Burke, Supervisor at Inland Steel in Indiana, deals with some rough-and-tough workers in his department. He feels that he must be especially careful in making disciplinary decisions. He said that before he does anything, he always asks himself three questions about his proposed decision. They are:

1. Have I made a decision based upon my best judgment or based upon the authority I have?
2. Will this particular decision be good as a general rule for everyone? Would I even want it applied to myself?
3. Would I make this same decision if I knew it would be publicized around the company? In other words, would I be willing to defend the decision in another department?

7.6 Understanding Decision-Making: Causes of Poor Decisions

Understanding what's involved in making decisions is of value because it will lessen the pressure on you when you must make a decision. By knowing the factors which affect decision-making, you can also improve your skill at supervising.

To learn the reasons why some supervisors are unable to consistently make good decisions, I consulted some industrial executives and managers. They told me that you, as a supervisor, can get in trouble with decisions because of one or more of the following:

- Insufficient or poor information to work with. Lack of information leads to guessing—you may guess wrong. Bad information leads to false conclusions—you decide wrongly.

- Not enough time to decide. If you have more time to get facts and consider them, you increase your chance to make a wise decision.
- Fear of the situation and the consequence of the decision. If you are scared and lack confidence, your decisions may be adversely affected.
- Concern with risk. You may be overcautious when the risk is great.
- Not enough authority. Responsibility without authority leads to weak, unenforceable decisions.
- Low importance. If you consider a matter not serious, you may not give it enough attention or ignore it entirely.
- Emotion. Emotions are behind bias and prejudice. Poor decisions often result when emotion rather than reason dictates.

7.7 How to Develop Snap Judgment

Supervisors sometimes unexpectedly find themselves in stressful situations which require them to come up with quick decisions. To ask for time in these situations is impractical, and to make no decision is out of the question. They must make a snap judgment, and they must be right much more often than they are wrong.

Experienced managers, those who have had to make snap judgments many times, say that being right when making them requires that you be talented in two ways. One is to have a good memory and the other is to be able to apply that memory to the specific problem or situation existing.

To develop the skill of making snap judgments, you must be very knowledgeable on all the aspects of your job. Each bit of information you pick up relative to it may at some time be important. By remembering bits of data, you can call on your memory when you need to make a quick decision. Thus, it pays to always be inquisitive and curious about all facets of your job.

Studying subjects which could be related to your work can sometimes prepare you for a snap decision. This is understandable if you realize that such a search is simply a part of an intensive study of conditions over which you have control.

Perhaps the most productive way of developing your snap judgment skill is to try making quick decisions without applying them. Making judgments just for practice, and then observing what happens later, can sharpen your decisive skill for the actual snap judgments you will be required to make in the future.

Although there is no benefit and many disadvantages to making snap judgments when there is time to do a thorough and rational study, you will be a better decision-maker if you develop the ability to make them. You will also remove some of the stress from yourself because, sooner or later, you will be called upon to make a quick decision.

7.8 How to Stay on Top of Problems

It's understandable that you might become upset if you are continually faced with problems, but remember that problems don't affect or interrupt your work—they are your work. If you didn't have problems, you wouldn't be needed as a supervisor.

Supervisors who stay on top of problems are skilled in overcoming trouble, delays, and the various roadblocks that prevent jobs from running smoothly.

To follow in their footsteps, *here's what to do:*

1. Handle problems as promptly as possible. Any delay on your part simply aggravates matters, upsets people, and increases costs.

2. Know when and where your presence is likely to be needed. Try to be there. Learn to supervise several jobs at the same time.

3. Split your attention among your people so that none are neglected for long. If any person runs into a problem, you will soon know about it.

4. Practice preventive action by doing things which avoid problems. Anticipate trouble and take steps to prevent it. You will have fewer problems and more time to work on those you have.

Case-in-Point: Dick Ryan, Plant Engineer at Hamilton Standard in Windsor Locks, Connecticut, says, "When it comes to decision-making on plant equipment and layout, the maintenance factor has too often been left out. The first opportunity the maintenance people have to see the extent of a project—construction or simple installations of new or redesigned units—is usually after all decisions have been made. Then they are 'stuck' with fixing any problems which occur and learning new systems without knowing the designer's background or intentions." Think how much easier a maintenance supervisor's job could be if maintenance people were consulted during the design stage of engineering projects at a plant.

7.9 Tips on Being Logical When Solving Problems

Supervisors should always try to be logical when solving problems. Being logical means not letting bias, prejudice, habit, or instinct be a basis for thinking and judging. Although this may be easier said than done because people usually are not aware they are being influenced, letting facts alone be controlling will result in better decisions.

To be logical in making a decision, you must follow a plan and watch your steps along the way. You must test the facts on which you base your decision and not let emotions, hopes, desires, and fears be a part of your thought pattern.

Avoid the urge to come up with a quick answer such as the first one that comes to mind. Be able to trace how you reason. Consider all the facts which could have a bearing on a problem and be unwilling to discard a fact without giving it more than a cursory glance. Doing some tangential thinking is good in that it helps to deter impulsiveness while at the same time possibly exposes an alternative solution.

Caution: Examine carefully any solution which very much pleases you or which you feel you were expected to come up with. In the same vein, beware of a solution to a problem which seems too easy.

In a last analysis, be willing to accept a solution based on facts alone even though the conclusion may be unpleasant or disagreeable.

Case-in-Point: Periodically supervisors may be told by their superiors that they've got to cut costs on their operations. "You can't argue about something like that," said a supervisor to me a few years ago. "The word came down from my boss that my labor costs were too high. He had the figures for comparing my costs with those of another department doing similar work. Upper management suggested to him that a cut of 10 percent be made in the number of people in my department. Well, I tried to find other areas where I could reduce our costs, but we had already gone over that a few months before. I finally had to sit down with my boss and decide which two people in my department would have to leave."

7.10 Guidelines to the Level at Which a Decision Should Be Made

Supervisors are usually required to make several decisions during a day on the job. At times they may question whether a particular decision is theirs to make, whether it shouldn't be made at a higher level of management. They need guidelines to help them with this problem.

When determining the specific level of management at which a decision should be made, two principles should be followed:

1. The decision should be made at the lowest level in the organization consistent with the functions of management position. If the problem requiring a decision fits into the normal, everyday duties and responsibilities of the supervisor, he or she should make the decision.

2. The decision should be made at a level high enough to include consideration of all characteristics that affect it. If the decision is unusual, may have a great impact, involves qualitative factors, may be difficult to reverse, or has a high degree of permanence, a management person at a level higher than the supervisor should make the decision.

Case-in-Point #1: Complaints and grievances of employees should be handled as close to their source as possible because supervision and employees involved are the people most familiar with existing conditions. When a complaint or grievance is settled between the parties involved, it seldom leaves after-effects or lasting animosity.

Case-in-Point #2: An employee's request for a leave of absence at a time when the employee's help is sorely needed should be answered by a management person at a level higher than the supervisor. The request, if granted, could have an impact on the quality or quantity of the department output as well as bring up a question of management control of operations and personnel.

7.11 The Psychology Behind Decisions: How to Use It to Advantage

There's more to making a decision than just deciding. Most decisions that supervisors make involve people. You've got to consider their feelings and their reactions. Timing is another matter which should be thought out. One time to announce a decision or take action may be much better than another.

Successful supervisors use psychology in making decisions. They also check their hunches and intuitions; they hesitate to make a decision if they instinctively feel it isn't right. Their decisions are usually better and more readily accepted because of these practices.

Always consider the people involved in your decisions. Is your decision good from their viewpoint? Could you do better for them? Are you going to have an enforcement problem? If people can participate in your decision you will probably have better acceptance.

Wait, if possible, for the occasion when you are rested and relaxed when making an important decision. Realize that you are unable to think and reason well when you are tired or depressed.

Don't let other people force your decisions. There's a good chance they may be working for their benefit, not yours. Besides, you must feel that you are making the decision, not them.

If you must make a quick decision, continue to investigate the facts afterward. You will be prepared if you have to reverse the decision and be protecting yourself from unforeseen consequences.

Don't feel that you must announce a decision just because you have it made. Pick the best time and place for that. Doing this will give you a little extra time for second thoughts and to make arrangements for steps which will follow the announcement.

7.12 The Importance of Following Up

You can't just ask someone to handle a complex job, and then forget it. Some kind of follow-up is required for the best results. But it's surprising how many otherwise capable supervisors fall down at this crucial point. They think well, plan well, make a good decision, and assign work intelligently. Then they sit down in their offices and are surprised when things don't work out the way they planned.

Following up, carefully and methodically, to check on how a decision is actually working out isn't nearly as glamorous as planning it. But it happens to be an essential part of being an effective supervisor.

Astute supervisors let people alone to do a job. But having assigned the work, they don't simply disappear. They stay in touch and keep in control by following the progress of the job.

All they may do on routine jobs is to stop by now and then to make sure the employee hasn't run into any difficulties. On big or complex jobs, particularly those that last for several days, they may ask for progress and status reports to keep them posted on how things are going. But they always know the score and will immediately take action if it is not to their liking.

7.13 How to Resolve a Bad Decision

It's inevitable that at some time you're going to make a bad decision. Even the most experienced and successful supervisors do it. Although having to reverse or change your decision may be distasteful and also leave you feeling weak, you must do what you can to correct your mistake.

An important matter to be concerned about is that you don't make another bad decision when correcting the first one. Put forth extra effort and spend additional time, if necessary, to be sure this doesn't happen.

When you are considering reversing a decision, get some help and advice. Talk to the person or persons who were involved or played a part in it originally. Do they agree that complete reversal would be wise? Do they have an alternative course to follow? Get an opinion also from someone you consider knowledgeable and experienced but who was not involved.

Decide what would be best for you to do. Before you act, however, explain to your boss what has happened and what's on your mind. Although your boss will probably back you up, you show that you respect his or her advice and you demonstrate that you consider it important to keep him or her informed.

7.14 Reacting to a Bad Decision: How to Handle Yourself

People expect something from you after they learn that you made a bad decision. They want to see how you react and they are interested in hearing what you have to say. Your credibility, reputation, and prestige are at stake. You show what type of person you are by what you do in this awkward and sometimes embarrassing situation.

Effective supervisors handle themselves well and don't lose the respect or admiration of their people. You should adopt their behavior pattern by explaining briefly and simply the reasons behind your decision to the people involved. But don't go too far with this or you risk sounding defensive.

Avoid apologizing for a bad decision. If it caused some inconvenience, a short, sincere comment of regret is enough. Never, of course, try to place the blame on someone else. Everyone knows it was your decision—own up to it.

Be sure to inform people quickly of a new decision if you make one, and explain it. Show that you are confident that it is a good one.

Case-in-Point: Bill Trent, supervisor in a meat-packing plant in Ohio, is quick to act when he learns that he made a bad decision. "I immediately get out in the plant to the fellows involved and say something like, 'Hey, guys, I goofed,' and then proceed to explain. I usually see a few smiles and seldom get a derogatory comment, so I guess they take it right in stride, which they should. Everybody makes mistakes, you know." Trent's philosophy on his and his people's reaction to a bad decision shows why he is an effective supervisor.

7.15 Answers to Having to Make Quick Decisions

Few people are not bothered by having to make a decision quickly or under pressure. You can be more sure of making a good decision if you can take the time to get facts, consider them, and choose between alternatives. Supervisors frequently are faced with making decisions with little time to think about them. How they handle such problems often decides how fast they grow on the job and move up in the company to positions of greater responsibility.

It's easy to lose sight of your objective when you're under pressure. Since time is usually the reason for pressure, your best bet is to try for as much as you can get. Look over the situation to determine if you really must come up with a decision quickly or if only the person presenting the problem to you feels that you must. A problem sometimes appears worse than it is; inexperienced people and people not familiar with a condition may view it with unwarranted alarm. Then, too, many people are impatient when things are not going their way.

Case-in-Point: Bob Tully, a 60-year-old supervisor in an automobile assembly line plant in Michigan, has been under pressure many times in his career. His advice: "I used to take the short-range view. To get people out of my hair I was inclined to make decisions in favor of the man who complained the loudest. I learned the hard way that in trying to get rid of one problem, I created three or four." Tully points out that you must keep in mind the big picture; avoid putting a lot of effort into solving a problem-of-the-moment at the expense of the overall job.

When you find yourself in a position where you must make a quick decision and you're not prepared to do so, look for an answer that can temporarily take care of matters. You can profit at least two ways with this move: 1) you buy yourself time for further investigation, and 2) you let events take place which might change the situation, making your decision easier.

If you cannot find a for-the-moment out, you must, of course, make the best decision you are capable of. At least, however, give yourself a few moments to think before you act.

7.16 What to Do When Your Decision Is Challenged

Not all of your decisions are going to be readily accepted because people have their own opinions, think differently than you, and may know something that you don't. Questions will be asked by your superiors, peers, or subordinates. You must be able to answer such questions and defend your decisions.

Successful supervisors do not become emotional when their decisions are questioned, regardless of how sure they feel they are right. Highly emotional behavior indicates a lack of stability and personal control which supervisors must have if they are to be effective on the job.

The proper way to respond is to calmly say that you may be wrong, that the person has a right to his or her opinion, and that you would like to discuss it. Then, ask why it is felt that your decision is not good. Recognize all the while that you may have made a bad one.

Case-in-Point: Once a supervisor, now a production superintendent, George Sanders told me, "One of the best ways to handle objections to your idea or decision is to listen to them. Not only will this help you to fully understand the objection, but, if a man's objections are weak, he may discover this for himself if he's allowed to talk freely."

In most cases your decision may be challenged because people do not understand it or why you made it. It's a matter of communication–people were not informed of something concerning them—you must now do that. When you explain, they often will be satisfied. If you've made a good decision you should have no trouble with this.

It stands to reason that a person will sometimes have a valid and logical reason for challenging your decision. If this is evident, say the person has made a good point and that you will reconsider. Be sure to compliment the person for recognizing the questionable decision; also thank him or her for telling you about it. Re-evaluate the decision as soon as possible.

It pays to personally keep the person who challenges a decision informed when you reconsider it, whether you make a new decision or not. You show that you recognize and value the person's suggestions and that you hope he or she approves of what you decide. If you reverse or make a new decision, go out of your way to see that the person is informed of this ahead of other individuals.

8

HOW TO HANDLE
PROBLEMS OF
COMMUNICATION

GETTING through to people is the most difficult part of the job for many supervisors. The matter cannot be taken lightly because no single aspect of the supervisor's job can contribute to career success as much as being an effective communicator. Since communication on the job is so important, it should be promoted and encouraged at every opportunity. To do so, supervisors should be aware of the barriers and how to overcome them. They must continually seek and practice ways to keep communication channels open. Being informal and available to discuss almost any problem has proven to be of value.

Supervisors need to know the answers to the many problems of communicating on the job, such as how to promote upward communication, how to carry on a conversation, what to do when they aren't being informed, how to avoid overcommunicating, how much people should be told, and how to deliver bad news to employees. Rumors should never be ignored; they require quick and positive action by the supervisor. The grapevine can be a good communication tool if handled properly.

Computers and electronic mail greatly facilitate company communications today, so supervisors should be familiar with these fast ways of communicating. Most important, supervisors need to be good listeners.

8.1 Uplift Your Personality: It Will Help You to Communicate

Personality plays a major role in spoken communications. In some situations, the impact of personality seems to be more important and lasting than the words you use. There is a great deal of evidence that the way you project yourself to others determines to a large extent how successful you are in communicating.

Yet personality is difficult to define, perhaps because it includes so many aspects of you. It is the type of thing you *feel,* but have trouble putting into words. However, one point is quite definite—you cannot adopt someone else's personality. Your personality must be your very own.

You must develop and perfect your own best self. This includes your way of speaking and listening. Your mannerisms, your smile, and your handshake are all part of your personality. It pays to reflect a positive attitude and an optimistic viewpoint. The degree of enthusiasm you display in the presence of others at least partly indicates how successful you are in these efforts.

Recognize how humor can complement and augment your personality. The right use of humor can create goodwill, increase your acceptance, break the tension of an embarrassing situation, and promote teamwork and cooperation. Of course, humor must be used thoughtfully and in good taste. Before you include humor in your conversation, make sure it is suitable for the occasion and that nobody will be offended.

Having a friendly way about you counteracts any tendency you might have to be overbearing or demanding when you seek cooperation. By refraining from acting superior, you can prevent barriers from coming between you and your people. Yet give your image the attention it deserves. Maintain a confident view of yourself as a person who is growing and improving in diverse areas, including the vital area of your personality.

8.2 Keys to Effective Supervisor-Employee Communication

Two findings of a Bureau of National Affairs survey of 219 big and small manufacturers and other businesses were: the most effective employee communication techniques are verbal, and the first-line supervisor is the key link in the communication process. The survey also revealed that among downward communication techniques, the bulletin board is used by nearly all companies. Then comes supervisor's meetings, followed by company publications and meetings of employees in small groups.

Supervisors communicate with their people to inform them, to influence them, and to support them. Successful communicators have learned, however, that it isn't wise to try to do more than one of these at a time. Doing so weakens the transmission of the message and also dampens the impact.

Good communication is simply effective passing of information by the most suitable means available. The result is more important than how it is done. The communicator must give some thought to communicating and not just trust it to chance. Although the keys to effective employee communication are simple, they are very purposeful. When you communicate, you must:

1. Have the receiver's attention. The receiver must be interested in you and what you have to say.
2. Have the receiver understand you. You accomplish this by using simple words, short sentences, and avoiding jargon.
3. Have the receiver accept your message. You succeed through reason, logic, and persuasion.

8.3 Information: The Essential Supervisory Tool

In carrying out their responsibilities, supervisors receive and transmit much information. How well they handle it affects not only their own productivity but also that of their people. Their skill with this facet of communication determines their success on the job and their promotability within the company.

Supervisors use information to spread the word and to generate ideas, both their own and of others. It is the basis for both upward and downward communications. Information helps in making decisions and in evaluating alternatives. Part of the authority and prestige of supervisors lies in what their people *think* they know.

Getting information is not always easy; you have to encourage people to give it to you. One way is by being friendly. Another is by keeping them informed so that they will realize the importance of exchanging news and data. Show your interest in them and their work. Be willing to listen to them, to hear their ideas and get their opinions.

Let people know, too, that you can take bad news without adverse feeling toward the bearer. Point out that without information, you can't carry out your supervisory responsibilities.

Information has become a source of power for all people in managerial jobs. But you cannot rely only on your position for this power. The type and amount of information you provide others greatly determines how they see you on the managerial ladder.

However, being a source of information does not guarantee that you will receive the information you need. It must come primarily from the rapport and camaraderie you develop with people. If you provide people with the information they need and want, you build their trust and loyalty to you. They will go out of their way to give you information, and they will do it because they want to, not because they have to.

8.4 How to Communicate Information About the Company

By giving employees information and facts about their company, you can develop their interest and their loyalty. If they are not given any information, they may draw their own conclusions from what they already know or have heard elsewhere. If they have false information they may develop a poor opinion, a feeling which doesn't bode well for the company.

Your company makes quality products or performs a good service. It would not be able to stay in business if it didn't. Pointing this out to your people helps them to develop pride in their jobs and their company. Surveys have shown that many employees do not know much about their company's products or service. If this is true of your people, you should make an effort to change it.

Always take advantage of opportunities to tell people when the company receives honors and awards, or makes a contribution towards a community project. Similarly, when one of your people makes the news, see that other workers know about it. The easiest way to do this is to put the item on the bulletin board.

A company should tell employees of its plans when acquiring and installing new equipment. The company should explain that the new equipment is being installed not only to cut costs but also to increase production and to boost sales which will probably increase jobs in the long run.

What about news concerning the company which isn't good? While it may not be wise to go out of your way to talk about things which make your company look bad, you still shouldn't hesitate to give bad news. Better that people hear it from you than from someone else.

If you are perceptive, you will be able to anticipate when you are going to get reactions from your people on announcements. Offer an explanation when you see that a company rule or policy is going to be unpopular. Although you may have to do a selling job, there is usually a good reason for rules such as prohibiting use of company refrigerators or ovens for handling food. If you explain such rules, you will find that people will go along with them better because they will see that the rules were made for their benefit.

Communicating information about the company prevents fears from arising about jobs and possible changes in working conditions. You'll find also that fewer rumors crop up when employees know what is going on.

Case-in-Point: Management of Tool Steel Gear and Pinion Company in Cincinnati, Ohio believes in keeping its employees posted. "Of most importance to our employees is the number of orders we receive," is the way they put it. Every day, order sheets that list all orders received the previous day are put up on various bulletin boards around the plant. In this way, the company says, it gives its employees a feeling of security by keeping them informed of upcoming work. a member of management says, "It lets them know they'll have a job tomorrow."

Case-in-Point: Instead of leaving just formally worded work orders for the night shifts, James Spies, Fine Chemicals Section Supervisor at Glidden-Durkee Division of SCM Corp., adds touches such as: "We're ahead of schedule and moving good. Keep it up." One of Spies' shift supervisors, Charles Fachko, says that such notes help tell the men how they're doing, make them feel like an important part of the company, and keep them from losing interest.

8.5 How to Promote Upward Communication

Your job of supervising is much easier if your people keep you informed. You will have the facts that will help you make decisions, and you will be able to foresee problems that could arise. For these and other reasons, it is to your advantage to promote upward communication from your people at every opportunity.

How does a supervisor promote upward communication? The best way is to always be available and receptive to people who want to talk. Listen to all your people's ideas regardless of how illogical or impractical they may sound. Listen also to their complaints, and answer them.

When people learn that you respect their opinion and are interested in their welfare, they will not hesitate to give you information, particularly if you show you appreciate it and tell them so. If they learn also that you are fair and honest, they will not hold back on telling you about mistakes rather than trying to cover them up.

To most workers, the supervisor will always be the boss, and it behooves them to say what the boss likes to hear and do what the boss wants them to do. It may be to some workers' interests to withhold certain information lest it be used against them or against others in the same work group. This psychological barrier to upward communication is simply fear. Successful supervisors do something about it by continually working toward ways to eliminate or reduce that fear.

How-to-Do-It: Be decisive on the job and confident that what you say and do is right. People usually have few fears when their leaders are positive in giving orders and directing work. When workers know that they are doing their work correctly and to their supervisor's liking, rapport improves and teamwork is given a boost. People just naturally communicate more when they feel secure.

Supervisors who want upward communication from their people to be good must keep up the morale. They must place a high value on the three strong desires of people: 1) to be recognized and given appreciation for work done, 2) to be kept informed so they are "in" on things, and 3) to receive friendly, sympathetic advice on personal problems. Understanding and willingness on the part of supervisors to meet these needs of their people will reduce communication fears and promote upward communication.

8.6 The Technique of Carrying on a Conversation Easily

Being a good conversationalist helps your image and makes you welcome at both business and social functions. It also makes it easier to communicate your thoughts and ideas because your listeners will pay more attention to what you have to say.

You can develop the technique of easily carrying on a conversation if you work at it. Here are a few dos and don'ts on the art:

● Be aware that an interesting conversationalist conveys a sense of leaving many things unsaid. Telling everything can be tiring for listeners.

● Never interrupt someone who is speaking. Waiting your turn makes what you say more interesting when the right moment comes.

● Add some body language occasionally to your words. You'll put some sparkle into your message and it will help you when you want to be emphatic.

● Refrain from raising your voice to get attention. It's a sure way to turn other people off.

● Ask a close friend if your voice is shrill, harsh, too loud, or too soft. Knowing about these faults makes them correctable.

● Avoid making remarks that make listeners uncomfortable. Think twice when you feel impelled to state unpleasant facts.

● Hold up when you sense you are monopolizing a conversation. Your listeners' minds may begin to wander. Worse, you will become boring.

● Minimize your use of slang and clichés. Although such words may make it easier for you to express yourself, they are dull to your listeners. They also convey the idea that your vocabulary is limited.

8.7 Ten Positive Ways to Avoid Creating Communication Barriers

Successful leaders are aware of the various barriers to communication that prevent understanding among people who work together. Here are several of the most serious ones. Experienced supervisors have learned to avoid them. To do the same, you must not be guilty of:

1. Failing to keep people informed. Supervisors may assume that because *they* saw something or heard something, *their* people also saw or heard it. Few people will admit that they do not know they have not been informed. Instead they tend to bluff, pretend, or just sit back and wait. Withholding information that people need to do a job robs them of dignity. Without knowing why, they not only lose contact, but also lose faith in the supervisor and the company.

2. Jumping to conclusions without evidence. People hesitate to communicate with a boss who jumps to conclusions without having the facts. They despair of the boss's ability to reason, decide, and solve problems. And they fear being blamed for something they didn't do.

3. Overlooking the impact of words. Taking a strong stand on a subject or making announcements which people take as threats may bring on severe reactions, with communications suffering as a result. Be careful in your choice of words when talking with people. Avoid being too positive if you want them to respond without fear.

4. Forgetting that how something is said may be as important as what is said. Your tone of voice may say more than your words. Voices can show irritation, hostility, and insincerity without the words suggesting these things. Body communication may also give a strong message. Whatever, how a supervisor acts when communicating may tell others that this is the time to be silent, with the result that communication suffers.

5. Failing to admit a mistake. People who feel that it is wrong to admit a mistake do not believe there is power in accepting blame for errors and strength in offering apologies for wrongs which involve other people. It is just about impossible to have any true communication with a person who looks for mistakes in everyone but himself or herself.

6. Preferring performance to people. A supervisor who gives the impression that all that counts are profit, production, and getting the job done fails to give credit to people. As a result, people will shy away from communicating with such a person on matters which do not apply to those things.

7. Being unprepared. Communication suffers when you try to discuss an important matter with people without having facts or information to offer. You look bad and you make others look bad by not being clear on what you're talking about, what you're trying to achieve, and what you expect from them.

8. Distorting ideas. Being overly pessimistic or optimistic solely for the effect that you think it will have on your people usually doesn't work because reality is always a matter for personal interpretation. Such tactics are recognized for what they are and simply discounted. But a damper is put on communication because of them.

9. Forgetting the importance of experience. A supervisor who is unrealistic in his or her demands hinders the inexperienced employee who needs help. When a supervisor expects immediate results, perfection, and no excuses, that is asking too much of inexperienced people.

10. Resisting change. If you are for maintaining things as they are, you probably stand in the way of good communication with creative people. They may hold back their ideas to avoid a confrontation with you. Everyone loses when there is no communication.

8.8 How to Improve Your Verbal Communication Skill

If you are concerned that you may not be fully accepted as a leader because your verbal communications are not as good as you'd like them to be, you can take a big step toward overcoming this problem. What you must do is work at improving your perception of what it takes to put your ideas across and to be understood.

One of the best ways to improve your verbal communication skill is to pick the words you will use in advance. Giving clear instructions will result in maximum comprehension by your listeners. You want to prevent their attention from wandering, and you want your message to be understood.

In trying to put across an idea or to persuade somebody to your thinking, recognize that people may be biased, prejudiced, and have preconceived ideas. These barriers to understanding complicate your efforts to communicate clearly because people may not listen carefully, if at all, to an idea, theory, or viewpoint they don't agree with.

It's better to avoid speaking rapidly when you give instructions because there are some people who need extra time to think about what they have heard, and to fix the information firmly in their minds. There are those who find it difficult to understand instructions unless the instructions are given slowly, even repeated. Some people also have poor retention abilities, so if you give them two assignments or more at a time, you run the risk of having them forget some parts of the jobs.

If you want to avoid any misunderstanding, try not to get too technical. Unless you are talking to a skilled technician, you are likely to lose your listener with your words and phrases. Using slang is one thing; using jargon that is unfamiliar to the receiver is a waste of time.

Many of your people want to be involved in any new job or assignment. They also want to know what goals they are expected to reach. These people will respond quickly if you give them more information relative to their assignments. They will listen intently, and they will absorb your instructions with less difficulty.

To get people into the proper frame of mind to accept and understand assignments, communicate frequently with them. Also, show a consistent willingness to answer their questions when they ask them. This paves the way for them to start listening as soon as you begin talking—thus the communication time can be shortened.

Try to pick the best time of day when you want to verbally communicate with individuals or groups. Mornings are usually best because by afternoon, your thinking and reasoning faculties can be dulled from several hours of hard work. In the morning you will be fresh and your listeners will be more receptive.

8.9 Evaluation: A Major Barrier to Communication

One of the major barriers to effective communication is a person's natural tendency to evaluate, judge, and approve or disapprove a statement of another person. Although evaluating is common in almost all interchange of thoughts, it is much greater in situations where feelings and emotions are involved. The stronger the feelings, the more likely it is there will be no mutual agreement of two persons in their communication with each other. There will simply be two viewpoints, two feelings, and two judgments, with no agreement.

Case-in-Point: On more than one occasion I have listened to a heated discussion between two individuals in which both expressed strong feelings about a matter. After the two individuals had left each other without reaching an agreement, I thought a bit about the discussion and realized that they weren't talking about the same thing. Each was making a judgment from his own frame of reference. There was really nothing which could be called communication in their meeting since neither accepted the other's points.

If some time you sense that you are in a discussion which is not going to turn out in agreement, stop for a moment to consider your position. Do you see and understand the other person's view? Are you giving the person credit for it? Could you compromise the issue in some way? Try to reach at least one point of agreement before you leave each other. Your future communications will probably be better if you do.

8.10 Lose an Argument: It's Often Better

Successful supervisors usually possess the judgment to back off most arguments because those arguments are baseless in addition to being stressful. Although sometimes an argument is difficult to avoid, that doesn't mean you must go all out to win one.

When arguing, it's often better to lose than win. The argument you win can cause you to ruin a relationship with an important person. Here are some questions you should ask yourself before you decide to put a lot of effort into winning:

- Is winning more important than being on good terms with your opponent?
- Is the argument actually a matter of defending your ego?
- How much will I gain if I win?
- What will be my loss if I lose?

Be honest with yourself in answering these questions. You'll find that it's often better to lose an argument than to win one.

8.11 Answers to How Much People on the Job Should Be Told

Today's employees want to know how what they do contributes to the whole of their company. They also want to know what people in other departments are doing. And they like to be "in" on things whether or not they are involved.

Most people in management positions recognize that knowledge is a good motivator and morale-builder. Still, the question remains of how much people on the job should be told. While everyone agrees that communication is good, it takes a lot of time, and time is money.

You can't tell everybody everything. It's not necessary to give people a lot of unwanted details. Information can be put into three categories when deciding what to pass on to your people.

1. That which they should have to properly do their work, such as how machines function, where supplies are, what forms should be used, when jobs must be completed, and similar information which relates to their specific job.

2. That which they should know because they might be affected, such as an expansion in the department or company, a rearrangement of work areas, or an increase in a production quota.

3. That which they would find helpful in relating to their position and contribution to the organization, such as information about the company's goals and achievements, sales, new products, and profits.

Generally, supervisors should see that their people are given information in the first two categories. The amount of information of the third category which should be told depends on the interests of the individuals. Those who are creative and innovative, such as research and development people, would welcome news about new products or services the company offers. Almost everyone should want to know how the company is doing profitwise and what the future looks like. Most employees are more interested in their company than their supervisors suspect.

Case-in-Point: In a personal interview with Richard Hammonds, Factory Manager, J. Strickland and Company, Memphis, Tennessee, he said, "Complete, constant, and thorough communications with every one of our personnel, all the way down the chain of command and all the way back up that chain, are the keys to loyalty of personnel and efficiency of production of our big line of toiletries and cosmetics. Those communications are particularly important because we are turning out many products including sizes, and the sales department so often calls for different quantities of items as demands fluctuate, making frequent rescheduling necessary on the production lines.

"When some change in procedures is indicated, or when a new product is added to those to be produced, we not only tell each employee concerned with the change what is needed, but also discuss with them our planning for production, tell them what they are expected to accomplish—what quantities of inventories are required at the start and also later on.

"We find that this complete openness keeps morale high. The employees appreciate it."

Case-in-Point: Several years ago, the chemical division of a large rubber company in Akron, Ohio undertook a waste control program in an effort to reduce raw material cost and thereby improve profits. The cost of individual chemicals were posted in the various process areas of the plant. Signs were posted also asking workers to avoid spills and use care in handling these materials. In some areas, the installation cost of new equipment and facilities was also spelled out to tell employees what it took in the way of investment by the company to run the plant.

Over a period of months there were no significant signs of less waste or carelessness on the part of employees, nor were employees impressed to the extent that their treatment of facilities improved. Should the company have reached the conclusion that employees felt the company could afford small material losses? Did the profit information that was published in the company newspaper tell the employees that the company had plenty of money for new equipment?

The company did not continue its cost information program after that experience, one reason being given that cost and profit information isn't understood by most employees.

8.12 Overcommunicating: A Habit That Is Hard to Break

Some supervisors, in their eagerness to be clear and completely understood, may overdo it and thus cause themselves other problems. It's easy to keep talking past the point of accomplishing your objective, especially when you are explaining something or giving instructions. Talking too much can become a habit that is hard to break.

Overcommunicating is undesirable for two reasons. First, it diminishes the interest of your listener in what you are saying. Second, it tears down all of the communication gains you have achieved up to that particular point. Thus, by talking too much, you become ineffective in a skill that all supervisors need.

People overcommunicate when they excessively repeat themselves and when they adorn or expand their messages beyond what is necessary. The problem with saying too much is that it confuses your listener. This happens when much of your explanation is unnecessary. Because you continue to explain, your listener attempts to attach some additional significance to your words.

Although it's dangerous to assume people know what must be done, at the same time you don't want to endlessly repeat something which they already know. Instruction time can be reduced by checking beforehand to ascertain whether or not something is already well-known to the other person.

8.13 Four Ways to Avoid Overcommunicating

What are the cures and remedies for overcommunicating? There are several things you can do that will help you overcome it. If you sense that you are doing too much explaining—repeating or expanding your messages—try doing the following:

1. Work at expanding your vocabulary. Better word usage will cut down the time and words you need to make your point. In addition, very few of the words you use will go over the heads of your listeners. If you find that people frequently have many questions to ask you after you've talked to them, it's a sign that you have not been understood.

2. When faced with the need to pass on a great deal of information, spread it out over a period of time. Your listener will more easily understand it and remember more; sensing this, you will not feel that you must repeat it. This is especially appropriate with technical discussions that you might have with staff people. While some of your data or information may be of value to them, overdoing it may simply be wasting their time.

3. Organize and arrange your thoughts before you express them. If you fail to do this, it is likely that you will use many more words than are necessary. Extra explanations may be required also if you don't present your material in a logical order.

4. Consider the possibility that you could put across something more effectively and faster with a picture, drawing, or some other type of visual aid. You should try to use as many such aids as possible because, in addition to

reducing the amount of talking you must do, they often are much easier to understand.

8.14 How to Deal with Defensive Communications

Defensive communication hurts the innovativeness, creativity, trust, and morale of a company's employees. Supervisors should be able to recognize the problems of defensive communication and know how to deal with them.

Defending yourself when you are attacked is a normal reaction. When you sense a physical threat, your biological self tells you to either flee or fight. But defensive communication is different. It doesn't involve a physical threat. It is the response to a psychological threat, one to your ego and self-esteem.

If, for instance, you feel that you are tolerant, reliable, responsible, and of high integrity, you become defensive if someone challenges one or more of those attributes. Faced with the challenge, you may respond destructively or constructively. To respond constructively, you must understand the scope of defensive communication and know how to contend with it.

Defensive communication occurs in one of three ways: with the person speaking, the person listening, or the message between the two. The person speaking is often more important than what he or she says. An example of this is a person whom you have learned not to trust. For whatever the reason, this person makes you defensive whenever he or she says something. Since experience and past treatment tells you to be careful when this person communicates with you, you can justify being defensive in your relations although you should try not to show it.

You probably also know people who frequently respond defensively to whatever is said to them. They are inclined to take almost any statement, question, or remark and turn it into a criticism or an insult. Such people can be classed as defensive listeners.

Defensive listening is bad because it discourages ideas and opinions that are vital to the growth of employees and companies. With chronic defensive listeners, pleasant and harmonious relations may be just about impossible, regardless of how hard you try. To make matters worse, many defensive listeners are good at sidetracking and at making you feel guilty after a conversation. To avoid such incidents, talk to such individuals only when your job requires it. This approach will help to relieve the frustration and guilt feelings you may experience when meeting and working with them.

A defensive message is one that disregards the feelings of others and challenges their competence or worth. If you are sensitive to other people and are tactful in what you say, you are not likely to make them defensive when you talk to them.

8.15 Withholding Information: Why It's Something Necessary

Although much communication between supervisors and their people is a sign of good management, there are times when information should be withheld and not made public. A supervisor should not pass along everything he or she knows when the following conditions exist:

1. Management has not finalized its plans. Rumors may be rampant when management is thinking about an expansion, a cutback, or a merger. Yet, the change may never go through. Usually management does not want information on such matters made public until its plans are finalized or close to it.

2. Information must be passed through regular channels. People involved in a change should be told before those who are not involved. Also, disclosing facts or change too soon to too many people may interfere with management's plans for publicity and promotion.

3. The information is related to security. Contracts or negotiations with the government, for example, often require secrecy. Other matters of security which are not discussed are those which involve the police, such as property damage and theft investigations.

4. Revealing the information may hurt the company. Formulas, designs, and new procedures not protected by patents must be kept secret to prevent competitors from taking advantage of such information.

8.16 The Technique of Asking Questions Properly

Supervisors need lots of information to carry out their responsibilities. Although there are numerous ways they can get it, many supervisors overlook the simplest and quickest way—asking questions. Asking questions is a basic fundamental of learning which you experienced in childhood. In those days, you were not concerned with how you asked questions, and you learned much.

Yet, asking questions is of most benefit when it's done properly. In fact, done improperly, asking questions does more harm than good. You can hurt someone's feelings, find fault, belittle, or insult someone if you don't think before you speak.

A good way to learn how to ask questions properly is to examine the various types of questions you should avoid. Here are a few illustrations of questions that fail their objectives along with some suggestions on how they could be improved:

Condescending questions: For example, "Do you know how you solved the problem, Frank?" Such a question is patronizing in that it implies that Frank may have come up with the answer accidentally. A better question is "How did you go about solving the problem, Frank?" This allows Frank to say as much or as little as he wishes; it also gives credit to Frank for his accomplishment.

Leading questions: For example, "Linda, aren't you in favor of . . .?" Such a question is usually phrased in a way that it suggests the right answer. When you ask Linda a leading question, you literally put words in her mouth, forcing her to agree with you whether she feels that way or not. The best question to ask Linda is simply, "Do you agree?"

Pressure questions: For example, "Bill, what do *you* think we should do?" This question shows that you are anxious and even worried, but it also puts stress on Bill. A better question for you to ask is, "Bill, what would you do *first?*" Bill would then think about a plan rather than feel he had to come up with a complete answer.

Loaded questions: For example, "I thought he was wrong. What do you think, Tom?" This question anticipates agreement. But it also contains an uncertainty. Tom is never sure what impact his answer will have. Also, he may answer the question the way he thinks you want it answered. An improved question would be, "What do you think of that answer, Tom?"

8.17 What to Do When You Aren't Being Informed

No executive or manager wants to hear, "Why didn't you tell me?" from one of the employees. The question is a tip-off that a misfortune has occurred, such as a lost sale, production delay, or customer complaint, which might have been prevented with better communication.

Supervisors seldom complain about being given too much information. To the contrary, many of them feel that they are not being kept informed on matters which they should know about. The problem is a serious one with supervisors who work night shifts and are out of close touch with their superiors.

If you need more information to do your job satisfactorily, ask for it. If you don't receive it, then you have a real problem and had better look into your relationship with your boss. Before you do, however, think a bit about your situation.

Is your boss really at fault, or are you, perhaps, not reading all the memos sent you, listening carefully when the boss talks, and keeping your eyes open? If you decide that you are not at fault, let your boss know, doing it in a way that has impact and gets results.

How-to-Do-It: Discuss with your boss one or more recent problems or events that did not turn out well. Point out that if you had been informed, you could have handled them to his or her, and the company's, advantage. After hearing this, the boss will certainly take steps to see that you are kept up-to-date on matters in which you could become involved.

Case-in-Point: Effective communication with and between maintenance personnel is an essential ingredient for the successful maintenance program at the Globe Battery Division of Globe Union, Inc., Milwaukee, Wisconsin. Clyde Cheney, Maintenance Programs Coordinator, confirmed this when he said, "Too often, sophisticated systems which appear flawless from an 'ivory tower' standpoint fail miserably because we didn't get all the people who could do something about problems involved. To 'get the word' to our maintenance people in our battery manufacturing plants, we now use an inexpensive and well-received *Maintenance Memo.* The frequency of an issue is tied to anticipated usefulness and the need as a practical consideration, instead of adherence to a rigid schedule. This permits us to get timely information to the reader quickly. We are firmly convinced that our *Maintenance Memo* is here to stay as an effective but inexpensive communication device."

8.18 How to Deliver Bad News to Employees

Supervisors now and then find themselves in the uncomfortable position of having to be bearers of bad news. Human relations experts believe that supervisors in that position are likely to suppress their feelings of sympathy towards employees as a way of overcoming their own guilt at having to give them the bad news. Thus they tend to be cold and indifferent at such times.

However, the experts say, supervisors can feel less stress, and, in some cases, soften the blow if they go about it properly. Here are their suggestions on how these situations should be handled:

● Always deliver bad news face-to-face. Written communications of this type, in addition to being callous, are also brutal.

● Use a group meeting or discussion only when the news primarily affects more than two or three workers.

● Avoid building an employee up with praise or compliments before breaking the news.

● Get to the point immediately. Small talk only builds tension.

● Be assured that violent reactions to bad news are relatively infrequent and predictable. Thus, there is no need to be prepared to protect yourself.

● Encourage employees to express their feelings, but don't take what is said personally or try to defend anyone's position.

● Make some positive comments about the employee *after* you have broken the bad news.

8.19 Four Tips on Using the Company Grapevine

Employees like to have information that relates to their work, their company, and the people who manage it. They particularly want to know about company plans and proposed changes that could affect their economic status. They will get this information one way or another.

If they receive it from official company sources, they will get facts and reliable information. But, if the company doesn't keep them informed, they will turn to the grapevine rumors. Unfortunately, the latter may provide them partial truths, distortions, and misinterpretations.

Some authorities say that a supervisor must never use the grapevine either to disseminate information or receive it. They claim that "the grapevine, so often rife with rumors and lies, seldom carries the exact truth, although it sometimes carries enough of the truth to be quite believable and attract widespread attention." They say that the supervisor who uses the grapevine is asking for trouble.

Other authorities aren't so contrary about it. They say that the grapevine, properly used, can be an aid to communications. Clever supervisors can get things done and get touchy matters handled simply by planting information in appropriate areas. Of course, such means of communicating are not always sure-fire, but if you can't get a job done through usual channels, you might try it. If you are so inclined, here are four tips on using the grapevine as a means of communication:

1. Never try to use the grapevine to gain an advantage over someone. If you don't have trust, you won't get communication. You could also lose your credibility.

2. Make sure you understand the situation, have the facts, and know the people involved. Don't try it if there's a big unknown matter which could disrupt everything.

3. Avoid letting the grapevine dictate to you. Be sure your people don't use it to convert you to their thinking on some matters on which you have a different opinion than they.

4. Learn who the talkers are and how they spread the news. Realize that there may be more than one way of getting the word around.

Caution: Be wary of an upper level grapevine. A grapevine in top management circles can be complex and vicious.

8.20 What to Do About Rumors

Since one of your responsibilities is to keep your people informed, dealing with rumors is one of your jobs. If rumors are ignored they can hurt morale, cause hard feelings, and result in foolish behavior of gullible individuals. You must do something when you suspect you've heard a rumor.

Here Is What You Should Do

1. Learn more about the rumor by asking your people what they've heard and where. If you can find out where the rumor started it will be easier to do something about it.

2. Tell people that you're checking. Suggest that they not be concerned until you get the facts.

3. Talk to your boss about the matter. He or she may know the truth or, if the rumor is true, why no statement has officially been made.

4. If you are unable to learn anything from your boss, begin checking with authorities. Ask them for guidance on what you can tell your people.

5. Give your people the facts. If there is no truth to the rumor, say so. If you have no information, tell them that. The most important thing you can do is to show that you care and that you want to do all you can to keep them informed.

8.21 Positive Ways to Fight Computer Fears

Do you worry about having to use a computer? Don't let it bother you. Most of your fears and worries are probably untruths. Computers help you and others by simplifying routine procedures and organizing complex information. They save you time and enable you to get your work done faster and better than ever before. Yet not everyone welcomes the computer, primarily because it involves change.

Getting to know and understand a computer is easier if you compare it to a new phone system, for example. It may be strange and appear difficult to get used to, but you will experience these feelings only for a short time. Realize too, that many people enjoy using a computer—they consider it fun when playing video games.

Some people may worry that the computer will catch every mistake they make. The truth is that computer systems are used far more often to keep them from making mistakes instead of to keep track of the ones they do make. Most of the software (instructions and programs) written for computers today is designed with the operators in mind. Computers really are "friendly" in that respect.

A friendly computer is one that is easy to operate and almost impossible to break. It provides simple and easy-to-understand instructions to operators, points out errors when they occur, and tells how mistakes can be corrected. A computer that is friendly also alerts operators to trouble. For example, if it is overloaded or unable to respond to an inquiry, it will report this situation with a message or at least beep or blink.

People lose much of their fear of computers when they understand what they can and can't do with them. A recent survey of computer owners revealed that knowing how to run a computer gives a person an ego boost and a sense of power.

A computer can function as a typewriter, a calculator, a clock, a calendar, a worksheet, and a filing cabinet, among other things. In addition, a computer can help you to become organized and to pace your workflow. You can keep track of large amounts of information, and you can get it quickly by just touching a few keys on the keyboard.

A word processing program can make your computer a high-speed, electronic typewriter. With it you can create letters and reports quickly and efficiently. What's more, you can revise your work without retyping and store it for future use. The best way to not let the computer bother you is to use it as much as possible.

8.22 Electronic Mail: What It's All About

Business and industry are continually finding ways to improve communications—particularly where the amount of information is large, must be transmitted great distances, or doesn't require simultaneous exchange. Electronic mail is such a system.

Electronic mail provides communications between a sender and a receiver where at least part of the transmission of the message or document is distributed electronically. Electronic mail is known also as computer mail, an electronic message system, and a store-and-forward message system.

Unlike the telephone where you and your party have to be connected at the same time, with electronic mail you can be somewhere else when your party gets the message. To better understand electronic mail, compare it to paper mail. The differences are that it operates with electronic rather than paper-based media, and instead of delivering paper envelopes of mail to mailboxes, it delivers "envelopes" of electronic data to computer files which are the "mailboxes." You don't need to print the message on paper after getting it unless you want to.

However, there is more to electronic mail. When you communicate in this manner, you can edit your message before or as you send it. In addition, the system has the capability of permitting you to respond in several ways to the messages you receive. You can either file the information for future reference or answer it with another message or by voice. With electronic mail you can hold conferences with people in different time zones, you can follow up on projects, or you can collect data and report on what you learn and know.

8.23 Five Ways That Electronic Mail Pays for Itself

Many companies are seeing the advantage of electronic mail systems in the conduct of daily business. While some businesspeople feel that the postal service isn't very reliable and is too slow, others point out that there are other good reasons why companies are more and more using the electronic mail system. Here are five ways that electronic mail is paying for itself. You can:

1. Frequently send many letters to many people.

2. Send important information such as price or model changes, engineering or design change orders, product information, and shipping instructions.

3. Distribute reports that need to arrive in time for important meetings.

4. Communicate with people who work in different time zones.

5. Eliminate spending time returning calls, missing your party, and being missed yourself.

8.24 Teleconferencing: A Group Communicating Technique

Teleconferencing is becoming more and more popular as a way for groups to communicate with each other, particularly with large companies having several offices or plants across the country. It is used primarily for business meetings where a number of people can assemble for the exchange of information without being together physically.

There are three types of teleconferences currently in use by companies for group-oriented business communications. Each has its own requirements in equipment and facilities:

● Audio teleconferencing, the least expensive of the three, operates with telephone connections. Unfortunately, telephone handsets are not designed for long conversations, and speaker phones need improvement in sound quality.

● Video teleconferencing uses television images in addition to sound. It requires modification of the telephone system or satellite transmission—and, unless expensive, low-light-level cameras are used, special lighting is also required.

● Computer teleconferencing involves transfer of information from data bases or from one computer directly to other terminals. Yet computer teleconferencing actually has few similarities to traditional meetings. It is more like exchanging memos or letters.

8.25 Three Benefits of Teleconferencing

There is no question that teleconferencing offers several benefits to business and industry. Here are some of those benefits along with an evaluation of them. With teleconferencing:

1. You are able to have shorter, more efficient, and more manageable meetings. Routine matters and simple problems can be solved more quickly because there is little small talk going on.

However, teleconferencing may not result in complete and efficient communication if the participants are strangers. A session may be more productive if you get to know people beforehand by meeting them face-to-face or have a telephone conversation with them before you participate in a teleconference.

2. You have more control over the proceedings. Teleconferencing works well for making assignments, exchanging opinions, conducting briefings, interviewing, and making decisions. By being independent of distance and time, teleconferencing extends your span of control. You can be in many places at once.

Yet there are times when you miss the personal approach that you are accustomed to when giving orders or handing out assignments. Also, when events and decisions come rapidly, the experience can be tiring and demanding.

3. You can reduce your need to travel. By leasing equipment, teleconferencing is almost always less expensive than travel. Without the costs of air travel, hotels, car rental, meals and the value of travel time, companies can afford a considerable investment in teleconferencing equipment and facilities.

The biggest drawback of teleconferencing is its price. Establishing a network in a company having many offices and plants can cost millions, but the savings in travel expense and increases in executive and managerial productivity may be worth it.

8.26 Listening: The Communication Tool That Also Motivates

To motivate your people, you must develop in them a spirit of wanting to work and wanting to do a better job each day. A way to do this is to listen to them when they talk about their jobs and their problems. For proof of this, look at the persons in your group who have come up with ideas and suggestions. You will find in most cases that innovations and improvements came from persons on the job who were encouraged and listened to.

People who work for the old-style, autocratic type supervisor seldom offer suggestions or are motivated to improve themselves. The autocratic type supervisor *tells* people what should be done, *how* it should be done, and *when* it should be done. Although the job gets done, it rarely, if ever, is in a manner better than the supervisor could do it. Individuality, originality, and initiative are stifled because the supervisor is mostly telling and seldom listening.

The democratic supervisor believes that people can and will make intelligent suggestions and decisions if they are permitted to do so. This happens if the supervisor trains them, helps them to develop, and listens to them.

Case-in-Point: John Sisty, Chief, Engineering Division, Veterans Administration Hospital at Oteen, North Carolina is a strong advocate of listening. He told me, "When I first took over our Engineering Division, my people came in a steady stream to present their problems. It was almost painful to watch their reaction when I would ask for their recommendations. They had very few answers to their problems because they had never been asked before. The ones they had were generally poor, but I listened. Within three weeks they had answers. I kept listening and their answers kept getting better and better. When they knew they would be asked, and their answers *listened to,* they started to study. A year later, 25 percent fewer men were doing 30 percent more work.

"As the men continued to improve themselves, I became enthused, continued to listen, started to study motivation, and developed the following practical guidelines. I say practical because they worked. Later, I learned from the experts and the psychologists why they worked. To motivate your men, listen to them and convince them:

1. That they are important members of your team, that their job is important, and that it is important that they do a good job.

2. That you are interested in them personally.

3. That you recognize their years of experience as valuable assets to your organization.

4. That their ideas and suggestions are wanted and welcome, that they can come to you with their ideas, and that you will listen to them and help them put their ideas into practice.

5. That you will back them up, support their interest, fight for them if necessary, and praise them.

8.27 Tips on Being a Better Listener

Being able to listen well depends on how you prepare for it, your skill in attentiveness, and your attitude toward the speaker and his or her subject. Here are some tips on what you should do to be a better listener:

● Think about what you will hear and the discussion beforehand, if you can. Prepare yourself both mentally and physically to listen.

● Give the speaker your full attention, trying not to relax. By concentrating and not letting your thoughts wander, you will be able to catch every word.

● Suppress any negative thoughts toward the speaker and the subject. Decide you want to hear him or her out. You can evaluate and judge everything later.

● Call upon your empathy to help you clearly understand the speaker's feelings and perhaps even why he or she has them.

● Relate what you hear to your own interests and knowledge. In striving to do this, you will listen more closely.

8.28 Proven Ways to Develop Good Listening Habits

Supervisors must be good listeners. Active listening on their part encourages workers to speak freely and explore problems. When employees see they are listened to by their supervisors they are more likely to listen more carefully themselves. This makes the supervisor's job of giving instructions and explaining work situations much easier.

Good listening habits can be acquired with practice. Here are the ways to go about it:

1. Listen with an open mind. Try to avoid mental blocks based on emotions. Hold off making comments until you've heard everything about a situation and had time to think about it.

2. Avoid interrupting anyone. Be an advocate of the doctrine that big people monopolize the listening and small people monopolize the talking.

3. Learn how to screen out noise and distraction so that you can concentrate on what is being said. When someone speaks to you, give the impression that what he or she has to say to you is very interesting and you want to hear more. It will make you listen more closely.

4. File away in the back of your mind the important points of what is being said while the other person talks.

5. Don't let highly charged or emotional words bother you. Keep your mind on the facts.

6. Avoid appearing and acting overly knowledgeable. You may turn off the speaker. Besides, you may miss something of value if you listen with the feeling that you already know what is being said.

9

PROVEN TECHNIQUES
THAT MAKE
GIVING ORDERS EASY

SUPERVISORS communicate with their people when instructing, training, and giving orders. Although all three functions require special skills, giving orders is the most important from the viewpoint of what is accomplished on the job. Supervisors who are adept at giving orders are better accepted by their people, and their people make fewer mistakes. Being aware of the pitfalls to avoid and the technique to follow makes the job of giving orders easier and simpler.

There's only one right way to put across management's decisions to employees and that is to give them as if they were your own. You strengthen your position as part of management and you demonstrate your ability to take on responsibility when you do this.

Avoiding misunderstandings is the major problem to be concerned with when giving orders. You can adopt proven practices to help you with this, one of which is to get feedback. Verbal orders have many advantages over other types but some orders should be put in writing. Recordkeeping is a vital means of control.

9.1 Seven Tried-and-Proven Pointers on Giving Instructions

Supervisors manage and direct people in being productive and doing work in the proper manner. Even enthusiastic and efficient people need guidance if the maximum is to be realized from their efforts. How much gets done is usually up to the supervisors and the effectiveness of their instructions.

When supervisors are skilled in giving instructions, jobs are handled promptly, work is done correctly, and people get satisfaction from accomplishment. Here are some pointers on the art:

1. Decide beforehand who you are going to ask to do a specific job. Think about how you're going to explain it to the person. Consider the timing—one time may be poor while another very appropriate. Decide where the job should be done, and determine if tools and materials are available.

2. Promote receptiveness for your instructions with preliminary remarks. Put your listener in a good frame of mind by first talking about things other than the job such as the person's hobby or a mutual interest. By asking a question or two, you can determine the person's attitude and emotional state. Knowing this helps in choosing your tone and deciding what words to use.

3. Be clear and specific. Use simple words and talk at a speed which gives your listener time to understand. Break up complicated and lengthy instructions into small steps and put them in logical order. Be consistent—if you call something by a certain name at one time, use the same name when you refer to it later.

4. Emphasize the positive. Tell a person the *right* way to do a job rather than *not* to do it the *wrong* way. When you instruct positively, you are more convincing and persuasive—what you say is more credible and authoritative. Positive instructions are more readily accepted than negative ones.

5. Favor optimism. Show that you are confident your instructions are clear and easily carried out. Indicate that you know your listeners have the capability and want to do the job. Wear a smile instead of a frown. Be interested instead of indifferent to how people feel.

6. Present ideas. When you instruct with ideas, you ask for opinions and you appeal to your listener's knowledge and judgment. Ideas make your instructions more interesting and cause people to think, thus promoting understanding as well as acceptability.

7. Point out benefits. Talk about gains to let listeners know what's in it for them. Do this by mentioning their benefits and the company's in the same statement. For example, tell people they will be safer, the quality of the product will be better, and the work will be easier if they use the right tools. Stating benefits results in better attitude, more cooperation, and higher productivity.

9.2 Mood and Temperament: Factors That Affect Your Receptiveness

You will be more effective in giving instructions and orders when you are in a good frame of mind because your mood and temperament will show in your words and actions. Conversely, you must be careful if you wish your orders to be accepted willingly and without question when you're not at your best. Here are a few precautions to help you handle your mood whatever it might be.

Although you might be charged up with energy and ambition, recognize that other people may not feel this way at the same time. Be considerate and reasonable in what you expect someone to do for you. Requesting a large amount of work to be done in a short period of time may cause people to think you unfair. It's better to challenge someone to do a bit more with occasional encouragement and praise for what has been done. The unreasonable approach can result in gripes, complaints, and slowups.

Avoid being sarcastic. Your listener may not understand why you are in this mood and may also resent such treatment, feeling that is is unjustified. Sarcasm certainly will not cause a person to do a better job—if anything, it will only cause hard feelings.

Losing your temper does not help to get things done either. It may make the other person lose his or hers, and result in an argument. Angry people don't get the work out. Besides, the instructions you give when you are angry will not be your best. People misunderstand the meaning of words said in anger.

Being sympathetic, considerate, enthusiastic, and cheerful influences people to be that way themselves. When you wish to stress the importance of your instructions, you can convey the point by being concerned, serious, and earnest. Remember, though, that your listener will perceive and accept your intentions only if you are sincere and honest.

Case-in-Point: Tom Gordon, Electrical Supervisor at The Goodyear Tire and Rubber Co., Akron, Ohio, told me, "A friendly and confident 'I know you can do it' comment on my part gets my instructions accepted and carried out faster than a sour 'this is probably too tough for you' remark. My men seem to sense how I feel about their capability to get a job done. Along the same line, I've noticed that a smile instead of a frown, and patience rather than anxiety, will get things done faster in the long run. You've got to be interested instead of indifferent to how your people feel. And always remember, it shows."

9.3 Tips on How to Give Orders

Supervisors are constantly communicating with the people on what's to be done and who is to do it. The more adept they are at doing this, the more they get done. However, they can be highly successful day after day only if they have people who willingly cooperate. How supervisors give orders often determines how much cooperation they get.

A good supervisor seldom should have to command someone to do a job. The message can be put across by asking that the work be done. Sometimes a supervisor can present a problem, discuss it, and then suggest that someone "take care of it." Another discreet way to ask for a job to be done is to suggest an action "we" should take, thus implying that other people are involved, even though the employee alone does the job. Ideally, the supervisor should help people analyze a situation in such a way that the situation itself dictates the order.

Managers at all levels should try to get subordinates to feel that they have the right to make suggestions and express their views on the ways jobs are to be done. People on the job are closer to the work than anyone. Over a period of time they get to know what a machine will do or how something can be simply accomplished. It pays to take advantage of such knowledge and experience.

Most people prefer *not* to be told to do something. Taking an order puts them beneath the person giving the order. The more you can put yourself on an equal level with your people, the more success you'll have in getting their help and cooperation.

Supervisors should realize that orders can be given in many ways, and that the best way depends on the specific situation and the individual involved. Experienced supervisors usually follow a procedure of first trying for agreement on what is to be done. If this doesn't work, they try suggesting. Failing at this, they try asking. As a last resort, they issue a direct command.

Case-in-Point: "I may give orders to do a job a certain way and have one of my men come up with an idea he thinks would do the job quicker and better," says John Chase, Line Superintendent with the Bangor (Maine) Hydro-Electric Co. "A man in a supervisory position must have an open mind and be ready to accept ideas, even if they may be contrary to his thinking," he said.

9.4 Tested Steps Which Make Giving Orders Easy

Giving orders that are always clear and completely understood doesn't come naturally to most supervisors, primarily because they are not aware of what is required to do so. Several factors affect understanding in most situations. Questions to be answered include: How much is taken for granted by the people who give orders? Do the receivers of the orders see things the same or differently? Do personal feelings get in the way when giving orders? Successful supervisors take such factors into consideration. To contend with them, they give orders in three steps.

First, they present organized facts about a situation or condition before they give an order. Doing this enables them to eliminate assumptions. Then they say what they want done.

Second, they explain the reason why they are asking for something and why they want it done in a certain way. Doing this makes clear the necessity for the work and how they see it should be done.

Third, they check for understanding. Doing this enables them to learn if their message got through and to probe for feelings and reactions.

Successful supervisors always follow up to see if their orders were carried out. They learn if their requests were clear and understood, and if the work was done correctly. If something went awry, they investigate so they can avoid a reoccurrence.

9.5 Pitfalls the "Pros" Avoid in Giving Orders

Because the "pros" know the ins and outs of giving orders, they stay out of the kind of trouble less experienced order-givers get into. Here are a few of the most troublesome pitfalls they avoid:

1. Giving conflicting instructions. Telling your people to do something that isn't standard practice or against company rules can get you and your people into real trouble. The same advice applies to telling one person to do a job a certain way and the next person a different way.

2. Being inconsistent. You can't be wishy-washy one day and stubborn the next. If you are easygoing one time and tough another, you cause uncertainty and anxiety among the people who work for you.

3. Acting important. Inexperienced supervisors may try to show their authority to get jobs done. The "pros" know they can gain their people's respect and compliance without coming down hard on them.

4. Showing favoritism. You must distribute the work fairly and not give the easiest work to the same people. Also, be sure the difficult-to-handle people get their share of the tough jobs.

5. Giving too many orders. Too many orders or too many details at one time confuse people. Limit your orders and make them short and specific.

6. Assuming understanding. Get the person to ask questions about the order or repeat it back to you in different words. You cannot assume anything.

7. Being offhand. Give your orders in a serious manner if you expect your people to take them seriously. Every order you give should be important.

9.6 How to Improve Your Order-Giving Technique

Although telling your people to do something seems simple enough, there is more to the art than is apparent. If you are an expert at giving orders, you probably are also skilled in planning, motivating, and persuading because those endeavors are prerequisites to giving good orders. Since giving orders is one of your main responsibilities, your success as a supervisor is measured by how skilled you are at it. You can improve your technique by adopting the following suggestions:

● Promote team effort when you give orders. Point out that the person's contribution is part of a total effort in which other people also contribute. Explain how what the person does will benefit other people and why his or her cooperation is needed. Say that it takes people working together to reach the company's goals, and illustrate your statement by giving examples of it in your own department.

● Make your order appropriate for the person and the situation. Use different approaches depending on the workload, the mood of the individual, the importance of the order, and the urgency with which it should be carried out. A request is always better than a command because it makes the person feel that cooperation is being asked for rather than demanded.

The suggestion is another type of order which is usually effective. Its success depends on the initiative and cooperative attitude of people. Although the order is implied, it brings a positive response from conscientious individuals.

Because of its demanding and authoritative tone, you should seldom use a direct order. Limit its use to times of emergency to indicate the urgency of the situation or when working with people who don't respond to any other type of order.

● Make your order clear and complete. Keep it as simple as possible, but be sure it includes all the information needed for it to be carried out quickly and efficiently. If more than one person is involved, clarify who is responsible for doing what. If time is a factor, say when the job should be started.

Check for understanding of your order by asking that it be repeated back to you. Go over how the most difficult part of the job will be handled. Confirm that you have provided the information needed.

● Give your order at the opportune time, such as when the receiver is most receptive. Avoid giving an order when the person is very busy or engrossed in another matter. If an order is complex or detailed, give it when the person is fresh and alert—there will be less chance of misunderstanding. Be aware that an order given just before lunch or at quitting time might be forgotten when the person resumes work.

Deciding when to issue an order can be just as critical as the order itself, especially if the order involves a major change. Experienced supervisors analyze the timing of their orders as to whether the greater risk lies in waiting or in acting immediately. They consider the probable outcome in each case and act accordingly. But they also recognize that many things take time and that mistakes are likely if they're impatient. Impatient people often make poor decisions in trying to settle matters quickly.

Case-in-Point: "Any damn fool can give orders," says Jean Richer, Manager of the Champlain Area for Canadian National Railways (Montreal). "A good supervisor coordinates the work. He gets the work done through others by picking the right man for the right job and by giving encouragement and support to his people to do a good job."

9.7 How to Raise and Improve Team Spirit

Promoting a team spirit is a major job for many supervisors, and it's getting to be more difficult as new factors and influences appear in the workplace. Pressures such as the push to achieve greater productivity, the introduction of new technology, and the constant need to train and retrain affect the desire and ability of people to work together efficiently and with a common goal in mind.

Yet there are answers to these problems. Knowledgeable and astute supervisors have found ways to overcome them. Here are some of the ways they've done it. To follow in their footsteps, you should:

● Be aware that many of your people may know little about the technical aspects of the department's operations, and they may occasionally have problems because of this. Encourage them to ask questions when they don't understand something.

● Realize that they may not ask the questions that they should to get answers to their problems. Also, they may be poor listeners. Train them to think before they speak, to phrase questions clearly, and to hear everything that is said to them.

● Recognize that tension and stress often result when people make errors. Try to console and sympathize with individuals on such occasions. Remind them that no one is perfect. Refrain from fault-finding, and be positive with your remarks.

● Note that you can't realistically expect everyone to like each other and be good friends. But if you demonstrate a team attitude and get your people to listen to you when you're talking about a common objective, you can go a long way toward raising and improving team spirit.

9.8 The Right Way to Put Across Management's Decisions

The supervisor who is skilled in giving orders has a great advantage over one who doesn't have that ability. The skilled person issues orders which are easily understood and don't result in hard feelings or resentment. Such a leader also does not use a higher authority's name in order to gain acceptance and compliance.

To put across management's decisions properly you must give and be responsible for them as if they were your own, whether you wholeheartedly agree with them or not. A weak supervisor says, "*The boss* would like you to . . ." A strong supervisor says, "*I would* like you to . . . ."

Case-in-Point: "Although I didn't agree with upper management's decision on what we were going to ask the operators of the new machines to do, I knew that, being a member of management, I had to follow the procedure we had agreed to and not let my people know how I felt." So spoke John Teller, supervisor in a fabric mill in Alabama, when telling me about how a new process was running. "The plant manager was right, as he usually is. I would have looked bad if I hadn't given him my support. Besides, we have a much stronger management team when we are in agreement on our policies and procedures. We do our best to make things work the best way possible."

9.9 How to Avoid Misunderstandings

We would be much more efficient and make fewer mistakes if we didn't have misunderstandings. Unfortunately, there are many ways that misunderstandings occur and conditions often are such to make them likely. The best way to avoid them is to recognize a situation where you might have a misunderstanding, and take steps to prevent it. Here are some tips on how to do that, both on your own and your listener's part.

A common kind of misunderstanding results when you assume a person attaches the same meaning to certain words that you do. The way such misunderstanding can be avoided is for the listener to repeat the message in different words, asking if that is what is meant. Another way is to ask a question pertaining to the message.

Misunderstandings also occur when someone simply doesn't hear certain words. Failure to hear *not,* for example, can cause a person to do something by mistake. It pays to repeat a message of this type using different words but emphasizing the *not.*

Many misunderstandings result from a person's poor choice of words. The words that you use in giving an order to someone may be taken as mandatory or discretionary. *Shall, will, is to,* and *must* are words which order action, while words such as *may, recommend,* and *suggest* do not require action. The word *should* may be interpreted either way.

You can make your message clear and help a person to better understand it if you come right to the point when you start talking. If you begin by asking a question which the listener doesn't know the reason for, you put the listener at a disadvantage. It's better to start by saying what you want or why you've come to talk.

When people don't speak the same language in the terms they use to describe something, they are very prone to have a misunderstanding. Make sure when you talk about a quantity or use numbers that your listener really understands. Use a written note if you have any doubts.

Case-in-Point: A supervisor in a small machine shop in Canton, Ohio told me of a misunderstanding that embarrassed him. One of his machinists had told him that the last box of a special fastener was used from the storeroom and that more should be ordered. The supervisor asked the company buyer to order "a box" of the fasteners knowing that they were packed 12 to a box and there were few calls for them. The buyer, accustomed to ordering material of this type in gross lots, placed the order with the supplier for "a gross." The shop still had many boxes of the item in the storeroom several years later.

Case-in-Point: A supervisor in a plant in Chicago was involved in the loss of 200 gallons of a chemical a few years ago through a misunderstanding. He had phoned a pipefitter to "remove the bottom valve on #60 tank so that it could be repaired." The pipefitter understood the supervisor to say #16 tank, and the spill resulted. Shortly after this incident the company adopted the use of A.V.O. (Avoid Verbal Orders) forms for transmitting such instructions.

9.10 Feedback: The Sure-Fire Way of Assuring Understanding

Since communication between people sometimes is a stumbling block in putting a plan or order into action, effective leaders have devised a way to check that the information and instructions they give are understood. They need to because many employees do not let their supervisors know of their ignorance by asking questions or by saying they do not understand.

Feedback has been proven to be the best way to assure understanding of your instructions or message. You get it by asking your listener to repeat your message back to you. You get it also by asking questions and listening.

Case-in-Point: At the Chemigum Plant of the Goodyear Tire and Rubber Company, Akron, Ohio, supervisors use a questionnaire to get feedback on safety. "We have a group of general questions which we ask a man after he has become familiar with the plant, his job, and the Safe Practice Manual," reports John Haynes, Maintenance Supervisor. "If he can't answer the questions, we know that he needs more training on safety. We try to see that he gets the information and learns the safety rules."

Feedback takes place between a supervisor and his or her superior when the superior requests reports on the status and progress of work projects. The superior learns from the report if management's decisions are being carried out and if agreed upon procedures are being followed by the supervisor.

If you want to feel more certain that your instructions and orders to your people are understood, get feedback from them in one form or another.

9.11 Effective Feedback Techniques

Feedback plays an important role in communications between supervisors and people on the job. One of your supervisory responsibilities is to provide feedback to the people who work for you. They, in turn, provide feedback to you when they tell you how they feel about you or what they think of their job. However, feedback is of most value when it is handled properly by both parties. Here are the techniques that have proven to be most effective:

When You Give Feedback

• Do it at an appropriate time, not just any time. Give it in private, whether it's praise or criticism. Be careful to avoid remarks that might make you appear biased or prejudiced.

• Decide what you are going to say beforehand, and try to match the style of the person you're talking to. Say, "It's my opinion that . . . ." rather than, "The fact is that . . . ."

• Refer to the person's performance, not to his or her personal qualities. Tell the person without being vague what he or she has done wrong.

• Describe rather than judge. Words like *good* and *bad* say little, while words like *consistent, complete, insufficient,* and *weak* have more meaning.

• Include both positives and negatives in your remarks, but try to give more positives to avoid hurting the person.

When You Receive Feedback

• If you ask for feedback, ask for it from someone you trust and respect. Feedback is more likely to be accurate and relevant when you receive it from those who know you quite well.

• Feel that you understand what you are getting, that you can accept it, and that you will be able to do something about it.

• Ask for feedback in a neutral and impartial way. Try to not put someone on the spot.

• Tell, if possible, your suppliers of feedback what benefit they may get from the communication. You want them to feel that the risk of providing it is worth it.

• Make it a practice to paraphrase what you've been told. This avoids the possibility of misunderstanding a person's meaning.

- Maintain a nondefensive attitude. You'll be less concerned if people judge you as a success or failure.

9.12 When to Put Your Orders in Writing

It's much easier to give instructions and orders orally than in writing. Face-to-face communication is faster, more direct, and often more clear since you can add tone and feeling to your message. However, some orders are better put into writing. Here are a few examples of such cases.

If an order must be carried out in steps and the sequence is important, put the order in writing. The person carrying it out can refer to the order as the job progresses. Similarly, if an order is complex and includes quantities, having it in writing will help prevent omissions and mistakes.

Whenever you change an order that was in writing, put the new order also in writing. If an order must be passed from one person to another, such as from one work shift to another, it's a good idea to have it in writing. Put it in the department log book or in a memo to be passed on to the people.

If your order has a high degree of permanence to it and may need to be referred to in the future, having it in writing will expedite and facilitate that.

Caution: Written communications have a big weakness—the reader can't ask questions. Consequently, a written message which is unclear, incomplete, or poorly written for some other reason may not accomplish its objective. When you write an order, read it back as if you were the reader to make certain that it conveys the request or information you intended.

9.13 Recordkeeping: A Vital Means of Control

Keeping records is one of the responsibilities of people who make decisions and give orders. Supervisors must not only document most of their work but also see that much of the data gets into the files. Maintaining an up-to-date set of records is the only way to keep track of production operations, maintenance, service, and procedural changes of a business.

Most supervisors dislike paperwork, preferring instead to spend their time with their people to see that problems are solved and work accomplished. Yet records must be made and kept if costs are to be controlled, operations conducted at optimum efficiency, and the business properly managed.

Although some supervisors may have relatively few duties involving records, the ones they do have are vital. Unless other people are assigned to the task, they are responsible for the time spent by their people on the job and records of absenteeism. In the office a supervisor may be expected to see that accounting records of various types are kept including purchasing orders, invoices, insurance and tax documents, wages and salaries, and the many fringe benefits which companies give their employees. In the plant a supervisor may need to keep records of machines, parts, equipment capacity and rating, preventive mainte-nance, raw materials, finished stock, inspections, accidents, and the various process data relating to the products manufactured or the service the company performs.

Accurate data and records are a "must" in today's business and industrial operations for several reasons. Data is needed for making management decisions and to measure operating efficiency. Good records are needed to support pro-posals for capital expenditures or for improvements in existing systems. Records are also needed to supply the various local, state, and federal governments the many types of information and data they want.

The best way to handle records is to keep up with them as you create them. Postponing making a record can lead to stress to do it later when you may be busy with other matters. There is always the risk, too, that you will forget to make the record. This can lead to criticism as well as frustration when the information is needed later.

10

GUARANTEED METHODS
FOR GETTING
COOPERATION

SINCE cooperation of people makes work easier and gets more done, supervisors should continually be looking for how to get it, both from their people on the job and from their peers. Fortunately, there are many ways to promote cooperation and bring about good employee performance. Successful supervisors do it by building a close rapport with people, keeping them informed, helping them with their problems, and showing appreciation for good work, among other ways.

But supervisors must be aware of the roadblocks to getting cooperation. A major pitfall is attitude. Effective supervisors have the right attitude toward their people and the job to be done. Also, they are able to influence the attitude of their people.

Cooperation from people on the job must be augmented with cooperation from peers in order to maximize productivity. Communication plays a big part in getting along with other supervisors in solving problems and reaching goals. Meetings provide the setting for supervisors to show responsibility and cooperation. Participative management has been shown to have many benefits.

10.1 What People Like About Their Supervisors

Surveys of people on the job reveal that liking the supervisor is one of the reasons most frequently mentioned for liking the job. This finding explains why a person may do a good job for one supervisor and a poor one for another.

Workers can give you many reasons why they prefer one supervisor to another and why they respect one and not another. If you want to be in the select group, you should think about some of the characteristics that people like to see in their supervisor.

Case-in-Point: John Chance, Warehousing Manager of Diana Stores Corp., North Bergen, New Jersey, says that without respect a supervisor might as well "pack in the job." "Being a boss means giving, receiving, even demanding respect of the people you supervise. And when you give it, there's no doubt you'll receive it," is the way he puts it.

Today's workers are good judges of their leaders. Workers hope that their supervisors:

1. Show a concern more with them than their output. Workers want their supervisors to be friends, not bosses who threaten them or demand work from them.

2. Are devout and dedicated planners and organizers. They should guide and train, investigate problems, and improve working conditions.

3. Show them how to do a job correctly when they've done it wrong. They should not bawl out people who make mistakes nor should they demand obedience.

4. Have trust and confidence that their people can do the work. Supervisors should give their people authority and responsibility as well as freedom in how to do a job.

5. Act and talk positively. Good leaders praise and compliment people for their accomplishments. They also boost morale and promote teamwork.

Caution: Although being friendly with your people can gain you their cooperation on the job, if you extend the friendliness off the job, you could be in for trouble. "A supervisor must be careful in his social dealings with his men," says John Butler, Dover Division Line Supervisor, Public Service Co. of New Hampshire. "Too much socializing can create on-the-job problems that can affect the supervisor's control and hurt his effectiveness. I don't think a man in my position can socialize with a man one minute, then expect him not to think he can't have special considerations the next just because he's close to the boss." Butler's observations might be summarized as: be friendly, but discreet.

10.2 Getting Cooperation by Asking Questions

When you ask one of your people for help, you inflate the person's ego because you indicate that he or she has the capability to help or the knowledge which is of value to you and the company. Asking for help, therefore, is a good way to compliment someone.

You have three objectives when you ask a person a question: to get information, to tell the person of your needs, and to get cooperation. Here are some examples of how to use questions to gain these benefits. Ask questions in order to:

- Call attention to a problem. You ask why a procedure isn't working right.
- Get agreement. You ask if everybody feels the same about what should be done or if somebody has doubts or disagrees.
- Provide reasons. You ask why a job has been done a certain way when searching for a better way.
- Receive suggestions. You ask for ideas to solve problems or to do a job safer or faster.
- Promote thinking. You ask if the cause of a condition or situation is known as an approach to doing something about it.

Caution: Once you ask for suggestions, ideas, or help, you must be ready to accept and adopt them periodically. If you establish a pattern of not doing this, you take the risk of not getting them in the future.

10.3 How to Use Self-Interest to Advantage

Psychologists tell us that people spend more than 90 percent of their thinking time speculating and reflecting on their behavior. Sharp supervisors take advantage of this fact to get cooperation from their people. You can do it too.

How-to-Do-It: Before issuing instructions or giving an order, ask yourself how a person can gain by doing what you want. Then put your instructions or orders in terms of what's in it for him or her. Here are a few examples of the words to use with this technique:

"You won't risk getting the dangerous chemical in your eyes if you wear your goggles whenever you handle it."

"By getting that dirty job done today you won't have to put those clothes back on again tomorrow."

"If you'll help me with this work today, you can take off early tomorrow."

Try this technique for getting cooperation. You'll find many opportunities where you can use it. And the good thing about it is that it usually works.

10.4 Ten Sure-Fire Ways to Win People's Cooperation

Good supervision is the art of getting others to do what you want, when you want it and how you want it. But such response from people doesn't come automatically to a supervisor. You've got to build up your relations with people and earn their cooperation. Here are ten ways to promote and kindle their feelings to the point where they will willingly cooperate with you:

1. Stress team effort when you communicate; use the word "we" frequently.
2. Make an effort to reward people who do more than you ask of them.
3. Set practical and realistic goals for your people; discuss the goals, making sure they understand and accept them.
4. Praise maximally and criticize minimally; never embarrass a person in front of others.
5. Supervise by persuasion rather than by force or pressure.
6. Help people when they need it; respond to their desires and needs.
7. Be honest about problems and issues; show that you have people's interests at heart.
8. Give people a chance to express their opinions; let them participate in problem-solving and decision-making.
9. Sponsor and promote training and development programs.
10. Demonstrate by what you say and do that you consider loyalty and integrity to be important virtues.

10.5 Roadblocks to Getting Cooperation

Most people on the job react adversely to weak leadership. They do it by failing to cooperate. Many people also are critical of poor managing. If you supervise in a manner they don't think is right, you create roadblocks to gaining their cooperation. Here are some supervisory actions which disappoint people and turn them off:

● Not recognizing extra effort. When people go that extra mile, they expect you to notice and give them credit for it. If you ignore a special effort, you may not receive it again.

● Being fair in judgment. When you make a statement that shows you overlook both incompetence and superior performance, you suggest that whatever people do makes no real difference to you. To be fair with people, you should give criticism as well as compliments when they are due.

● Passing off your own importance. Being meek and humble doesn't fit your position. Your people know you are in charge and have the authority to make decisions. Pretending that you are not important for any reason weakens your credibility and attacks the intelligence of your people who know better.

● Being indecisive. If you aren't sure whether you want or don't want something, you cause confusion. When people don't know what you really want, they may suspect you are trapping them and will try to play it safe.

● Using fear and intimidation. People don't work willingly for someone they fear. When people respect their supervisors they plan and discuss problems with them. They go along with their supervisors, not fearing them or looking for ways to betray or defeat them.

10.6 How to Remember People and Their Names

Of all the skills that lead to admiration and success, one of the most desired by supervisors is being able to remember people and their names. Although some supervisors believe they have a poor memory and not much can be done about it, this is not true. You can learn how to remember people and their names.

You gain two benefits when you remember a person's name:

1. You pay him or her a compliment. If you don't address a person by name, you imply that you don't consider the person important enough to go to the trouble of remembering his or her name.

2. You are more likely to get the person's help and cooperation. Use of such words as *buddy* or *hey you* are blunt and crude. Moreover, they don't show respect. Many people are reluctant to respond if you show that you haven't bothered to learn or remember their names.

Remembering people and their names can be easy if you put some effort into doing it. Here's how you should proceed:

● Make sure you hear and learn the person's name when you first meet. If you fail to hear a person's name when you are introduced, ask for it to be repeated or even spelled. This interest on your part impresses people.

● Look at the person's face. Most people remember what they see better than what they hear. When you look at someone's face, search for a feature that is most memorable such as dimples or a scar. Although you may feel that it's not right to stare, remember that it's good manners to look at a person's face while listening to him or her. Take advantage of this listening time to observe details of the person's face.

● Connect the name to the face. Since faces are easier to remember than names, use the face to remind you of the name. Then whenever you see a familiar face, it will remind you of the name.

● Repeat the name at every opportunity. Do this when you talk to the person, and whenever you talk about the person to someone else. Also, always use the name when saying goodbye to the person. This enables you to confirm that you have the name right, and it also fixes it in your memory.

10.7 Making People Defensive: A Major Barrier to Cooperation

Supervisors must be careful to avoid making their people defensive if they want to have their cooperation. When people are on the defensive, they are concerned with avoiding blame, being uncommitted, not getting involved, and just "watching out for themselves." In your relations with your people you should try to put them at ease.

How-to-Do-It: You can overcome this barrier with empathy and sympathy for people and their problems, by showing respect, and by recognizing that people have a right to their opinions.

People don't go on the defensive when they are shown consideration. Take time to talk with them, especially when they have problems or are making mistakes. They will usually feel better and try harder. Idle people are usually ignored people.

Case-in-Point: Many years ago the Martin-Decker Co. adopted a program called Operation GIT (Get It Together), in their main plant. This was a positive action program to reduce errors and boost production. Whenever any employee observed an error in equipment assembly, calibration, instructions, specifications, or simple written communications, the person tagged the mistake with a GIT sticker. By concentrating on fixing the problem, not fixing the blame, the company eliminated "finger pointing" and encouraged cooperation among workers.

10.8 How to Avoid Being a Grouch

Some people are always complaining. They seem to have the knack of being able to find something that isn't to their liking and then griping about it. Do you complain frequently?

What is your tolerance for others' complaints? Here are the ways you can avoid being a grouch:

● Monitor your attitude and feelings with extra care on days when nothing seems to be going right.

● Have the courage to keep your troubles to yourself.

● Be generally patient with people, even when they go against your wishes.

● Pause a few moments before passing judgment on a grumpy person.

- Counter stress by exercising, getting enough sleep, and adopting good eating and drinking habits.
- Give people who are not feeling well a little extra consideration.
- Steer clear of an individual when he or she apparently is in a bad mood.
- Realize that when you are having trouble with people, they are having trouble with you.

10.9 Five Pitfalls to Avoid when Seeking Cooperation

Since cooperation among people on the job is so important, supervisors need to be constantly alert to combat anything which discourages it. Experts on human relations say there are five major behavioral characteristics which inhibit cooperation. I have listed them in a special way to make them easy to remember.

Watch out for and try not to be guilty of these P's:

Prejudice—Having a preconceived opinion resulting from past experience. People and issues should be evaluated on their own merits. Keep an open mind to avoid being biased.

Preoccupation—Being so busy with other matters that you don't devote enough time to people. You've got to listen to people and show an interest in them if you want them to cooperate.

Premature judgment—Accepting first impressions or incomplete information. Obtain more data before you criticize, condemn, or reach a conclusion on a person's behavior.

Predisposition—Hearing what you want to hear and seeing what you want to see. Avoid making up your mind and then looking for evidence to support it.

Projection—Attributing your motives and faults to others. If you tend to be slow and need motivation, don't think that other people are necessarily also that way.

10.10 Three Ways to Bring About Better Employee Performance

If employees always willingly did their work to the best of their ability, supervisors would have a much easier job. Unfortunately, all people don't have this temperament. Some need to be motivated and others need to be encouraged. Some need close supervision while others go ahead well on their own. Successful supervisors have learned that they need to give of themselves if they expect to get good performances from their people. Although there may be several ways they can do this, three are especially effective. You should practice them to get the best from your people.

1. Most people like to be in on things; they like to know what's going on, and even more, they like to have a voice in decisions about their work and the job. If you give them a chance to participate in these matters, they're more likely to do a better job. Even if you don't adopt every one of their suggestions, they appreciate it when you give them the opportunity to discuss a matter and when you listen to them. Keep them informed. Let them know what's expected of them and why. Most people want to help but sometimes they need to be told how they can.

2. If you let people work out rules and regulations, they'll abide by them more. People are often more strict in this role than you would be. What's more, they'll make it rough on anyone who gets out of line. Be warm and friendly in your approach to people. Avoid trying to push them. Talk *with* them rather than *at* them.

3. One of the best ways to bring out better employee performance is to treat people as individuals and to give them everything possible to show your appreciation for their efforts and achievements. If you can make them feel they are working *with* you rather than *for* you, you stand to get a maximum of cooperation. Give them recognition. Tell them you consider them important and depend on them.

An expert's comment: Phil Ensor, Director of Employee Relations at the Goodyear Tire and Rubber Co., wrote a paper on in-plant communications. He said, "The type of relationship which exists between the management group and the employees cannot be overlooked with respect to the extent communications will change organizational effectiveness. If the relationship is rigid, authoritative, and adversary, messages passed downward from 'the bosses' will be viewed as propaganda and will be for all practical purposes disregarded. None of us have a tendency to pay close attention to individuals and groups when little or no basis has been formulated for mutual trust and concern."

10.11 Reasons Why Some People Don't Come to Work

One of the biggest problems that supervisors must contend with is absenteeism of their people. It has been reported that almost 2 million employees fail to show up at their jobs each day. Why does this happen? Are there answers to the problem? Here is a list of the reasons why workers take time off from the job along with some possible solutions:

• Inability to get along with fellow workers. Unless a supervisor handles personality clashes quickly, conflicts can develop into feuds with everyone losing.

● Having to put up with poor working conditions such as inadequate ventilation, bad lighting, and a dirty environment. Pleasant surroundings can make coming to work more agreeable.

● Being bored. When jobs are very routine or repetitive, job enrichment is the only answer.

● Finding the work too difficult. Supervisors should be alert to recognize when training or retraining is needed by a worker.

● Feeling that they are not needed. Motivated people are turned off when their efforts are not rewarded with increased responsibility.

● Uncertainty of transportation. Absenteeism tends to rise if public transportation is infrequent or unreliable. Some companies solve this problem by encouraging and coordinating car pools.

● Poor supervision. Uncommunicative or surly supervisors can create absenteeism by what they say and do. Make sure you are not guilty of such offenses.

10.12 Advice for the "Do-It-Yourself" Supervisor

If you are singlehandedly trying to conquer all the challenges thrown your way, you're overlooking the major responsibility of your job as a supervisor. As a member of management, you are expected to get work done through others. Although a do-it-yourself supervisor may have good intentions, he or she should realize that a person has limitations, and that the company doesn't expect a supervisor to handle all matters by himself or herself. The supervisor who tries to handle a job without help may get only half the facts about a situation and consequently correct only part of a problem.

Today's total business needs are met best by a concerted team effort. Industrial supervisors, in particular, almost always have available to them staff support, both technical and administrative, to help work out problems. Office supervisors also have such support and can consult with department managers, their superiors, and officers of the company. When supervisors are faced with other-than-routine problems, they should ask for this help.

If you are a do-it-yourself supervisor you are jeopardizing your future with the company because your actions suggest that you do not know how to delegate. When you can successfully delegate, you demonstrate that you are capable of moving up the management ladder to a better job.

10.13 The Importance of Talking Positively About Peers

The supervisor who always speaks positively or complimentarily about another supervisor finds it easy to get along well with him or her and with other company management people. The temptation to criticize or blame someone at your level to promote yourself is often hard to resist, but you're better off if you absolutely avoid it. People on the job don't get ahead by tearing someone else down.

Disparaging remarks about a person's dress, manner, or behavior gain nothing and only make you appear biased and prejudiced. People are different, have different viewpoints, and different standards. Simply because you see things differently is no reason for you to condemn or ridicule people who look and act differently than you.

Saying a good word for another supervisor when you have the opportunity shows that you recognize the capabilities and attitudes of other people, that you are not self-centered, and that you give credit when it is due. You'll find that it also gains you cooperation from the person you compliment.

10.14 How to Keep Communication Channels Open with Other Supervisors

Mistakes and failures to get jobs handled in the plant or office can sometimes be traced to lack of cooperation between supervisors. The situation may be difficult to remedy when the company operates with two or three shifts. Management needs to take steps to improve communications among its supervisors in such situations.

You can do something about the problem by upgrading your relations with your fellow supervisors. Get to know those people on other shifts and in departments with which you work. Make friends with them and take time to discuss mutual problems. The rapport you have with your peers will help to improve business communications.

Don't assume that other supervisors know something about a job or work in progress simply because you know it. Ask them if they know about it. If you must report on a plant or office problem to a supervisor on the next shift, use a notebook or the department log book. That prevents you from forgetting to mention it at shift change.

Consider other supervisors' points of view. Don't get so involved in your own problems that you forget ones that they may have. They may need some of the information you have to do their job. Adapt your communication style to the needs of the supervisors involved, allowing for their experience, knowledge, and capabilities. If details are necessary in your communications, by all means provide them.

Never pass the buck or blame something on a supervisor of another shift. You may get out of trouble for the moment, but you'll lose the trust and respect of people for the long term. Show appreciation for help received. Be quick to thank people for information which they didn't need to give you.

Avoid indifference and lack of interest when working on problems which other supervisors could solve. To keep the communication channels open often takes patience, persistence, and tact. Be sure you're long rather than short on these things if you want to get cooperation from your peers.

10.15 Five Guaranteed Ways to Gain the Cooperation of Your Peers

Any supervisor who attempts to run a department without working with other supervisors is likely to get in trouble. Teamwork is necessary to solve today's personnel and labor problems, keep up with technology, and control costs. All these things must be properly managed if a company is to be profitable and grow.

Effective teamwork in the department and among other departments of the company requires good communication among supervisors and willingness to cooperate in working toward goals. You can help to develop cooperation with your peers by improving your communications and by adopting a spirit of understanding. Here are five ways of doing this:

1. Consider how your actions affect the operation of other departments. Make decisions that will benefit rather than hinder them.

2. Recognize that other supervisors have goals to meet and commitments to honor, and realize they have problems just as you do. Treat them as partners rather than opponents. Offer to help whenever you have an opportunity.

3. Do everything you can to eliminate friction between your people and other supervisors' people. Promote friendly relations and compromise, if necessary, on differences in order to achieve compatibility.

4. Explain and give reasons when you ask another supervisor to do something for you. Point out benefits from going along with your request.

5. Distinguish the difference between cooperation and interference when it comes to the performance and behavior of other supervisors' people. Try to always deal with supervisors rather than their people when you want help.

Case-in-Point: John Beers, Supervisor in the Roger Mills Co. in Alabama, found two people smoking in the cotton stores area one afternoon when he was checking inventory. One of the men was his utility man, the other a warehouse man from the shipping and receiving department. Beers reported the incident to the Plant Safety Director and then told his own boss how he handled the problem as follows: "I was first concerned with the danger of fire in this 'no smoking' area so I stopped that. Then I told my man to get back to work and that I would talk to him later. Lastly, I spoke to the other worker's supervisor about the violation because I realized that it was up to the Warehouse Supervisor, not me, to discipline that man." Beers was complimented by his boss on how he handled the incident on both communication and cooperation with other management people.

10.16 How to Hold Meetings That Count

In your career you will probably attend some meetings which will be a waste of time. Successful supervisors are seldom guilty of calling unnecessary meetings. If you hold a meeting, you should have a good reason for it to justify taking busy people from their work. You must also be sure to conduct it properly to get the most from it. Meetings are good for identifying and recognizing problems. They are not usually good for trying to solve them.

The people who should be invited to the meeting is a matter for the person calling the meeting to decide. Obvious choices are those who will be asked to contribute to reaching the meeting's objective. People who will be affected by decisions made in the meeting are others who you may want to be present.

If you are to lead the meeting you should have as much information as you can gather to facilitate the discussion. To enable the participants to also come prepared, notify them sometime in advance of the meeting time. You can help matters by including a brief explanation of what the meeting will cover in your notification.

The first matter you should handle at the meeting is to state the reason for getting together and what you hope to accomplish. Resist any attempt of people to confuse the objectives or to broaden them, even though this may introduce complications since the participants will be looking out for their best interests. People at meetings usually try to be constructive but their motives may lead them to obstruct as well as introduce side issues.

To conduct an efficient meeting you must see that the discussion stays on the subject. Do this by immediately interjecting a question or statement relative to it whenever someone starts to stray. Another control you should exert is to exclude matters of implementation from the discussion until what has to be done has been decided.

Problems often encountered in a meeting are those concerning when and what decisions should be made. Members usually have several courses of action available to them, any one of which probably would lead to the desired objective. In such situations, it is better to select one and go ahead with it rather than continue the discussion in hopes of finding a perfect answer.

Try to keep the meeting moving along so that you don't lose the interest of the members and also that you cover all items you planned to discuss. One hour or less is an ideal time for the meeting to last. It's better to have a second meeting than to go beyond two hours.

When to close a meeting is another matter for you to decide. If you have an agenda to work from, you simply adjourn after you have handled the last item.

Without an agenda, it's not so easy because people are inclined to go on until the leader announces that the meeting is over. You can signify the end by saying, "That's all I have to discuss today. Thanks for coming."

10.17 Participative Management: What It's All About

When a company adopts the principles of participative management, it encourages and promotes participation of its employees in decision-making on matters relative to how the company should be operated. True participation means more that just physical involvement in a work situation. It is involvment of the employees' minds in their thinking and opinions of the work and how it should be performed.

Case-in-Point: Marvin Runyon, President and Chief Executive Officer of Nissan Manufacturing Corp., recently said, "Our system is structured to max-imize interaction between management and employees. We only have five levels of management, whereas the traditional automotive company has 10 to 12. By decreasing the number of levels involved in the communication process, we've made it easier for ideas to flow back and forth throughout the company.

"Nissan needed the cooperation and enthusiasm of its employees. We needed their commitment, and that was something we knew we'd have to earn. So we started by getting them involved in deciding what kind of company Nissan should be."

It is easy, however, to be misled into thinking that employees are participat-ing when you see them attending meetings, asking questions, and seemingly agreeing with an activity that has been decided for them. But only if they make suggestions or contribute some ideas can they be said to be truly participating.

Supervisors should realize that true participation isn't achieved easily. Besides, there are limits to how far management can go with it. For one thing, it is more difficult to get the participation of a large group than a small one. For another, the procedures of attaining participation are not always clear-cut and straight-forward.

If you try to accomplish too much in one step, some people are likely to hold back and even withdraw entirely. It is best to use participation as a way of encouraging contribution and teamwork.

10.18 Seven Benefits of Participative Management

There are many benefits and advantages to getting employees involved especially if you can persuade them to contribute on matters which usually are considered only the responsibilities of management. It should be noted, too, that both the employees and the company gain. Here are seven of the most important benefits that result from effective participative management:

1. It gives people the right to be creative members of a cooperating group.

2. It leads to new relationships being formed between employee and supervisor, and between an employee and other employees.

3. It can spur less skilled employees to greater effort, and it encourages them to accept responsibility.

4. It usually results in more job satisfaction and greater output of employees.

5. It helps to improve job performance. When employees have a say in how their work should be done, they feel the need to prove that their way will enable the job to be performed more efficiently.

6. It raises human dignity and interest in what other people are doing.

7. It enables change to be accepted much more easily, particularly when those affected by it have participated in deciding its extent and how it should be implemented.

The truth of these words is illustrated by the number of displeased and unhappy customers who find that they have bought a poor quality or inferior product. If, for example, you find that you have been stuck with a lemon, aren't you likely to say, "I wonder who worked on this one—nobody in his or her right mind could have considered it okay," or "Who was the day-dreamer who filled this order?"

Supervisors should think about what their people are doing personally to improve or destroy the company's image. Employees must be supported and commended when they make an extra effort to improve the quality of the product or service they are involved with. If they try and are ridiculed for what they have attempted to do, they will be turned off. Doubletalk on quality is an effective damper. Show that you place quality of workmanship above quantity of output with what you expect from your people.

11.7 Positive Ways to Get Workers Concerned with Quality

You can't control quality all by yourself—you need the help of every person on the job. If your people don't seem interested in quality, you must tackle the job of selling them on its importance.

To make people conscious of the importance of quality, you must stress it on their first day on the job and bring it to their attention frequently afterward. Explain what good quality is and what the company strives for with its products or service. Show what kind of work is acceptable and what does not meet specifications.

Another way to impress upon employees the necessity of doing quality work is to convince them that their failure to do so makes problems for other employees, their fellow-workers, and eventually the customers. When people know the reasons for doing their jobs a certain way, they are more likely to be quality-minded than if they are told only how to do their jobs.

You can get people to be concerned with quality by talking about the cost of poor quality and how quality actually is the determining factor in whether the company is profitable and stays in business. When you tell people their jobs are at stake, you hit home with your selling of the importance of quality.

Perhaps the best way to sell quality is to point out the benefits of it. You can tell people, for example, that quality:

1. Reduces cost of rework as well as waste of time and material.
2. Meets competition and increases sales of products and service.
3. Builds pride in workmanship and satisfaction in accomplishment.
4. Gains recognition and enhances job security.

A Personal Viewpoint: Irving Bluestone, Vice-President of the United Automobile, Aerospace, and Agricultural Implement Workers of America made some statements about quality to UAW local unions in the General Motors section of his union that are worth repeating. He said, "Good quality isn't the concern of General Motors alone. It's important to us workers, too! It can affect the security of the workers. Poor quality cuts down sales. Then it cuts down jobs. So good quality enhances the product—and the job security of the workers who produce it.

"We have always insisted that GM must recognize the interrelationship between quality performance and work pace. An overloaded worker can't give quality performance. Workers want to produce quality products. They must be given the time and the opportunity to do so. Workers want to take pride in the jobs they do.

"We urge each worker to pay close attention to the quality of his work. For when quality workmanship is the rule, the job security of workers is strengthened. Workers and their families benefit."

11.8 How to Build Enthusiasm for Quality Performance

Every supervisor wants high quality products or service to come from company employees. Quality workmanship is vital to a smooth-running department and plant. But all employees are not quality-minded. You need to motivate some people and you must create enthusiasm for quality performance with others. Companies through their supervisors practice several ways of doing these things.

One way they do it is to conduct a program or contest to name the "Employee of the Month," the person in the department or plant who contributes the most to quality for that period. To get people interested you must provide an incentive such as a bonus, time off with pay, or some other inducement. Although praise for doing good work on the company bulletin board or in the newspaper spurs some individuals, most people want both praise and money.

Taking time to discuss quality with each employee is another way to get across its importance. When you spend your time doing this and are sincere about it, the employee will see that the company puts high quality workmanship high on the list of the responsibilities of his or her job.

Since liking one's work and getting satisfaction from it shows in the quality of one's performance, supervisors should try to match their people's skills and preferences to their jobs. If a person expresses repeated interest in another job or department, the company and the person will probably gain if a switch is made. A supervisor may not want to lose a good worker to another department, but if the change increases the quality of the person's workmanship, it's worthwhile. The supervisor who is flexible in this respect promotes and gets better quality performance from employees.

11.9 How to Make It Easy to Control Quality

One of the skills of successful supervisors is their ability to consistently keep up the quality of the products or service of their department. Part of their success with this can be attributed to the way they promote workmanship of their people. You can follow their lead on your job.

How-to-Do-It: Set up work procedures that make it easy for people to do good quality work. Then *recognize* and *comment* on the good quality work when they do it.

Most people like to feel that they are on top of their job and that what they do helps the company. You can boost this feeling and promote its continuance by not letting their efforts to meet or exceed the standards of the work go unnoticed. Tell your people you appreciate it when they do a good job.

All employees must accept the responsibility for controlling quality and meeting standards. Quality control isn't only a management function. Control requires detecting signs of poor quality and taking corrective steps immediately. You can't wait until the product or service drops below an acceptable level or specified standard. The way to keep in control of quality is to constantly stay on top of it. You do it by reacting as soon as you become aware of a downward trend in the condition of material, tools and equipment, or workmanship. A major deterioration in any one of these elements can cancel the satisfactory character of the other two.

Case-in-Point: The operator of a packaging machine in an office supply house noticed that the glue used by the machine was not resulting in complete closures—some of the packages were coming open after leaving the machine. His immediate response was to increase the amount of glue applied by the machine. He then notified his supervisor of the situation and both of them observed the operation to see if this adjustment corrected the problem. The supervisor also began to look for other causes such as misalignment of the glue applicator or poor quality glue. With both people working on this quality problem, it was soon solved. The packages sent out by the company continued to be tight and neat in appearance.

11.10 Personal Control: Key to Good Job Performance

Some of your people may feel that they are working for an impersonal company which has no control over the quality of their work, and that it's your job to make sure they do a good job. You should point out to these people that they are *employed* by "the company" the same as you, but they are *working* for you and responsible to you. With this approach you can develop personal control and achieve better performance from them.

You can accomplish this by letting them know they are people you respect and depend on. An employee who responds to your personal appeal will see a difference between letting "the company" down and letting you down. A person's pride in turning out quality work is reflected in your recognition and appreciation of his or her skills. But, in the same manner, a person who turns out poor quality work fails you as one who is depending on him or her.

By displaying personal interest and control you can develop a close relationship with your people. You can also make the need for quality a challenge to people to create personal pride in their efforts.

Case-in-Point: "I think a healthy pride in the work we are doing is very important," Ruth Berkey tells all her new employees. Berkey is office manager in a large chemical firm.

"Pride, the right kind of pride, increases our mental and physical powers, and keeps building up our self-confidence. Of course, pride in our work can come only with experience and skill. But if we do our work in a don't-care, slovenly manner, we'll never enjoy the benefits of pride."

11.11 How to Get Help on Quality Problems

Companies who are concerned with the quality of their products or service often try to learn what their customers think about them. They then are able to handle quality problems and thus keep their customers and get new ones.

Perhaps the most well-known practice of this is that of requesting a customer to comment on the product or service. If you have bought a new car recently, you may have received in the mail a questionnaire about how the car is performing for you and asking if the service the dealer has given you has been prompt and satisfactory. If you eat many of your meals away from home, you have probably noticed that some restaurants ask you to comment on the food and service in a space on the bill. These organizations want to know if the quality of their product or service pleases you. They realize the importance of quality, and they want to be aware of instances where they failed to provide it or could have done a better job. Some companies ask their own employees for help on improving quality.

Case-in-Point: Because they wanted improvement, Western Electric's Hawthorne Works conducted a survey of about 200 questions for their maintenance craftsmen. The craftsmen were asked to rate such things as the accuracy of engineering instructions, the availability of tools, the cooperation of fellow-workers, and other job site activities. By studying the responses, management determined where changes needed to be made. Consequently, innovations occurred at Hawthorne and better communications resulted.

Consultants are frequently hired today to provide direction and assistance to a company in solving operational problems. This is particularly true when management feels they need help to reduce costs. Experts in various types of manufacturing and business can help a company reduce waste and inefficiency as well as improve the quality of their product or service.

Case-in-Point: Two of the major rubber companies in Akron, Ohio in past years contracted with The Emerson Consultants, Inc., New York, to study their engineering and maintenance functions. In both cases, the companies were able to reduce operating costs and improve work procedures by adopting the recommendations of Emerson. Planning and scheduling, preventive maintenance practice, and better supervisional control were the outgrowths of the help provided.

11.12 What to Do About Poor Workmanship

By eliminating or reducing the causes of mistakes, you can increase the quality of output of your people. This is true in the office as well as on the production line because the results of a clerical or typing error can be just as costly as a tolerance error on a product.

Attitude toward the job is a big factor in workmanship quality. People who are interested in their work and like their company make few errors. One of your supervisory objectives, therefore, should be to promote interest in the job. Another should be to set a good example by being extra careful in your own work. A third should be to let everyone know that you believe it is within their capabilities to do error-free work.

Boredom is a common cause of poor workmanship, particularly with repetitive jobs. The best you can do to overcome it is to rotate people in different jobs to provide them some variety. You can also make certain that the right person is on the right job—a person doing a job that requires only a small portion of his or her abilities becomes bored quickly. Learn to recognize when a person is bored so you can try to expand the work, vary it, or add responsibility to it.

Some people find it difficult to do good work when there is a lot of noise or distraction in their work area. Ringing phones, noisy typewriters, and people talking can be distracting to efforts which are other than routine. You can solve such problems by seeing that noisy machines are individually enclosed or put in separate rooms. You can also relocate people away from the noise. Discouraging unnecessary talk and visiting in work areas are other ways to improve workmanship and raise the efficiency of employees.

Misunderstandings are sometimes the cause of poor workmanship. Study the incidents of misunderstandings which your people have experienced. Were your instructions too complex? Did you use technical terms that were unfamiliar? Did you tell them everything they needed to know to do the job? People may say they understand rather than admit they don't. You can overcome this problem by asking them questions or encouraging them to ask you questions. Whatever, let your people know that it's much better to ask questions than to make mistakes.

11.13 Tips on Solving Workmanship Problems

When you find that a quality problem is the result of poor workmanship, you must look for the cause immediately. You can do this by getting the answers to the following questions concerning the employee involved:

1. Does the employee need more training? If so, the training should be undertaken as soon as possible.

2. Does the employee understand the close tolerance or limits required? Nobody can consistently meet job specifications unless they understand them.

3. Is the employee careless? The person may need to be counseled on his or her work habits and shown why they must improve.

4. Does the employee lack the ability to do the job? If so, it would be better for everyone if the employee were given a job more in line with his or her ability.

A supervisor cannot tolerate poor workmanship on the job. You must determine the reason for it and do what is necessary to correct it. This step may include going to your boss for help if it appears that a major change is needed.

11.14 How to Combat Poor Quality Excuses

Some of your people may be reluctant to put forth extra effort on the job to maintain or assure quality. They will, of course, have excuses for their behavior. For one thing, they may not understand why quality is so important. For another, they may say that other people aren't going out of their way or working extra hard on quality, so why should they?

You have a job on your hands when you encounter such excuses because you've got to justify quality and get those people to agree.

How-to-Do-It: The way to combat excuses is to eliminate the logic behind them by establishing practices conducive to good quality and seeing that the practices become standard procedures. You can accomplish this in several ways:

1. Make sure that shortcuts are not taken on operating procedures.

2. Don't permit improper or defective tools to be used.

3. Have a definite policy on what is to be done with defective material.

4. Give recognition to quality workmanship.

People will not be able to come up with excuses for poor quality if you take steps to always promote it and literally make it a way of life.

11.15 Stress: A Factor Affecting Quality

Quality of your product or service won't maintain itself. You've got to continuously work at it. You've got to put the pressure on both yourself and your people if you expect to keep quality under control.

There's nothing harmful about some pressure or stress on the job. If people are not occasionally under pressure, they simply don't produce to their ability, much less give you a high level of performance. But the stress must be the right kind.

Stress which induces fear, anger, or frustration is wrong and usually results in more negative than positive effects. People who fear making mistakes, being criticized, or even losing their jobs waste energy and drive in combating this fear. The quality of their performance usually suffers. People who are angry from a feeling of injustice or frustration similarly do not perform well. They may simply refuse to be productive or their efforts may become destructive.

The right kind of stress is that which challenges, which encourages initiative, and which raises competitive feelings. Such stress is positive in its effect. People who feel called upon to use all their knowledge and skill on the job to compare favorably with others will put quality into their efforts. They will not waste time on thoughts of resentment and actions of retaliation.

11.16 Five Mistakes to Avoid in Quality Control

Some management people consider quality control a necessary evil. They see the persons who practice it as do-gooders, narrow technical specialists, and police-type checkers. The reasons they give for such dim views of quality control people deserve examination since they contain a few truths about the way some supervisors handle quality control. But since these methods of checking on quality are faults and weaknesses, you should consider them as pitfalls. The effective quality control supervisor avoids:

1. Relying too much on statistics, not enough on good judgment. The problem here is that technical data are often not available or cannot be obtained fast enough when a decision must be made. Decisions should be based on the information that is available plus use of good judgment.

2. Spending too much time trying to find defects, not enough time trying to prevent them. The job of quality control involves more than just preventing poor products from leaving the company. It includes preventing their creation. You may be handicapped in this inclusive effort if you don't know how to go about it. You may need to learn more about the process or service of your company so that you can be of greater value on the job.

3. Paying too much attention to the technical aspect, not enough to cost. You must be more concerned with the practical side of the function. Analytical evaluation is only as good as its ability to get results with the least cost.

4. Doing too much nit-picking, not showing enough concern with major issues. Too many quality control people believe that if they solve most of the quality problems they are doing a good job. They could contribute more if they solved the major problems even though those may be only a small percentage of the total.

5. Dealing too much with things, not enough with people. The quality problem which causes the most trouble usually involves people. Therefore, if you usually concern yourself more with things than with people, you fail to do your best on quality control. Being aware of what's happening on the production line is more important than knowing what the quality control figures and charts say.

An Expert's Comment: "A crucial question in American industry today is whether companies will listen to and support their quality control specialists," said Robert Reece, President of the American Society for Quality Control. Reece pointed out that industry wastes over $100 billion a year correcting sales of defective and unsatisfactory products. "Our best estimate is that 15 percent of net sales of all these companies is spent on this 'fire fighting' activity, whereas competent 'preventive' quality control programs could reduce that figure to 2 percent of net sales," he said.

"If you're in charge of quality control," Reece commented, "you cannot be inflexible, but you've got to be willing to make decisions and stand by them. It's no surprise that sometimes the goals of sales, marketing, and production people are going to clash with those of quality control."

12

SURE-FIRE WAYS
TO CONTROL
COSTS

EVERY employee must participate in controlling costs if a company is to prosper and grow. Supervisors can't do the job alone. But they can get help and cooperation in the effort by selling their people on why costs must be reduced and controlled. Workers need to be convinced that their company must make a profit. It will follow logically that profits will be better when costs are lower.

Supervisors prove their worth when they become interested in cost control and keep costs down. They become experts at the job by learning how to attack specific cost problems and how to prevent little costs from becoming big. Proving one's worth in this respect is not difficult because almost everything that a supervisor controls is a cost to the company in one way or another. The ways by which costs can be controlled are many and varied.

Efficient use of labor, care in the handling and use of material, reduction of waste, and minimizing overhead charges are the main ways which a company adopts to control its costs of operation. The supervisor has a responsibility in all of these areas in that he or she can promote productivity of employees, control the amount of overtime they work, and see that utilities, operating items, and supplies are used with discretion.

12.1 Communication: Key to Selling Cost Reduction

When your company is making an effort to reduce costs, one of the first things you must do is pass this word to your people. It's only with their cooperation that you can accomplish any significant reduction except for layoffs or shutdown of your department. Although your people may see the situation as beyond their control, it's up to you to convince them otherwise. The way to do this is to explain how they are directly involved and what they can do to help.

Consider how you would feel if someone in authority were to talk costs to you, and let that guide you in what you say to your people. Obviously, you are going to suggest operations that should be looked at and changes that should be made. You're also going to talk about why costs must be reduced.

Point out that reducing waste and scrap is one of the most logical ways of cutting costs, and that employees are in good positions to do this. Tell people that doing their work safely avoids accidents which are costly; add that good house-keeping promotes safety. Be sure to get across that extra effort on their part benefits them as well as the company, that they will be cutting costs for the sake of their own jobs rather than being cooperative with you or the company.

People on the job often do not understand why their company makes changes in equipment or procedures because nobody takes the time to explain such matters to them. The key to selling cost reduction is to give people the facts and to point out how raising the profits of the company helps them. You should talk to them in words and terms they understand.

Quote figures on how the cost of the raw materials they use have risen. Tell them about the production schedule, what it was last month or last year, and what it is now. Mention who the company's competitors are and what they're doing in the market. Explain that making a profit is necessary if the company is to stay in business and provide jobs for people.

Your goal in talking to your people about costs is to be sure they get the facts and that you clear up any misconceptions they may have about how much profit the company makes.

Case-in-Point: Frank Mahney, President of the Stationary Power Tool Equipment Division of Black and Decker, said, "Planned cost reduction programs in some companies have not achieved their potential because they were not the primary goal. Therefore, the first step in establishing an effective cost reduction program is to clearly communicate from the top down that cost reduction should be a primary objective of each employee. It sounds obvious, but it's surprising how many firms never do it.

"Next, all of the company's resources—its people, its capital, its equipment—must be geared to making cost reduction a way of life. Then, there must be an overall plan to release these resources fully and effectively and then sustain momentum."

12.2 How to Get Across the Need for Profits

Louis H. Meyer, President of the Material Handling Institute, said, "There is a great deal of evidence to indicate that the most misunderstood subject in the United States today is profits." He went on to give facts and figures that are needed to deal with this problem. He said that leaders should pass along such information to their people on the job.

Supervisors should do this to convince people that their livelihood and their future depend upon a system that permits the company to make a fair profit. You can sell the need for profits of all businesses by pointing out some reasons such as:

1. Profits create more than a million new jobs in the U.S. each year.
2. They provide federal, state, and local governments more than $40 billion in annual tax revenues.
3. There are over 30 million shareholders in the country who depend on profits for part of their income.
4. There are over 33 million workers whose retirement funds are invested in stocks and bonds, and who depend upon the profits these companies make to increase investment values.

This kind of information relates profits to people. The supervisor's task is to get the message across to those who do not understand the relationship. Profits are vital to all of us—people on the job and management, alike.

12.3 Five Painless Ways to Sell People on Cost Reduction

You've got to have the cooperation of your people when you set out to reduce costs. Unfortunately, you may encounter some resistance because cutting costs often means getting along without some things, eliminating some expenses, doing more work, and doing jobs differently. People naturally resist change even when it is for their good. Here are five ways to overcome that resistance and sell your people on cost reduction:

1. Ask for their help and cooperation. Let them know you appreciate their suggestions and recommendations. Get them interested in finding ways their work can be performed at lower cost. Compliment them on their efforts to do so.

2. Set specific goals to shoot for. Don't just ask for cutting costs as much as possible—set a figure or amount such as "25 percent less overtime this month," or "10 percent less waste of materials this week."

3. Point out costs of specific items. Many employees don't realize what various items cost the company. Explain what the company pays for utilities, telephone service, and such items as stationery, work gloves, and tools.

4. Talk about company profits. Get their point of view on these matters and straighten out any misconceptions they have. Explain that wages and salaries can't be maintained or increased if the company isn't profitable.

5. Give reasons why the company has made changes in procedures to cut costs in the past and what they might have to do in the future. Compare the company's ways to what employees do personally under similar circumstances. Give examples such as turning off unneeded lights and fixing leaks.

12.4 How to Become an Expert at Cost Control

You might think that you as a supervisor can't do much about cutting costs significantly short of suggesting a major process or equipment change. Although it's true that big cost reductions can result from such changes, it's also true that real cost saving can be made by conscientious supervisors in their daily routines. You can become an expert at cost control if you want to be one and put forth the effort to do so.

How-to-Do-It: Study and learn about costs from the purchase of raw materials to the selling of the finished products, from the training of personnel to the doing of the work in the plant or office. Investigate the various costs of the company. Most important of all, familiarize yourself with cost areas where you have direct or indirect control.

By understanding the overall picture, you can see where your efforts may be applied. You can study those areas in particular so that if those costs start to rise you know what to do in order to control them. Get in the habit of applying value analysis in your decisions.

Case-in-Point: At a Philadelphia electrical products company, the value engineers studied switch and battery housings and found them to contain many nonfunctional and marginally functional components. They were simplified with an annual cost and labor avoidance estimated at $11,650.

Plant and office procedures were analyzed similarly. Each step was challenged by the question: "What if this were eliminated? Would it make any difference?" In many cases, steps were eliminated, and in one case, an entire operation was discontinued.

Don't wait for your boss or other people to push you into cost control. Develop the skill and knowledge on your own. You will be a more effective and successful supervisor as a result.

12.5 Seven Tried-and-Tested Ways to Control Costs

Since almost everything you do as a supervisor has an effect on costs, you must be constantly aware of the value of material, labor, equipment, and supplies. Every good supervisor knows ways to cut costs and realize savings on the various operations he or she controls. Here are seven such ways which successful supervisors use to keep their department costs in line:

1. Plan and schedule work. By planning you can eliminate idle time, avoid duplication of effort, and handle job steps in proper sequence. Scheduling enables you to avoid waiting for materials, tools, and instructions. Jobs take less time and are done more efficiently if they have been planned and scheduled.

Case-in-Point: A tire plant maintenance engineer had difficulty in scheduling preventive maintenance for the busy production lines until it was suggested that the production department notify the maintenance department prior to the scheduled shutdown of any production line and indicate approximate duration of the shutdown. After this was done, the planner/scheduler had no difficulty in having the production lines inspected and minor repairs made.

2. Become adept at recognizing wasteful practices. Resist assigning too much labor to a job, such as putting two people on when only one is needed. Be aware when machines and equipment need maintenance or repair. Notice when more material is being used than required.

Caution: Simply reducing the amount of something that is used on the job may not necessarily reduce costs—it could actually be a wasteful practice. For instance, saving material may not be economical if you increase your labor costs. Similarly, saving labor is worthwhile provided it does not excessively run up your equipment or material costs.

3. Remove material, supplies, and equipment that aren't being used in the work area. Such things hinder safety, make housekeeping difficult, and cause inefficiency. Their value is probably also deteriorating by being idle; see if they could be used elsewhere.

4. Study processes and equipment, the flow of material, and the use of labor in order to find ways to eliminate procedures and get optimum performance from people.

5. Work at reducing tardiness and absenteeism. Talk to your people who have those problems, explaining the difficulties and cost to the company of their not being on the job on time and every day.

6. Eliminate high cost operations and overtime. Adjust operations to fit the standard workday. Simplify jobs to get them done faster.

7. Eliminate duplication of effort. Combine operations and jobs. With job enrichment you can get more work done by one person while at the same time making the work more interesting.

12.6 How to Attack a Specific Cost Problem

If you have been asked to work on a cost problem, you had better try to do the job quickly. Your boss will be looking for an answer to justify assigning you instead of someone else to the job. Upper management may also be aware of the problem and your involvement. They are expecting you to deliver.

If the cost problem is a major one, you should plan your attack and how you'll proceed so that you'll get the most from your efforts. Decide, too, how to keep management informed of your progress. Set your mind to stay on top of the project to a successful conclusion. Here is how to go about it.

First, find out what you are expected to accomplish. How serious is the problem? How much must costs be reduced? Your boss should give you a clear goal to shoot for.

Second, accept the fact that you must make some changes. Costs will not automatically drop just because word gets around that you are assigned to the task. You are expected to eliminate something or introduce a new technique that will result in lower costs. If your people are aware of the situation and your role, they may suggest some changes you can make.

Third, set up a course of action to reach your goal. Make it as detailed as possible. Get your boss's approval, and make your people aware of what you hope to do. Ask for their cooperation.

Fourth, make periodic reports on your progress. Management is concerned, and they want to know where the project stands even if you haven't made a lot of progress. The briefer your reports, the better. You want mainly to keep management up-to-date.

Fifth, evaluate the changes you make. Don't hesitate to alter them if they don't work, but be sure of a failure before you make a new decision.

Last, show progress and success with evidence of improvement. Wrap up the project with a report documenting your accomplishment.

12.7 Eliminating a Procedure: An Easy Way to Reduce Costs

Most companies have standard procedures which have been in effect a long time. They may be inefficient and uneconomical, but because "they have always been done that way," nobody questions them. It pays to study procedures periodically to see if they are practical as well as necessary. More often than you think, you may be able to change or eliminate one to achieve a significant savings.

A common example of a wasteful procedure is the large amount of paper-work generated in many offices. Surveys show that companies turn out many unneeded reports, memos, letters, and other papers. The low, per-copy cost of putting out paper is a trap. Overlooked are the costs for distribution, filing, storing, retrieval, and eventual disposal.

You can cut paperwork costs in several ways. Start by taking an inventory of all the reports and documents routinely and repetitively produced in your department to see if they are essential. If you can't eliminate a report, try cutting down on the number of copies produced. Also, don't issue a lot of detail information if summary data will do the job.

Another way to reduce a procedure cost is to review work assignments after a process or equipment change is made in the plant. Such a change may cancel the need for a continual inspection or eliminate the need for periodic adjustments or cleanup operations.

Case-in-Point: Benson Wayne, Plant Supervisor in Mahwah, NJ, wrote an editor of *Supervision* magazine, "I've found in my experience that a careful time utilization analysis periodically conducted on an employee-by-employee basis invariably pays off." In one of Wayne's recent studies, he found that an inspector's actual working time amounted to less than one-half of his shift. The rest of his time was spent waiting for production to be ready for inspection. His supervisor assigned him compounding jobs which reduced the need for compounding personnel from three employees to two. The move saved the company considerable money.

12.8 Four Ways to Hold Down Labor Costs

Any cost-cutting program must include examination of how labor is handled. If you are not getting the fullest potential from your people, you are wasting one of the costly items of running a business. Here are four ways you can hold down your company's labor costs:

1. Use only as many workers on a job as are actually needed.

2. Give on-the-job training to all workers. They will be more efficient, make fewer errors, and create less waste.

3. Assign skilled people to skilled work and unskilled people to unskilled work.

4. Provide enough people on the job to assure that overtime work isn't necessary.

The proper use of labor is a key responsibility of a supervisor. Labor costs can be minimized if you get the most from each worker's ability, knowledge, and experience.

12.9 Overtime: Overlooked Reasons for Reducing It

Working your people overtime is costly to the company in salaries and wages. It's costly to the company in other ways, too. An enigma is the fact that the more you use overtime, the greater the problems become which you use it to solve. Four reasons other than direct cost for reducing overtime work are:

1. Quality suffers and there are more mistakes and errors made when people work overtime.

2. The efficiency of people working overtime drops each hour they continue to work.

3. Worker's efficiency will be lower than normal the day after they work overtime, especially if the overtime was considerable.

4. Constant, day-to-day overtime will often cause an increase in absenteeism.

Note that every one of these effects of overtime increase a company's operating costs in one way or another. If you're out to cut costs in your department, reducing overtime work is one of the sure places to start.

12.10 Reduce Waste: A Positive Way to Cut Costs

One of the quickest yet effective ways to cut costs is to reduce waste. Many wasteful practices go on in today's factories and offices. Supervisors are often unaware of them or simply ignore them under the pressure of other problems. When ways to reduce waste are being sought, the prime areas to look at are idle people and machines, underutilized skills, and mishandling of materials and supplies.

To reduce waste you must apply controls and set up standards for people and machines to meet. Do this where mistakes are being made, high scrappage is occurring, and maintenance is lagging. Check the reasons for high overtime, inventory problems, and production delays.

Case-in-Point: Leaking hydraulic systems are responsible for the worst lubricant waste in industry, according to Mobil Oil corporation engineers. The solution to the problem is to train oilers to look for leaks and to keep track of hydraulic oil makeup machine by machine. Another answer is to put the job of checking and tightening of the system on the preventive maintenance or lubrication schedule to be sure it's done regularly.

Excessive wear of tools and equipment shortens their life. You can slow the wear as well as prevent it by making frequent inspections and by promoting preventive maintenance. See that tools are not abused and that the right ones are used on the job. Tools should be cleaned and stored at the end of the workday.

Wasted time probably costs a company more than the waste of anything else. Although unforeseen events will always result in wasted time, you can plan and schedule many jobs so that people, material, and equipment are coordinated to save time.

12.11 How to Cut Material Handling Costs

A recent study revealed that the cost of handling materials amounts to between 25 and 40 percent of the total cost of manufacturing. If you review the material handling operations in your company, you likely will be able to find ways to cut the costs by improving the work flow, adopting better inventory control, and reducing waste. Here are some ways to do it:

• Examine where materials are stored in relation to where they are used. The farther they are from their point of use, the more they must be handled. You'll find that materials and products may not follow the most direct route in manufacturing unless your plant is a new one. When processes are changed and steps added or removed, relocating materials accordingly can reduce handling costs. Any time a step in handling can be eliminated, the work flow will be improved.

• Make supplies handy for the people who use them. Also, make sure your skilled labor don't waste their time in looking or traveling for material if such things can be done by unskilled labor or if material can be better placed.

Case-in-Point: A large petrochemical plant in Houston, Texas provides pipefittings, gaskets, nuts and bolts, and the like in bins and cabinets close to the process piping and equipment. Maintenance craftsmen needing these items in their work save considerable time in not having to go to the maintenance shop or the storeroom for this material.

• See that the best equipment is available for moving materials and that it is used properly. For example, drums can be moved faster and more efficiently than by use of hand, manually operated trucks if forklift trucks are equipped with drum-handling attachments.

Case-in-Point: Joe Heffernan, Manager, Material Handling Engineering Dept., Ford Motor Co., said, " 'Learn to do the job the correct way' should be everyone's theme. There are many causes of equipment damage that can be easily eliminated. For example, running forks through the side of a wire mesh container, or failing to close a down gate on a container before lifting, are nothing more than sloppy handling. Damage to racks and pallets can be eliminated by making sure the truck forks are the correct length. Similarly, when lifting long items from the side, there's less chance of dropping the load if the forks are properly spaced."

● Have planned procedures and assign specific employees to receive materials as well as ship them. Demurrage charges can be avoided on receipts by being prompt and efficient in handling them. Also, people trained and experienced in shipping and receiving procedures take better care of materials.

12.12 How Just-in-Time Operations Reduce Costs

Just-in-time (JIT) procedures are a relatively new way of handling materials. All industrial supervisors should be aware of its principles and how they are implemented. JIT cuts costs by combining inexpensive, low-tech products like containers, racks, and casters with improved methods like storing tools and material near the point of use.

The material costs of a production operation are a matter of how much is handled, how often it is handled and what it is handled with. JIT manufacturing methods have a great impact on all of these considerations.

Companies that operate their production facilities in conventional ways have raw material in storerooms and warehouses *in case* it is needed. Companies that operate under JIT procedures have inventory in sub-plants and supplier's storage facilities *because* it is needed. This reduces material cost because less material is stored and because it doesn't have to be moved far to the point of use.

In addition, companies with JIT operations organize the production equipment to reduce in-process inventory. Instead of doing one operation on a lot of parts and then storing them, all operations are done on a single part and the completed part sent to assembly. There's nothing to store.

The JIT operating approach requires that materials not be issued and production not started because a schedule says the time is right. Instead, activity is controlled by demand from the next operation.

12.13 Avoid Losses: The Big Answer to Lower Material Costs

The objective of a supervisor who tries to lower material costs is to see that material is used productively and that losses are minimized.

How-to-Do-It: Develop standards for the handling and use of materials plus train people to meet them. Although training and instructing people in the proper handling of materials may take time and cost money, the benefits will far exceed the costs. For instance, here are a few losses that can be avoided when people are careful in handling material:

● Damage in the warehouse and storeroom, in receiving and in shipping.

● Damage from poor stacking, inadequate protection, and failure of racks and bins.

- Spillage and loss in handling.

- Spoilage from aging or contaminating.

- Taking more material than needed for a job.

- Waste from rejection of off-quality finished product.

To do a good job of controlling material cost, you must continually stress three matters with people: care in handling, value, and conservation.

12.14 How to Keep Little Costs from Becoming Big

If you take the time to study your areas of responsibility where costs have increased, you should be able to spot the time when the increase began. If you had been aware of what was happening at the time, you might have been able to prevent it from going so far. However, with matters like this you don't just give up and accept them—you may still be able to take corrective action or at least stop further cost increases.

Alert and experienced supervisors are aware of how little costs become big. When they observe a change in operations, a slowing down or speeding up, a decrease or increase in a function, an omission or inclusion of a factor, they immediately investigate to see if costs will be affected. Here are some examples of such incidents along with advice on what to do if they happen to you:

1. An increase in operating costs occurs which is not explainable by current trends, rate increases, or new acquisitions. Look for work being repeated because of something wrong with either equipment, materials, or workmanship. Check also on customer complaints and returned goods.

2. An operation or process slows down for no apparent reason. Since there must be a reason for it happening, and it probably will get worse, you must find the problem. Search for it and take corrective action.

3. A small increase in the use of a supply item takes place without an accompanying increase in work output. Since it is a single item, tracing it should be easy. The task deserves your attention to determine if a more serious problem is behind it.

Cases-in-Point: Dennison Travis, Works Superintendent at a Rhode Island metal foundry, makes a pertinent comment on the matter of costs when he says, "Employees who are trained to be less wasteful of so-called trivial items will be more careful of costly items as well." Travis's company monitors the use of virtually everything issued in the office and plant from paper clips and ballpoint pens to precision equipment costing thousands of dollars.

A New York laundry posts on its bulletin board a total expense account of low-cost supplies. The figures show dramatically how nets, pins, aprons, coverings, pads, and other items which some people may consider insignificant add up to $500,000 a year.

A west coast aircraft manufacturer points out the high cost of everything from paper towels to memo pads by giving usage and cost figures in the company publication.

4. The accounting department bills your department a new item in the overhead area. Has your department picked up a research or development charge? Has a new tax gone into effect? Whatever, a call to the accounting department is in order for an explanation.

5. You have a feeling of something not being right and you've sensed it more than once. Don't pass this off lightly because your experience on the job is telling you that a problem is developing. Talk it over with people who could be involved. Observe how individuals are doing their work. Be alert for abnormal behavior and unusual remarks. The quicker you can learn what is wrong, the quicker you can do something about it.

12.15 Tips on Cutting Overhead Costs

Every business has its overhead costs. These are the costs which are not affected by variations in production volume or service performed. Whether the office is operating or not, whether the plant is producing or not, costs such as insurance, taxes, maintenance, and the salaries of management and staff continue to be incurred by the company.

Before studying them, you might think that overhead costs are beyond your control—you would be only partially right. Certain overhead items are within the responsibility of supervisors. The problem is that some of these costs have been accepted for so long that no one thinks of trying to cut them.

Although many overhead costs are minor, they add up to rather large amounts of money, particularly when they are not controlled. Some costs of this type are: utility leaks, overuse of air conditioning, poor housekeeping (which runs up janitorial costs and accident costs), inadequate fire protection (which causes high insurance rates), extra telephones and extensions, and rented equipment not being used. Larger overhead items which supervisors share some responsibility for and can do something about are pollution control, energy conservation, spill prevention and control, safety controls, and the training and instructing of workers.

Case-in-Point: An energy survey conducted by the Goodyear Tire and Rubber Company at six of its plants revealed that much could yet be done to conserve energy. Thomas Leary, Manager of Corporate Engineering, pointed out that some plants are only interested in energy conservation if they can get $500,000 in savings through 10 to 20 big items. They overlook the fact that they can achieve those savings by correcting 500 smaller items.

12.16 How to Avoid Overlooking Areas Where Costs Can Be Cut

You can expect that you will periodically be asked to cut costs in your department. It happens in even very efficiently operated companies, and usually is an indication that you are not carrying out your responsibilities to the best of your abilities. Although you prefer not to suggest that the number of people working for you be reduced, what else can you do?

A good way to cut costs when you can't do it by reducing your unit labor and unit material costs is to work on the methods your people use in putting out your products or supplying your services. As a result of improving a method, you can achieve savings on total labor and/or total material costs.

Your viewpoint on method improvement should be that any procedure or process can be updated, even though it may have been changed recently. Don't be swayed by remarks from people like, "We tried that once before and it didn't work." Also, ignore the person who has a negative attitude because one of his or her suggestions was at one time rejected. Consider making a value analysis of your product or service. By eliminating something, you may be able to save both labor and material.

Look closely at your department procedures, too. Investigate layouts of the work area and the facilities. Study the ways that materials are moved. Decide if adopting ergonomic principles would be of benefit.

By improving a work method, you enable your people to be more productive. The payoff with this is that better productivity results in lower costs.

13

TESTED WAYS FOR
EVALUATING PERFORMANCE:
HANDLING APPRAISALS
EFFECTIVELY

PLANNING and preparing are necessary if you want to conduct an effective performance appraisal. You will learn more about the person and be better able to help him or her if you know what you are going to talk about. Employees need and want to know their strengths and weaknesses, and what they should do to improve. A number of benefits to the company and the person result from a frank and friendly discussion.

To be able to evaluate performance and do a good job of counseling, the supervisor must know much about the person and how he or she is doing on the job. During the interview, the person should be encouraged to talk about the job and problems concerning it.

An interviewer needs to be adept at asking questions and listening for the answers. To be effective, you need to know what to say and what not to say to motivate and encourage a person. For the company's benefit as well as the person's, you should also be consistent in your evaluations. Evaluating on points is a common method for comparing the performance and the accomplishments of employees.

Successful appraisers are aware of the pitfalls to avoid when interviewing people. They see why personnel records must be kept up-to-date and confidential. They also realize the importance of following up after interviewing.

13.1 Tips on Preparing for an Appraisal Interview

A performance appraisal interview will be easy for you to handle, and you'll do a more extensive job if you prepare for it. Here are some tips on how to do this:

● Review the record and personal history of the person by collecting all the information you have, including that from other people. Look into the person's background, service-time with the company, previous jobs held, and what progress the person has made since being hired. Study any notes made of previous appraisals with the person.

● Consider the job the person is doing. Become familiar with the standards and responsibilities of the job in order to judge how he or she is doing. Determine what a person in that type of work must do to be a success.

● Decide where you will talk with the person. You must have a place where you have privacy and your conversation cannot be heard; this is important to the person. Recognize that a place other than your office would probably put the person more at ease and would therefore be preferred.

● Pick a time for the interview. Avoid scheduling it for when you or the person might be very busy or could be interrupted. Plan to not start the interview unless you're fairly sure you can finish it.

13.2 How to Get Started Right

The secret to a good performance appraisal interview is to have the interviewee at ease, willing to discuss the job, and wanting to learn how to improve. To put the person in this frame of mind, you should begin by explaining the purpose of your meeting. Say that you are talking to all your people, and that your main purpose is to help each person. Tell the person that you want to talk about the work and how it is going, and that you also would like to talk about any problems the person may have.

Case-in-Point: Roy Leedy, former Manager of Engineering at Goodyear Tire and Rubber Company's synthetic rubber plant in Akron, Ohio, told me how he began an appraisal interview. The words he used after greeting the individual and putting him or her at ease went something like this: "We see each other several times every day but in the rush of doing our work we do not have much of an opportunity to talk. So I plan to take some time now and then to sit down with you and with every other person in the department for a personal talk.

"I would like you to tell me how you feel about your job. Also, I want to give you a chance to talk about any ideas you have about your work and problems that have come up. At the same time, we can talk about the work you have been doing. We can probably help each other."

13.3 Guidelines for Handling an Interview

When you counsel with your people, you let them know how they are doing and what they can do to improve their performance. Since an appraisal interview is like a progress report, most people consider it important and will take it quite seriously.

The interview is equally important to the supervisor because it presents an opportunity to learn more about the person and to motivate him or her through encouragement and praise. Because both of you have a lot to gain from an interview, it's essential for you to do the best you can with it. Here are some guidelines to help you:

1. Listen carefully when the person talks. This may be difficult for two reasons: first, you may already think you know what the person is going to say, and second, while the person is talking, you may be thinking about how you will respond. Remember, however, that if you don't listen carefully, you may not understand completely what the person is saying. Consequently, you'll be unable to provide the right motivation for better performance.

2. Allocate equal time to praise and criticism. Resist the inclination to spend a lot of time discussing a person's weakness or area of below average achievement. Recognize that too much finding fault can cause resentment.

3. Be friendly and sincere. You are trying to help the person, not tear him or her down. Be encouraging and positive when suggesting how performance can be improved.

4. Limit the goals and objectives you set for the person both in number and degree. Recognize a person's capabilities in anticipating what can be accomplished. Don't expect a complete change of behavior during or immediately after a single interview.

13.4 Ways to Encourage a Person to Talk

Successful interviews require an exchange of ideas between participants. Unfortunately, many supervisors find it easier to talk than to listen. You must realize that you are not learning anything when you are talking—you need to get the other person to talk. Here are some good ways to do that:

• Listen intently when a person is talking. Nod your head and encourage the person without interrupting except for saying, "I see," and "Mm-hm."

• Repeat the person's words in your own: "Let's see if I understand you."

• Persuade the person to explain further or in more detail. "Tell me more." "That's interesting. What else?"

• Turn the person's questions back with "What do *you* think?"

Be friendly and reassuring in what you say because the person is much more conscious than you are of your difference in rank. By all means, be yourself. Any person who knows you well on the job would be quick to see any falseness in your manner and immediately be on guard.

A good way to measure your success at getting the other person to talk is to watch how much you're dominating the conversation. If you're talking less than half the time, you're on the right track. Try to keep it that way.

An expert's comment: A personnel manager for a large chemical company once gave me a tip on talking during an interview. I had expressed a fear that I and the person I was interviewing would run out of something to say. He replied, "Don't panic if the conversation stops during the interview. Be glad of the silence and use it to think a bit. Rest assured, the interviewee will think of something to say."

13.5 Asking Questions: The Sure-Fire Way to Get Information

An interview may be difficult for you and not seem to go as smoothly as you'd like it to if the interviewee is nervous and hesitates to say much. What can you do? First, try to put the person at ease. Talk about a subject that you know the person is interested in, such as a hobby. The person should soon be more relaxed because you'll be talking his or her language. You can then go on to talk about the job.

An excellent way to get a person to talk is to ask questions. Most of your questions should be ones that cannot be answered with a yes or no. Here, for example, are some which would be appropriate:

About the job: What part of your job do you find challenging? What parts do you consider the most important? How do you feel about the job overall? What suggestions do you have for improving our department?

About performance of the work: What part of your job gives you the most satisfaction? What part do you find easiest? How can I help you to do a better job?

About ideas or problems: What is your biggest problem on the job? What are your goals with the company? How do you feel about the other people you work with? What do you think about interviews like this?

Caution: Try not to fire one question after another to avoid making your meeting seem to be a simple interrogation. Mix in a few comments such as how you would answer the questions and what your experiences have been. You'll put the person more at your level when you do so, and talking will be easier on that basis.

13.6 Three Questions You Shouldn't Ask

The supervisor who is skilled at performance appraisal interviewing avoids asking certain questions because they don't help in getting information and may also be disturbing to the person being interviewed. The most annoying and troublesome of these are questions which put the other person down in some way or set the person up for embarrassment. Here are three types of questions which a good interviewer doesn't ask:

1. The leading question. This question is phrased in a way that it suggests a correct answer. Examples are: "You agree that ... don't you?" "Aren't you in favor of ... ?" "I'm sure you like ... don't you?"

When you ask a leading question you put words in the interviewee's mouth, literally forcing him or her to agree with you whether the person feels that way or not. You can't learn how a person truly feels with a leading question. Many people will agree so as not to put themselves in jeopardy, especially if their job is important to them.

2. The loaded question. This question is closely related to the leading question in that it also anticipates agreement. The loaded question, however, has an added feature—the person answering it is never sure what impact, if any, his or her answer will have. Examples are: "That isn't a very good reason for acting that way, is it?" "When did you stop wasting time on the job?" "I thought he was wrong. What do you think?"

The loaded question is a poor one for several reasons. The interviewee may not know the answer, may resent you asking the question, or may answer it the way he or she thinks you want it answered. Whatever, the result is the same; you learn nothing new about the person. Like the leading question, it only stifles communication.

3. The stress question. This question puts the interviewee under tension because of its grilling connotation. Examples are: "Are you positive that ... ?" "How do you explain ... ?" "Why didn't you ... ?"

Stress questions often are leading or loaded questions, asked to test how sharp and alert a person is. But they don't always reveal that. Instead, they put the person on edge. They also tend to break any trust you may have attained. Another fault with stress questions is that since they make you appear as an authority figure as well as a judge, they simply hurt any communication link you may have established.

13.7 Tips on How to Appraise Fairly

Although most companies today have personnel appraisal systems, too many supervisors fail to use them to best advantage. There are certain steps which should be taken by a supervisor that will ensure an employee is given a fair appraisal. Following these simple steps helps the employee, the supervisor, and the company. Here are some tips on what you should do:

● Take individuals aside and tell them whenever they surpass expectations or whenever they fail to meet standards. With the former situation, people are pleased when their good performance is noticed. With the latter, they learn where they are falling short and how they can improve. It can be very devastating to a person to be allowed to perform poorly for a long period of time without a single word of correction from his or her supervisor.

● Evaluate people on the basis of actual results and not on how the job was accomplished, provided, of course, the means used were ethical and efficient. An introverted person who can achieve goals in his or her own quiet way should be graded just as high as a gregarious and aggressive person who does the same.

● Rate each person as objectively as possible. This means that you should be aware of your prejudices and set them aside. When criticizing an employee, you, preferably, should be able to relate more than one incident that backs up the criticism.

● Do not color the achievements or cover up the shortcomings of persons who are your friends or who have pleasant personalities. If you are partial to some employees, you seriously damage both the morale and productivity of the rest of the work force as well as the usefulness of the appraisal system.

● Keep a log of employee performance to which you can periodically refer. To make sure that the log accurately reflects each individual's performance, remember that appearances are not always what they seem. For example, when someone usually seems busy and periodically works overtime, he or she may be inefficient rather than industrious.

13.8 How to Use the "Sandwich" Technique

Experienced and effective counselors often use the "sandwich" technique when talking to someone about the person's behavior or performance. They are careful to make an unfavorable comment only after giving a compliment, and they follow it with a favorable remark. In this way, they soften the blow of criticism while still getting it across.

For example, if you were to use the technique when talking to one of your people, you might say, "John, I like the way you tackle a job without delay. It shows me you've got the right attitude about the job and want to do your share of the work. But, you should try to cut down on the amount of waste you make because that runs up our costs. I'm sure you can do this because you're one of the most skilled people we have in the department."

Astute supervisors look for opportunities to use this technique in handing out their work assigments to their people. When they find that they must give an employee a distasteful job, they fit it in with easy or pleasant tasks. They've learned that a person is more willing to accept a dirty job under such circumstances.

A word of caution: You must be careful in your use of the sandwich technique—don't become so predictable in your approach to people that they become suspicious whenever you compliment them, expecting that a criticism will follow. The way to avoid this is simple enough—be more liberal with praise and appreciation for work done as you go along.

13.9 Answers to What to Say to an Outstanding Person

It's relatively easy to talk with a person who is doing well on the job because your attitude toward the person is good and your compliments are very sincere. As a result, your conversation will be high-key and positive in almost all respects.

Although you may be tempted to talk about achievements, you should resist this. Your responsibility to the person should be with his or her future. The greater the person's abilities, the greater the obligation you have to see that these skills and attributes are directed to the advantage of both the person and the company.

Talk to the person in a way that shows you appreciate his or her talents and good performance. Say words such as "How can I help you rise to a better position with the company? Tell me what your goals are—I want to help you reach them." An outstanding person appreciates such comments and will continue to do a good job for you. You will also be able to work together toward the advancement of the person with a corresponding benefit to the company.

13.10 How to Talk with a Failing Person

Nobody likes the job of telling someone that he or she is not doing well on the job and that something will have to be done about it. Yet, it is an obligation that should not be put off by the person's supervisor. You should face the problem early while there still is some hope of saving the person. Because of that, do not postpone the task to the time when you normally conduct appraisal interviews with your other people.

Don't be surprised to learn that the person is aware of his or her failing on the job. He or she may even welcome the opportunity to discuss it with you. Both of you will likely feel better after talking about it whether or not you find an immediate solution to the problem.

Sometimes you can help a person to find a job more suitable to his or her talents and liking. You seldom do a man a favor when you keep him on work he cannot handle. You should be helpful rather than critical when you talk with a failing person. Say, "How can we solve this problem together?" Never say, "Here's what's wrong with you," or similar faultfinding words. Get the person to talk and to offer an answer to the problem. Don't try to solve it yourself. You can't do it unless you simply transfer the person to another job or take action to terminate his or her job with the company.

Caution: Avoid getting involved in emotional problems when you counsel someone who is failing. Leave such matters to psychiatrists and psychologists— you do not have the proper training unless this is your field. Besides, it is very easy to become trapped by your own feelings which then add to the problem. Only if you can tactfully do it should you recommend that the person get professional help. The best person to suggest this should be the company doctor or a very close friend of the person.

13.11 Handling an Appraisal with an Angry Person

Talking constructively with an angry person is difficult if not impossible. If a person becomes angry or emotional at an interview, you must listen, not talk. Let the person get rid of the emotion. If you become angry, you will fail to learn much about the person. You will also not be able to suggest ways that the person's performance may be improved because you cannot do your best thinking when you are upset.

An angry person is expressing one or more feelings which include resentment, frustration, fear, prejudice, and disappointment. The person may not mention these feelings but they will be apparent to you if you listen carefully. Only by listening and trying to understand can you have any hope of helping.

Don't try to explain, persuade, or convince a person of something while he or she is emotional. Nor should you suggest that both of you talk about something else. When a person is emotional, his or her mind cannot be put on any subject.

If you see that a person continues to show emotion after a few minutes with you, it may be wise to give up the interview attempt for the moment. Tactfully suggest that you meet again sometime soon, assuring the person that you understand the feelings he or she presently has. Show an interest in the person the next few days and express your desire and willingness to again sit down to talk.

13.12 How to Be Consistent in Rating People

One thing you want to be sure of when you rate your people is that you are fair. Don't let bias or prejudice influence your thinking. Just as important, and a way of being fair, is being consistent.

To be consistent, rate your people on only one factor at a time. For example, if you're rating them on their attendance, rate the person who is never absent as excellent, the person who misses a day every three or four months as good, and ther person who is absent more than once a month as unsatisfactory.

Resist the tendency to let one favorable or unfavorable trait of a person affect your feeling toward the person as a whole. For instance, because a person may have a poor attitude should not cause you to forget that the person's workmanship is excellent. Along the same line, a perfect attendance should not impress you so much that you overlook an inability to get along with other people. You do your best rating when you rate all your people on one factor before going to another factor.

You can check your ratings for consistency by observing whether you have a variation among your people on each of the factors. You should have a range on each factor such that the great majority are in the middle of the range with lesser numbers at the top and at the bottom.

13.13 Evaluating on Points

The way to make an evaluation of people specific and relative is to rate them on points. Some companies do this as a means of determining the amount of pay increase they award to their people. Others use a point system for advancing workers to higher classes.

A typical evaluation system may contain more than ten traits or perform- ance items. Depending on the responsibilities of the people being rated, the items would include: accuracy, alertness, attendance, creativity, courtesy, de- pendability, drive, friendliness, housekeeping, job knowledge, personality, personal appearance, quantity of work, safety, and stability. If the person were in a supervisory position, you might include the items: control of costs, control of waste, company/union agreement, handling people, meeting the schedule, and specifications.

To convert these performance items to points, the usual procedure is to use a scale of 1 to 5 points for poor, fair, good, very good, and excellent. Evaluation and judgment of performance of an individual is based on the total number of points the person is given on the selected performance items.

Caution: A common problem some supervisors have in rating their people is their proneness to rate nearly everyone as good or average on every item instead of being more critical in judgment. People are not this similar in actuality. To be realistic, you should use the ends of the scale as well as the middle.

13.14 Repeat Interviews: How to Handle Them

After you've gotten into the routine of having periodic appraisal interviews with each of your people, you may wonder what you should talk about at subsequent meetings, especially in the case when a person is doing all right and nothing of importance has happened to change the person's situation.

You may make a repeat interview brief and very informal under such circumstances. But, take heed: the other person may not see it as the routine matter that you might assign it. For one thing, you probably have not talked about the person's accomplishments or goals for a long time. For another, the person's viewpoint about the job may have changed. You must again persuade the person to talk—don't assume everything is just as it was when you last met.

You're never out of style to thank a person for doing good work. And you can always talk about the future. If pays to tell a person that you appreciate his or her cooperation. You might also add that you hope the two of you can continue to work together in the future.

13.15 Evaluating Performance: A Prerequisite to Promotion

Although the most common use of a performance appraisal is to help a person develop on the job, appraisals are used also for determining rates of pay and promotions. You should know a person quite well when you promote him or her in order to be reasonably sure the person can handle more responsibility. You must also consider how the company and your department will be affected. Will productivity of the people involved increase? Will you have a smoother operating group?

Case-in-Point: "You should promote an individual only on the basis of frank, honest appraisal," says Clyde M. Hyde, Department Supervisor with Tucson (Arizona) Gas and Electric Co. "Your recommendations for promotion to your superior should be based on your knowledge of what is best for your department and the company irrespective of personal friendships. At times it is not easy to pass an unbiased opinion on the work of your men. Years of association with them will always tend to influence the decisions you make. Nevertheless, you must make an effort to be honest with yourself." Hyde's thinking is respected by management in his company. He's had numerous promotions since he started to work for them.

13.16 Five Pitfalls to Avoid in an Appraisal Interview

Several stumbling blocks are in the path of the supervisor who wants to get the most from an interview with one of his or her people. You can overcome them by thinking about what you are going to say before the meeting and by keeping in mind that your main objective is to help the person. Here are five pitfalls to avoid when you talk to a person about performance on the job:

1. Avoid comparison with other people, especially peers. Nobody likes to hear that someone else has done a better job. Say, "Here are some ways you can do better," rather than, "Here is what you have done wrong."

2. Don't dwell on a person's weakness. Focus on improvement in the future, not on past mistakes. Talk about what a person has done, not about what the person is. Speak more about the work than the person. Be constructive in order to motivate.

3. Be careful about discouraging a person by saying that his or her goals are impractical or impossible. You could very easily be proven wrong. If you feel you must say something about a person's goals, go only so far as to tactfully point out the difficulties which might be in the person's path.

4. Refrain from using words which connote poor performance or failure. Words such as *guilty, faults, mistakes,* and *weaknesses* are better left unsaid. Also, words such as *reasonable, common sense,* and *logical* are antagonizing to some people.

5. Do not make promises. You can't predict the future, and you shouldn't try. Never, for example, promise a raise or a job. Circumstances may change or events may occur which would make it impossible for you to deliver.

13.17 Follow-Up: An Important Part of Appraisal Interviewing

For everyone to gain from appraisals, you may need to take care of some matters after the interviews. The people you interview will gain more from it if you carry on after your talk by showing interest in them and their work. You have the responsibility also of following up on matters you discussed with them.

For instance, you may have promised to take action of some sort on changing the work assignments or responsibilities of an indvidual. The person will be expecting some word on this matter—you must not let him or her down. Or, you may have decided during the interview to look into the person's history or job experience in order to correct the record or add some information—this should not be allowed to drag or be forgotten.

A planned program of development and progress of your people often is an outgrowth of your appraisal interviews. Your people need your help if they are to advance in the company as well as get satisfaction from their work. They look to you for guidance and direction. Such developments and plans for the future should not be left to memory. Make notes immediately after an interview. You may put them on the appraisal form or on a separate paper for the person's record file. They'll be of value to you at the time of the next interview.

13.18 Keys to Efficient Handling of Personnel Records

Personnel activities such as hiring, transfers, promotions, and fringe benefit programs require that records be created and maintained. Although most of these actions are usually handled by the personnel department, supervisors frequently are also involved, particularly with performance appraisals. One of the responsibilities of supervisors is to protect the privacy of such information.

All personnel records must be kept confidential. This means that information and data on hourly pay or salary and performance on the job should not be exposed on your desk or left unattended even in a file or desk drawer. Such records should be kept in closed folders, filed when not in use, and locked when unattended.

Information in the file should be limited to that which concerns the employee's job, performance, pay, conditions of employment, and benefits. Any information that could create a legal liability to the company must not be filed. This includes data on race, color, age, sex, religion, national origin, ancestry, marital status, handicap, or military service. But since certain information may be pertinent to records such as insurance, benefits, or tax withholding, supervisors should get the advice of the company's personnel department on what information is permissible and what records should not be maintained.

It's good human relations to permit an employee to have supervised access to his or her own file if there is a question about the accuracy of the information in it. Some state laws require the employer to permit employee access. However, the important thing to remember is that all employment records have a high privacy priority.

14

PROVEN METHODS
FOR GETTING ALONG
WITH THE UNION

THE presence and influence of unions in business and industry make supervisors better leaders in that because of the union they become more aware of the needs of people on the job. Although the union may make their jobs more difficult at times, supervisors should realize that it is a waste of time and effort to fight it—they must accept it.

Knowing the agreement or contract as it is sometimes called, and what it covers, is a requisite for getting along with the union. Of great importance, in this respect, is the grievance procedure. Since grievances are costly in both time and money, supervisors must constantly work to reduce their number and frequency. Supervisors can take a big step in this direction by being on good terms with the union steward. Getting this person's cooperation in handling people problems means much because the union and management don't always agree on the best ways of working toward the company's goals.

While the company has the right to discipline employees for infractions of rules and poor performance, the union may express a different opinion on the discipline imposed. Arbitration by an umpire is the way such differences are settled. Supervisors should be familiar with the procedure and have proof to support any action they take since they may be participants in umpire hearings.

14.1 Collective Bargaining: What It's All About

Collective bargaining is a procedure. It's the getting together of representatives of management and the union to discuss and agree on wages, hours of work, and working conditions. Almost anything that affects people on the job is a fit subject for collective bargaining. The union bargains for something it feels its members should have. Management has to bargain in good faith on whether it can grant all, part, or none of what the union proposes.

Both the union and management present their arguments in attempting to reach agreement, the outcome of which depends on several factors: whether the company feels it can pay for its cost, how desirable it is to employees, management, and stockholders, and whether it is reasonable under the circumstances. Issues are often decided on the bargaining strength of each of the parties.

Collective bargaining usually starts when the union and management begin negotiating on the contents of the agreement or contract which they will eventually sign. Both sides hope a good agreement will be reached since everyone must live with it for its term like any other contract. Agreements between the union and management are seldom changed during its life but the contract by no means is a forgotten document. Supervisors, employees, and union representatives will refer to it many times during its term to carry out its meaning.

14.2 Answers to Why Employees Join a Union

Supervisors should know why their people may want to belong to a union. Such knowledge provides insight to getting along with it and an understanding of what people expect of the company they work for.

Most workers decide they want a union to represent them when they see that management doesn't listen to them and when they believe that management is indifferent to their needs. Employees show these feelings in many ways. Turnover and absenteeism increase, productivity is erratic and usually declines, scrap and waste are high, and safety records are poor.

Yet, discovering what the real issues or differences of opinion are may still be difficult at times. Management typically believes that money and benefits lie behind most dissatisfactions, but these things often are not the real problem. Money becomes the big issue when employees feel they are ignored. And that is the major reason why employees join unions.

An expert's comment: Psychologist Milton Blum in his book, *Industrial Psychology and Its Social Foundations,* admits the importance of collective bargaining in the formation of unions, but he points out, "Some employees also believe that membership in a union gives them an opportunity to develop more self-respect. The importance of this need must not be underestimated . . . 'Telling the boss off' is often a compelling desire, and a person sometimes avails himself of an opportunity to do so when he has a group, such as a union, in back of him."

14.3 Attitude: The Controlling Factor in Getting Along

As a supervisor, you must recognize that once your company has made a contract with a union, you will be working with it from then on. You may as well accept the union and do your best to get along with it. You will only cause trouble for yourself and the company if you fight it.

You would not be carrying out the responsibility of your job, however, if you gave up interest in your people and their welfare solely because they belong to the union. Management expects you to be a leader and to guide employees in their work. If management felt that union leaders could do this, you wouldn't be needed as a supervisor.

Employees expect their union to protect their economic interests, health, and safety, and to make their jobs more secure. You cannot fault your people for wanting this. An employee who works for a considerate supervisor, one who recognizes this relationship of the employee to the union, usually will be easy to get along with and will try to do a good job for the company.

14.4 How to Promote Good Union/Management Relations

A company's supervisors can contribute much toward achieving and maintaining good union/management relations. The relationship between the supervisor and the individual employee is critical because when employees think of management or the company, they think of their supervisor.

A poor supervisor can harm relations more than any other level of management because he or she is the closest management person to the employees. Thus, it is important that supervisors create and promote confidence and trust among their people. Supervisors can do much, for instance, to promote a team spirit by letting each employee know how valuable his or her contribution is to the company and how people working together in team efforts can improve productivity.

Another way that supervisors can help to maintain union/management relations is by being good listeners when employees are dissatisfied with their work, want something, or have other matters to talk about. This is not to say that supervisors should give employees whatever they ask for, but that they should try to understand employee problems and explain why not all of their requests can be granted.

Compatibility between the supervisor and an employee is a plus toward maintaining harmony because small differences of opinion can easily be handled when they arise. If you can resolve problems before they become grievances, you serve to cement the union and management relationship.

14.5 Knowing the Agreement: A "Must" for Supervisors

To get along with the union you must be informed on the union/management agreement and understand it. Without this knowledge, you cannot fully carry out your responsibility as a member of management nor can you always be right in how you handle and treat your people. Rest assured that your counterpart, the union steward, is well-versed in that document. To be his equal in the eyes of your people on matters covered in the agreement, you must be just as well-informed.

Most companies see that their supervisors receive training on the agreement. Such training and instruction is usually given by the industrial relations or personnel people in the company who know the contract provisions well. The training should include briefing on past practices and the unwritten understandings which the union and management have reached over the years.

The grievance procedure presented in the agreement is very likely the most important part of the document to the supervisor. As for other matters contained in the agreement, you will never regret taking time to study and discuss them with your peers and your superiors. As a result, you will have an easier time in getting along with the union.

14.6 How to Get the Cooperation of the Union Steward

It pays to be on good terms with the union steward. Although you may at times personally resent the person because of the problems he or she gives you, realize that the steward is the elected representative of your union people, a position which carries a lot of responsibility.

The key to getting the cooperation of the union steward is to treat the person with respect and show that you feel he or she is important. You can do this in several ways.

One way is to always let the steward know what's going on and keep him or her up-to-date. See that the steward is the first person to be told of changes that affect the union people. Another is to show the person you understand the problems of being the union representative. Always do your best to answer the questions that the person asks and to solve the problems that the person brings up.

Get to know the union steward as well as any other employee. The better you know the person, the easier it will be to get along with him or her. You and the steward will have many mutual problems in your daily work. Just as the steward will frequently come to you to straighten out matters, so should you periodically ask for his or her help on your problems. The fact that you do will help you to get the cooperation you need to be a successful supervisor.

14.7 How to Work with the Grievance Procedure

To get along well with the union, you must know how to handle a complaint. Once you acquire this skill, you will be able to resolve differences of opinion on the job more easily as well as carry out the responsibilities of your job with more authority.

The supervisor should not consider a greivance as a personal attack on his or her authority but as a way the union communicates to management a complaint or the existence of a problem. With this viewpoint, you will not be resentful or antagonistic when you handle grievances. It makes for a more equitable solution of problems for all concerned.

Winning a grievance is not as important as promptly settling it so that an employee can be productive with a minimum of dissatisfaction and loss of time on the job. A supervisor should recognize the need to settle a grievance as soon as possible. The longer it is put off, the more unhappy and discontented the submitter becomes. If a grievance is promptly and properly investigated by the supervisor, the chances of outside arbitration being required are greatly decreased.

14.8 Tips on Successful Handling of Grievances

If you can discern the nature of a grievance, you have taken the first step in successfully handling it. Although a majority of them will fit one pattern or another, two types are likely to occur more frequently than others.

The first type is imaginary or arises from a misunderstanding. Of course, it is real to the employee, and a supervisor should accept it as such. You should still give a grievance your full attention no matter how illogical or impractical it may appear. Be especially thorough when investigating a grievance which seems to be far out of line—it may be the surfacing of a serious hidden problem.

The second type is simply the expression of an employee asking that he or she get a fair deal. The person may be wrong and not sure, but wants to be checked out. Give the employee the facts and a fair answer. You may have to say that he or she is wrong, but the person will know that you took a personal interest and tried to help. If, however, you ignore or slough off the complaint, the employee will feel that it was not important enough to you. The disappointment and discontent resulting may bring you more trouble later.

14.9 Effective Ways to Contend with the Grievance Problem

Management hopes that employees will never turn in a grievance. Yet, few companies with unions have been able to completely eliminate them, try as they may. This is not to say that a lack of grievances means that everyone is pleased on the job. Frank discussions of problems are better than silent discontent.

When management receives numerous grievances, they must search for the reason or reasons. Disgruntled employees are not productive. The company is the loser when employees are unhappy or feel ignored.

One of the ways to avoid grievances is to discuss proposed changes in the work with the union before putting them into effect. Another is to ask for the union's help and cooperation in solving problems and resolving differences of opinion as soon as they become known.

Perhaps the most realistic approach to the grievance problem is to take a less rigid view toward the agreement, to be more liberal when interpreting it. Both the union and management should recognize that conditions involving people on the job change—the agreement must change accordingly. If the agreement is looked upon as a guide for solving problems and reaching decisions rather than as a group of inflexible regulations and restrictions, both parties may be more willing to concede on issues more often.

14.10 Three Mistakes Supervisors Should Avoid

A study of the grievances of employees that end in arbitration hearings revealed that about 90 percent of them reached that point because of mistakes made by supervisors. This indicates that today's supervisors need more instruction and training in human relations and in how to handle people on the job. The three most serious mistakes that supervisors make are:

1. Making light of or brushing off legitimate complaints. When an employee turns in a grievance, the matter is more important to him or her at that time than anything else. The employee will not be satisfied until the grievance is answered. Too often, a supervisor misjudges the seriousness of a person's complaint.

2. Handling a complaint without getting all the facts. This mistake is an outgrowth of not placing enough importance on the matter to justify a thorough study of it. The problem is aggravated when the supervisor isn't aware of the true feelings of his or her people and hasn't been interested enough to know their likes and dislikes.

3. Imposing severe discipline for a minor offense. The union often feels that discipline meted out by the supervisor is too severe. The problem of consistency must also be contended with. If you suspend one person for a rule

violation, you can't give a simple warning to another person for the same offense.

14.11 How to Interpret the Agreement on Discipline

Union/management agreements invariably give management the right to discipline or discharge employees for just cause. There has to be discipline, obedience to authority, and respect for the rights of others in any successful organization. Without them, order and efficiency would be impossible.

The supervisor fits into the picture in that he or she determines a person's need for discipline and metes out penalties for infractions. Through progressive steps of more and more severe discipline, the point may be reached where discharge is the final step. Supervisors who are concerned with the welfare of their people will counsel them and try to prevent this from happening, but they aren't always successful.

Under the agreement, employees have the right to protest disciplinary action they feel is unfair, discriminatory, or too severe, and they have the right to have the union represent them in these protests. Many cases of discipline or discharge of employees eventually reach the arbitrator because the union and management are unable to resolve them.

Case-in-Point: Grievance No. 3-1512-285-77, submitted to arbitration by the United Rubber, Cork, Linoleum, and Plastic Workers of America AFL-CIO-CLC, reads: The grievance claims that a 30-day disciplinary suspension imposed by the Company was unjust, and the Union requests that the grievant be made whole for all monies and benefits lost.

Arbitrator Peter DiLeone resolved this grievance after a hearing with both the union and the company. The Facts section of his analysis read, in part:

"The Union does not argue that the Company need negotiate penalties for any rules violation, nor does it even contest the point that discipline is warranted in this case.

"The thrust of the Union's case is that the Company can impose discipline only where there is violation of a reasonable rule that has been properly promulgated and that once a violation has been established, the penalty for such violation must be evenly applied. It is the Union's contention that the 30-day suspension imposed by the Company in this case is clearly excessive when viewed in the light of penalties previously assessed by the Company for the identical violation—fighting in the plant.

"To further buttress its argument, the Union submitted 17 variously dated suspension letters issued at this plant. All of the suspensions were for fighting, pushing, or threatening in the plant; out of the 17 suspensions, there was one 14-day suspension, the remaining 16 suspensions being for either a three-day or seven-day period.

"Therefore, the Union urges that the penalty be found to be excessive and it requests that the penalty be reduced so as to be consistent with previously imposed penalties for similar violations."

Also in the Facts section of the document was the Company's viewpoint, reported, in part, thus:

"The Company argues that the attack upon Supervisor Jones was without provocation or mitigating circumstances and that discipline must be maintained if the Company is to fulfill its obligation to provide a safe work environment free of both violence and threats to the well-being of its employees, be they supervisors or members of the Bargaining Unit.

"The Company also asserts that it was in compliance with Article V of the contract in that all the facts and circumstances surrounding this incident were properly considered, and further that the 30-day suspension imposed upon King was a proper exercise of its authority when viewed in the light of those facts and circumstances."

In the Analysis and Opinion section of the document the arbitrator stated the following, in part:

"The fact that this grievant received a 30-day suspension, while of the 17 suspension letters referred to by the Union, only one was for a 14-day suspension with the remaining 16 being for periods of either three days or seven days, fails to demonstrate an inconsistency, in the opinion of the Umpire. Any given suspension is meted out for very specific reasons and under very specific circumstances. The Union has shown the penalty in this case to exceed those applied in the past but does not demonstrate any equation between the facts and circumstances of this case and those of the previous suspensions referred. From what the Umpire can determine, the majority of those previous suspensions were for employees fighting in the plant; or pushing, shoving, or threatening a Supervisor, with varying degrees of provocation and mitigating circumstances present. Significantly, the 14-day suspension was imposed on an employee for striking a Supervisor.

"Thus, although the Umpire might find a certain consistency present in the handling of disciplinary measures, it is not found to be as urged by the Union. The only consistency or practice that can be solidly established is that the Company has considered each case on its individual merits and acted accordingly. The penalty for any given rule violation need not be *identical* to other such penalties to be *consistent* if the variation is attributed to differing facts and circumstances."

In the Award section of the document the arbitrator states: "The Umpire can only come to one conclusion in this case. The grievance should be, and is hereby, denied."

14.12 Tips on Providing Proof to Back Disciplinary Action

A large share of all arbitration cases today question the disciplinary action imposed on an employee by supervision for violation of plant rules or for poor work performance. In most cases, arbitrators consider what the degree of proof must be to support the supervisor's action. Some type of proof is usually a necessity.

The supervisor frequently is the star witness in such situations. The specific facts relating to the case must be established by your testimony and by the written record. You must be prepared to show, for instance, that your worker, Tom Johnson, was absent on specific days and that he was warned on particular occasions that his attendance would have to improve.

Nobody in a supervisory position likes to take disciplinary action with one of his or her people. But you must prepare to do that well in advance of the time that it becomes necessary. An efficient supervisor keeps a record of events and incidents at the first sign that disciplinary action may eventually have to be taken. Since the testimony of other people could be needed at an arbitration hearing several weeks or months later, a wise supervisor also records who was present and who witnessed a violation. Unless a record is made, one that identifies people with places and dates, time will obliterate the memories of everyone.

14.13 Proven Ways of Promoting and Transferring Without Hassles

One of the most difficult problems management has concerns the promotion of union people. Management needs the maximum amount of flexibility in selecting persons for promotion and also wants to avoid basing promotions on straight seniority. Unions often do not trust the judgmental factors involved with promotions; they prefer to base decisions on a known and measurable factor like seniority. Despite the opposing viewpoints, management and the union usually try to find a common ground on which to compromise.

The right of management to employ the most skilled and efficient people in key positions is one of the basic rights that must be understood in any contract with the union. Supervisors should always interpret the contract in that light. When a job applicant is rejected, it should be done on the grounds that he or she is not qualified. The ruling may be backed by the employee's personnel record which gives in detail the educational qualifications of the person as well as what his or her work experience has been.

Management should insist on proper qualifications also when an employee puts in a bid to be transferred. Many grievances are written on this matter.

Frequently an employee may claim the company is guilty of discrimination when his or her request is denied.

Case-in-Point: Tom Shannon, Maintenance Supervisor at Ace Products in Springfield, Illinois, was faced with a problem of job qualification when an utility worker left his department for another job. Following company policy, Shannon posted the vacancy on the bulletin board. The first person to bid for the job was Mary Campbell who at that time performed light maintenance duties. She was a slightly built, four-year employee in her mid-30s.

But before any decision was made on who would get the job, Shannon told Campbell that the job would be too difficult for her because it included handling crates and cartons that weighed up to 75 pounds. Campbell replied that if she needed help she would ask for it. Shannon said that too much time would be wasted doing that.

Mary Campbell told the supervisor that he was simply looking for excuses not to give her the job because she was a woman. "That is not true," Shannon replied. "We have women working in all kinds of jobs in the plant."

"Then there's no reason a woman can't do this job as well," said Campbell. "I may be small, but that doesn't mean I'm not strong enough to handle it. The union will back me at arbitration if you don't give me a chance."

Shannon went to his personnel manager for advice on how to handle the case. The manager supported him in his stand, saying, "The fact that we employ women in a number of jobs formerly held by men is proof that we don't discriminate. And the requirements of the job show that Campbell lacks the qualifications needed to fill it. Going out of our way to avoid discriminating against someone is one thing. Hiring a person who isn't qualified for the job would be going too far. I don't think that Campbell's claim that she was turned down because of her sex would get very far with an umpire. Apparently union officials agreed with the personnel manager's analysis because Campbell and the union did not take her complaint to arbitration when the job was awarded to another person who had demonstrated his ability to handle heavy cartons easily.

14.14 How to Handle a Promotion to a Supervisor

Management may some day ask you for your opinion on who of the union workers would make a good supervisor. If you are not prepared to recommend one of your people, you could begin your search by asking the union who they would suggest. Union nominees often turn out to be very capable individuals.

But be aware of your objective: to help the company achieve its goal by putting its most skilled and efficient people in key positions. If the union recommends someone whom you feel does not have the proper qualifications, don't accede without giving the matter considerable thought. You must rely on your own evaluation of the person's performance and your own estimate of the person's potential. Usually this is not easy to do because not all good workers make good supervisors.

To be able to make a good recommendation to management, you should evaluate your people for the qualifications of a good supervisor long before you are asked about it. Potential supervisors should be recognized early and be brought along on the job by guiding and counseling. It is also wise to talk with other supervisors about who has the capabilities for the job. You want to be sure you are not overlooking someone as well as confirming that your choice is a good one.

15

PRODUCTIVITY
AND WHAT TO DO
ABOUT IT

SUPERVISORS who put a sincere effort into improving the productivity of employees are a real asset to their company. A highly productive labor force means that people are efficient on the job, enabling the company to be profitable and keep up with the competition. Supervisors play a key role in productivity improvement programs because they are close to the workers and have a great influence on their performance.

The productivity of employees can be raised in many ways other than the obvious "making good use of time." Motivating and training people on the job are two of the most successful ways. Job enrichment is another. Supervisors contribute best when they spend most of their time in direct leadership working with their people. By planning and scheduling work, they can more fully use the skills of workers as well as assure that materials, tools, and equipment are available when needed.

Supervisors have other resources to call upon to help them do something about productivity. Those who understand systems and know how to handle fluctuating workloads are a great aid to management. With work sampling studies, supervisors can determine its levels and where they should direct their improvement efforts. A company that has a suggestion system and encourages employee participation usually reaps worthwhile benefits. Supervisors themselves should become skilled in presenting and selling ideas to their superiors.

15.1 How to Raise Productivity by Talking to People

Effective use of manpower and good productivity in the workplace require that people communicate with each other. Employees must work together to achieve company goals. Supervisors should stress the importance of communication when directing work activities.

Many employees want to know what other employees of the company do. They are interested also in the problems of other departments as well as how their company is doing as a whole. Giving them such information prompts greater interest in their work and leads to more cooperation among departments. The result is quicker and more effective handling of problems and greater productivity.

If you want your people to be more efficient, you should periodically talk to them about materials and equipment. Workers in the office and in the plant have ideas on how to do jobs quicker, where they run into delays, and how materials can be handled better. By discussing these things and taking corrective action where needed, you can raise the productivity of your group and help your company. Even the simple act of talking to employees about their work, how they feel about their jobs, and what they need will result in an increase in productivity on their part.

Case-in-Point: Back in 1927, Western Electric was concerned about the productivity of their employees. Management had tried everything it could think of to increase performance, but nothing worked. In desperation, one of the managers decided to talk to some of the workers to see if they had any suggestions. Although he didn't get many worthwhile ideas, a strange thing happened. Production rates began to increase and rejection rates began to go down. Overall performance was higher than it had ever been before.

Not knowing what brought about the change, the manager interviewed the workers once more. Again, few ideas came out of the talks, but production again improved. When the manager talked to some other departments, the same thing happened. Production increased and rejects went down whenever people were talked to about their work, their needs, and their attitudes.

Since 1927, Western Electric has conducted a formal program of talking to their employees, getting their opinions and suggestions, and listening to their complaints, followed by acting on them. Western Electric, as a result, is one of the most efficient industrial companies in business today.

15.2 Promoting Productivity Through Better Use of Time

The inefficiency of people on the job is principally the result of poor use of time. Recognizing this, supervisors should be continually looking for ways to get their people to put more of their time on the job and less on personal matters.

Employees today waste a lot of productive time with late starts and early quits, excessive rest and coffee breaks, long lunch periods, nonbusiness conversations, and just plain loafing. Regardless, effective supervisors combat the waste of time by their people in various ways.

How-to-Do-It: The best way to get people started on the job is to stay with or near them after giving them an assignment until they begin work. Of course, you have no assurance they will continue to work after you leave, but you can return a short time later.

About the only way you can control the time people take for rest and coffee breaks is to put in an appearance if the privilege is being abused. Although most supervisors dislike doing this, it provides the opportunity to inquire how the work is going, if assistance is needed, or to ask other specific questions related to the job.

One way to break up bull sessions is to join the group, asking if you can help. You imply that the persons have a problem they are discussing—you would like to help. Another answer to break up idle conversations is to approach the group and ask for the help of one of the members, help that requires the person to leave with you to go to a workplace or office. Removing one person from a group often gets the point across to the others that they should be getting back to their jobs.

Nonbusiness conversations have a place in work areas to promote good relations among employees and to relieve stress and tension on the job. You will find that people are more productive if they have a friendly, relaxed atmosphere to work in, one where they can freely discuss their families and their hobbies with their fellow-workers. You should participate in such conversations, too. When employees see that the company is interested in their welfare and personal lives, they are more willing to cooperate on the job and do a good day's work. However, you must guard against excessive visiting among employees which reduces productive time.

Case-in-Point: "The problem of people wasting time by visiting with one another can be handled by making it difficult or inconvenient for them to get together," says Eugene Sankey, former Section Manager of Factory Accounting for Goodyear Tire and Rubber Company. "I remember that we had this problem years ago before we remodeled the offices. A suggestion was turned in by a conscientious fellow who had, with others, a desk along an aisle between two departments. People going from one department to another continually stopped to talk with these employees. His answer to the problem was to have a 6-foot partition wall put on both sides of the aisle; so that the partitions were not too unattractive, the upper portions were constructed of glass. It took a lot of shouting if people tried to converse."

15.3 Job Enrichment: A Key to Increased Productivity

Although you may not read or hear as much about job enrichment today as you did a decade ago, that doesn't mean it no longer is practiced in our plants and offices. Job enrichment is the altering and expanding of a job to provide a worker with greater responsibility and more autonomy for carrying out that responsibility.

To adopt and implement job enrichment, you must put a lot of thought into the jobs you give your people. You should also consider the effect these jobs will have on them in terms of feeling of responsibility and pride. Job enrichment usually gives people more dignity and security. Many workers have reported that pride in their work increased after their jobs were enriched.

Before job enrichment came on the scene, management customarily broke down operations into parts and assigned a worker to each part. With this arrangement, responsibility and authority of each worker was limited, and few people were extended to anywhere near their mental or physical capabilities. When an organization practices job enrichment today, management looks at job responsibilities and task objectives differently. Supervisors try to broaden jobs and make them as meaningful as possible. An increase in productivity naturally occurs.

There's a possibility you will learn that some of your people are not willing to take on additional responsibilities. Such people are content with their jobs as they are. Still, you may want to try to sell them on the idea. To succeed, you must handle the situation carefully and be as tactful as possible. Explain fully what is involved in the step from a task to a project, why it's being proposed, and what is expected to be accomplished. Be sure to point out that people who adopt the principles of job enrichment usually derive much more satisfaction from their work.

15.4 Training: Supervisors Can Make It Pay Off

Training is probably the best way of helping people to perform well. Many companies could reduce their costs, increase safety, and improve productivity if they gave more of their employees training. Most workers really want to do a job well. A lack of knowledge and skill often prevents them from being as productive as they could be.

On-the-job instructing is the most common way that companies train their employees today, although classroom instruction and attending seminars also is popular. Training by supervisors is more practical than by professional teachers, administrative personnel, or consultants. Supervisors are in the best position to measure the effectiveness of the training and place emphasis where it is needed. Since most workers want to please their supervisors, trainees are more receptive and their retention is better when they are taught by their supervisors. Other advantages to using supervisors to train people are that the supervisors also learn from the program and are committed to it more than other instructors would be.

You should be sure to cover the basics when training on the job. Training which consists only of telling people what, how, and why to do something is usually not adequate. Many people need to do the job or task in order to learn it. Certainly, this is the only way for people to really become proficient and raise their productivity.

Day-to-day problems should not be permitted to interfere with training lest the participants see the training as unimportant. Training pays off the most when people are conscientious in how they go about it and put their full efforts into it. The optimum benefit is realized when the training is on how to do the job itself or closely related to the work to be performed.

15.5 How to Handle Fluctuating Workloads

It would be nice if we always received our work assignments and production schedules in a steady stream with no ups and no downs. That's probably one of the dreams of most supervisors. However, everyone knows that it rarely happens that way. Worse, sometimes the fluctuations are quite dramatic. Yet, if you are an efficient and knowledgeable supervisor, you can learn how to cope with this problem. Here are the ways you can do it:

- Ask your people how they would handle or eliminate peak situations.
- Determine if there is new equipment available that might permanently eliminate excessive workloads.
- Suggest that management make arrangements with retirees to come back to work temporarily when workloads skyrocket.
- Keep historical records to help you accurately predict peak and slack times and thereby avoid chaos.
- Be honest with your people about the potential of slack periods, thus giving them time to plan for vacations during those times.
- Train your people for more than one job so they can fill in where needed.
- Ask your boss to hire outside help during peak times using temporary services.

- Plan to make some procedural changes such as shifting some work to another department when your people can't handle all of it.

- Postpone some jobs temporarily while your people handle a peak load.

- Have contingency plans in place to assure your people will be kept busy if the workload drops without warning.

15.6 Positive Ways to Prevent Obsolescence of People

While aging of your people is natural and expected, obsolescence should not be. The company should be concerned and try to keep employees knowledgeable of developments which affect their work. Maintaining and improving the productivity of people on the job requires that they be kept abreast of technology in their type of work.

Most workers are interested in new ideas, new products, new tools, and better ways to do a job, especially if these things will make their job easier. You can prevent your people from becoming obsolete in the way they handle their work in several ways.

How-to-Do-It: Provide the appropriate training for them when a work procedure is changed or when new equipment is put in use. Usually the vendor or manufacturer of new equipment which the company acquires will provide instruction on how to operate and service it or will supply a manual which does this. See that such instructions and information are made available to your people.

Encourage your people to take courses at the high schools and universities in the area. If your company will pay tuition costs, you have a good selling argument. Emphasize the value of improving one's skills on the job and how such education can lead to a better position with the company.

Rent or buy films to show your people subjects of interest such as safety and health. Bring speakers and lecturers to the company to make presentations. And don't overlook payroll inserts, bulletin boards, and the company newspaper as other ways to keep your people up-to-date and informed on new products, new tools, and better ways to do a job.

15.7 Motivation: The Sure-Fire Way to Raise Productivity

Most management experts agree that motivation is the key to good productivity. The supervisor's task is to create the right atmosphere conducive to motivation, using all the resources and skills he or she has. This is difficult. It takes time, intuition, and a sensitivity to people to accomplish and maintain enthusiasm. You should never give up, however, even though you may often be discouraged and feel frustrated.

A way to motivate people is to see that they get satisfaction from their work. Try to provide the factors that fill their needs. Make the work challenging and interesting. Give people a reason for doing a job and compliment them upon its completion.

Believing in your people and having confidence that they can do the work will increase their level of performance because they will attempt to live up to your expectations and be worthy of your trust. Training is a motivational tool if your people want to learn more about the technical side of their jobs. This is particularly true with craftsmen.

Public recognition often maintains motivation. Formally congratulating skilled people after they successfully complete a demanding job is very effective. So is recognizing work done under unfavorable conditions such as bad weather, poor location, and hazardous situations.

A temporary promotion is an effective way to motivate a worker in many companies. Acting as a temporary supervisor, for example, will motivate a person to raise his or her productivity when the person returns to his or her job.

15.8 Recognition Pays Off

Recognition is more important to some people than are salary or working conditions; in fact, most people want to be given credit for their work.

Praise is another need. Everyone needs to occasionally hear that he or she has done a good job. Praise arouses feelings of competence and ability which, in turn, motivates or leads to future display of those skills. Recognition and praise invariably result in greater productivity.

Case-in-Point: Management of Diamond Fiber Products, Inc. was able to save $5 million in an 18-month period in the early 1980s at four of its plants by promoting The 100 Club, an employee recognition/involvement concept. The 100 Club is a people-oriented program without an incentive connection. Recognition is symbolized by the nominal value of the gifts employees may receive in contrast to so-called big awards.

When explaining the purpose and objective of creating The 100 Club, Dan Boyle, co-owner of the company, said to employees, "You become a member of The 100 Club when you earn 100 points. Becoming a member means you automatically are given a jacket which displays the company's logo. Then there are a variety of gifts available to you at additional 50-point increments. The number of points you accumulate is up to you. When you decide to cash in a certain number for a gift, those points are subtracted from your total, and then you start accumulating points for another gift.

"In order for you to get points in The 100 Club for attendance, you simply have to come into work. Points for on-the-job safety will be given to those who go a year without a lost-time accident. Some of the points you earn are determined by your personal performance. Others are awarded to you on a departmental basis. For example, if you work in the shipping department, and the shipments per manhour worked exceed a standard, everyone in the department gets some points for this. The same rule applies in the maintenance department where we've set standards for maintenance efficiency."

Diamond's first-year savings attributed to The 100 Club were $1,600,000. Savings on absenteeism reduction alone were $90,000. The largest gain came in higher productivity: an improvement of 14.5 percent. Simultaneously, a 40 percent reduction in quality related mistakes was achieved, and a 41 percent reduction in days of work lost due to accidents was noted.

15.9 Tested and Proven Benefits from Planning and Scheduling

To have high productivity, emphasis must be placed on the supervisional functions that promote efficiency and job accomplishment. Planning and scheduling of work is the way to go about it.

Planning determines what work needs to be done, when it should be done, and what will be required to do it. Scheduling assigns people to jobs at a specified time. The procedure involves coordinating people, material, tools, and equipment to assure that all are available at the time to start the work. Here are six proven benefits which a company gains from planning and scheduling its work:

1. Attention and action based on priorities. You can make sure first things come first. When supervisors consider customer orders, work situations, availability of labor and material, and the other factors which affect service and production, they can make decisions to get the optimum from their resources within the time available.

2. Better procedures for getting work done. Planning and scheduling prompts study of the job which results in finding the best method. If a supervisor gives a worker a job without instructions, the worker may do it in an inefficient manner as well as waste material. The worker may also run into a problem on the job and wait for the supervisor to come along to ask for help. When a job is well-planned, such waste of time and material is avoided.

3. Better coordination of labor and materials. Planning enables you to decide what materials and tools are required. You can then see that they are on hand before starting a job. A worker doesn't have to wait for material or be unable to complete a job because of the lack of it.

4. More efficient utilization of labor. When planning a job or project, you consider its scope and size. This prepares you to assign the optimum number of people and time to get it done. Estimating the time to do a job helps with scheduling people, thus improving their efficiency. It also enables you to avoid or minimize overtime.

5. Reduction of errors, mistakes, and omissions. Planning and scheduling permits you to provide written instructions for jobs, thus reducing errors which occur with oral orders. Drawings and specifications prevent omissions as well as result in better workmanship.

6. Better credibility of supervisors. Good personnel relations between departments of an organization promote more cooperation and teamwork, thus raising the productivity of all employees. Planning and scheduling enables supervisors to be more accurate with job completion promises. This enhances credibility and reputation along with confidence in ability to get the job done.

15.10 Systems: How They Work

Many of today's industrial and business operations are carried out through systems, a system being a planned and orderly procedure of accomplishing objectives. A basic requirement of a system is that it must be simple. Errors are less likely to occur if a system is easy to learn and use. Simplicity also promotes understanding as well as acceptance.

People, equipment, and procedures are the components of a system. Systems are created and developed with a purpose, the most common being to minimize the cost of accomplishing a job. Some systems promote company growth and stability. Others are concerned mainly with improving efficiency. But systems provide benefits only when people understand them well enough to make them work.

The features of a system must be such that its users have faith and confidence in it. People must believe that it can do the job for which it was designed. If a system is not acceptable, it will be misused or bypassed.

Systems must leave no doubt in the minds of users as to scope and coverage. The capability and range of a system should be spelled out in specifications which include a list of equipment involved. Systems are not truly usable, however, until what people do is clearly defined.

15.11 Answers to Why Some Systems Don't Work

Some systems work well while others don't work at all. Failure in any one of the following areas of communication and decision-making can result in a system which does not function effectively:

- The withholding by management of planning and financial data from operating people.
- The inability of operating people to provide accurate data to a consultant or systems supplier.
- The unwillingness of engineering people to discuss computerization with vendors.

- The belief of the purchasing department that a system can be bought simply by writing specifications, asking for bids, and awarding a contract to the lowest bidder.

- The shortsightedness of the systems supplier who works only with management and engineering, neglecting supervisors and people on the job who have to make the system work.

Making a system work is difficult without a cooperative effort and complete communication among all people in both suppliers' and users' organizations. That, plus a make-it-work attitude of everyone involved, are the most important factors in the implementation and operation of a system.

15.12 Three Pitfalls to Avoid in Keeping Productivity Up

Successful supervisors avoid the roadblocks in their procedure of attaining and maintaining high productivity of their people. Three pitfalls they are particularly alert to are:

1. Allowing employees to set their own methods for doing work and the time to do it. This practice can be especially unproductive with maintenance work if craftsmen are sent to a job site by their supervisor to see what the job for the day will consist of and what tools and materials will be needed. These decisions should be made by the supervisor before sending the men to the job.

2. Failing to consider time span and man-hours required to get a job done. The supervisor should know how long it will take to do a job and insist that employees meet the standards or come close to them.

3. Neglecting to place a value on cost in determining how work should be performed. Examples of abuse are assigning too many people to the job, using inefficient work methods, using more expensive material than required, and resorting to overtime.

15.13 Work Sampling: A Useful Tool for Measuring Productivity

Work sampling is a technique whereby supervisors or personnel department people observe workers to determine how productive they are. The principles of work sampling are based on the laws of probability. These laws conclude that a large number of observations made at random intervals and classified into distinct activities will provide a fairly reliable story of what percent of the time each activity is occurring. A key point is that activity observations must be taken randomly to assure unbiased results.

Work sampling procedures are designed to:

1. Measure the amount of control that supervisors have over their people.

2. Determine the percent of time people are working.

3. Reveal activities that are preventing people from putting more time into their work.

4. Provide a base against which future performance may be measured.

Caution: Work sampling should not be used to measure a worker's performance nor should it be used as a disciplinary tool. You lose the trust and confidence of your people if you use it for these purposes.

15.14 How to Make a Work Sampling Study

A definite procedure must be followed when work sampling if the information you get from it is to be valid and reliable. Here is how you should proceed:

1. Predetermine what activities you are going to look for so that you can classify your observations. The usual activities are: working, idle on job, idle away from job, traveling, getting instructions, and cleaning operations.

2. Make your observations in all areas of the office or factory where people may work, covering it entirely during one tour period.

3. Make tours on a random time basis throughout the workday. Determine the times by the use of random number tables.

4. Limit the tour period to 15-20 minutes. If you cannot complete it in this time, have another observer help you.

5. Include the canteen and lunchroom in the areas to be observed. Do not include locker and washrooms unless you have a problem locating people.

6. Know the total number of people to be observed on each tour and compare the number of observations you make with the number of people available. People not observed should be less than 10 percent.

7. Make a minimum of 12 observations of each person over the period of the study. The more observations you make, the more reliable the information.

8. Record your first impression when you observe a person. No additional observation time is needed.

9. Calculate the percent of time you found each person in each predetermined activity.

10. Summarize your study and put it in writing so that you will have it for comparison purposes on future work sampling studies.

15.15 Four Steps to Management by Objectives

A generally accepted mark of an efficient supervisor is a proficiency in setting and achieving his or her department's objectives. Management by objectives is a currently recognized and practiced procedure for carrying out the functions of management. It involves setting job responsibilities and perform-ance standards for each job in a department. Although each person has specific objectives, all persons work toward a common goal, directed by the manager or supervisor.

People do a better job if they are aware of the level of performance expected of them. Also, managerial functions are more efficiently carried out if respon-sibilities are understood by both manager and subordinates. The four procedural steps to management by objectives are:

1. Analyze the person's job responsibilities. Supervisors frequently are surprised to learn what subordinates believe their responsibilities are. The issue is best resolved by having both the supervisor and the person list them indepen-dently. When the lists are compared, agreement should be reached on those functions for which the person will be held accountable.

2. Specify the person's level of performance. People on the job need guidelines to enable them to determine how well they are doing. By setting standards for performance, the supervisor gives them a yardstick to measure the quality and quantity of their work. The use of standards makes possible an individual's determination of where more effort is required.

3. Set goals for the person to attain. The goals should be agreed upon by both the supervisor and the person. The supervisor may limit a person's goals to assure a good showing within a specified period of time. Discouragement because of failure can be minimized or avoided if goals are not set too high.

4. Assess the person's degree of accomplishment. Follow-up is essential to evaluating accomplishments. The supervisor should have an appraisal interview with the subordinate regularly to cover the objectives and goals previously agreed upon. At this time, the supervisor and the person usually set goals for the future.

15.16 How to Cope with a Shortage of Space

If your company is growing, automating, or adding a new process, the amount of workspace is likely to diminish substantially. This change causes problems for both workers and their supervisors. Production and maintenance people like to have room to move about as they do their work. When they see they don't have it, their morale suffers and they also feel unsafe.

With inadequate space, workers may be unable to place materials where they belong, causing double handling as they are set aside until space opens up. In addition, many workers can't find things they are looking for quickly, or see that items are inaccessible. Such conditions are bound to result in lower produc-tivity.

Safety is a matter of concern when workspace is limited. Also, people must be extra careful to avoid stumbling over or bumping into objects. Craftsmen working in cramped quarters are more susceptible to sprains, cuts, and abrasions since they may be unable to use their tools and equipment in a normal manner.

Since shortage of space may take some time to be corrected, you must make an effort to see that workers understand and adjust to it. Here are the ways you can do this:

- Discuss the problem openly and frankly so your people understand why it has happened. For example, you might explain that the purchasing department ordered a lot of material because sales forecasts indicate that there will be a big demand for these products in the near future.

- Make a study of how space is being used to see if shelves, racks, floors, and aisles might be cleared or used differently to cause less stress to people on the job.

- Survey the plant or office for obsolete or unused machines and equipment that can be removed and either sold or put in a warehouse temporarily.

- See if just-in-time practices can be adopted to minimize or eliminate material-in-process inventory. These procedures are becoming more and more popular because they save money and also provide more workspace.

15.17 Five Selling Points for Suggestion Systems

Every company should have a suggestion system if for no other reason than to raise the productivity of its employees. The Bell Telephone Laboratories in Raritan, New Jersey made a study some time ago of their system and reported that a good one will return from $3-$8 for every dollar invested in it. At that time, the average suggestion system plan cost about $28 per employee yearly. John Main of Bell said that the indirect benefits included:

1. Release of employee frustration and boredom.
2. The opportunity for employees to demonstrate their value to the company and their peers.
3. A sharpening of healthy competitive instincts.
4. The focusing of employee's attention on what is of primary importance in their jobs.
5. Involvement of employees in the firm's procedures and objectives.

15.18 How to Promote More and Better Suggestions

To raise productivity, you've got to think of efficiency and be cost conscious of all the operations and services your people perform. Why not ask your people to think about better ways to do their work?

You can start by explaining the company's interest in suggestions from employees. Suggestions from people on the job help to reduce costs and improve productivity. Point out some of the problem areas where improvements are needed. Mention the need to reduce waste, to overcome a bottleneck, and to simplify some of the work.

Build up enthusiasm for submitting suggestions by talking about the awards people are eligible for and how they have a lot to gain with nothing to lose by participating. Say that you're available to answer questions and to help anyone in writing up suggestions.

Case-in-Point: Dan Mills, General Supervisor with the White Manufacturing Co. in Edison, New Jersey, says, "Make your people feel they are working for a human organization, not some kind of impersonal machine. This can be encouraged by acting on employees' suggestions." He adds, "Don't ignore the ideas of subordinates. They can't identify with the organization and its goals if you won't let them. Unless they do, they won't produce any more than they have to, and you'll have to spend more time closely supervising them."

Caution: When you promote suggestions, be sure you make it clear that turning in suggestions is an entirely voluntary matter—suggestions are not a requirement of the job nor are you telling people that they should be submitted. Some people will find suggestions systems more palatable when they are presented this way. Also, you avoid any arguments that may arise concerning pay for time spent developing an idea on nonworking time.

15.19 Selling an Idea: The Positive Way to Do It

A sometimes heard complaint of supervisors is that their bosses are unwilling to listen to them or that they cut them short when they propose something. Although there are autocratic people in middle management jobs today, most managers are interested in their subordinate's ideas. Supervisors should not use the excuse of a nonreceptive superior to put off trying to sell an idea. Getting your boss to listen to you and accept your idea may not always be easy, but you can improve your chances of success if you go about it in the right manner.

How-to-Do-It: Whether you're trying to sell your boss or someone else an idea, the first thing to do is look for the feature or part of it which would interest the person. It's difficult to sell anybody anything if they're not interested or cannot see anything in it for them.

Think out your idea thoroughly. This means compiling as much information as possible about it and deciding what part you will present. Try to have facts rather than opinions for support.

Pick an appropriate time to do your selling. Don't burst in when the person is busy nor at the end of the day. You may decide to ask the person for a time to meet when it would be most convenient for him or her.

Be enthusiastic. You can't expect someone to accept your idea if you're only lukewarm or half-sure about it yourself. Present the benefits and the advantages. Include savings. Show that you have spent some time working on the idea, that it's not just a whim on your part.

Look for agreement and acceptance. If you have a good idea and present it well, you should get approval. Offer to take whatever steps are necessary to put the idea in practice.

15.20 Six Steps to Take for Improving Operations

If you are an astute and conscientious supervisor, you are continually looking for ways to cut costs and increase the productivity of your people. But are you aware that by following a definite procedure, you can increase your chances of being successful in improving operations? Here is a six-step procedure that has worked well for other supervisors:

1. Start by looking around and observing activities that are either time-consuming, inefficient, or very costly.

2. Think or conceive of one or more ways an improvement can be made in the activity. Visualize how the change could be made.

3. Do some research as to how other companies handle the same problem. Decide to either: recommend using their ways in toto; adopt the best of their ways to your idea; or reject their ways as not as good as yours.

4. Consider the practicality and cost of adopting and maintaining your idea compared to the present way the operation is being performed.

5. Discuss your way of improving the operation with the people who are performing it and with your fellow-supervisors. Get their views, and then reconsider your idea.

6. Assuming the idea still has merit in your opinion, plan how you will present it to your boss in written or oral form. Then make the presentation and offer to implement the idea.

15.21 Tips on Controlling Your Paperwork

One of the major stumbling blocks to being productive are the tasks you must perform that are nonproductive, such as paperwork. When you put in a lot of time on paperwork, you have less time to devote to your supervisory responsibilities. Although you'll never be able to eliminate all of your paperwork, here are some tips on how to get around much of it:

● Do the paperwork when it arises rather than postponing it. The papers and records won't accumulate and become a big job later.

● Handle the paperwork on the job whenever possible instead of carrying it to your desk or office. The quicker you can handle it, the less of a burden it will seem, and you won't have to handle the paper twice.

● Keep a minimum of records but know where you can get information if you need it. You'll avoid clutter and distraction, not to mention having to decide where to file something.

● Don't recopy records or forms. Avoid making duplicates of anything. The less copies, the less paper to keep track of. Most copies are seldom referred to again.

16

SUCCESSFUL WAYS
FOR GETTING THE MOST
FROM SKILLED AND
"SPECIAL" PEOPLE

PEOPLE on the job are different, one from another, in their education, skills, experience, and how they feel about their work. This is especially true with those who have the potential to accomplish much. Professional people look at their work and their jobs differently than nonprofessional people, and they expect to be treated in respect to their position. Creative people also view their work and perform it in ways that fit how they think and reflect their lifestyle.

Young workers and old workers also think about their jobs and perform their work differently compared to each other. Older workers in many cases have demonstrated a superiority over their younger peers by outperforming them. Supervisors often find that they get more cooperation and better performance from their older people.

To work successfully with the minorities, the handicapped, and other "special" people, you must care about these people and be patient with them.

They usually need more training than other workers in order to perform on an equal level. Once they have been trained, however, they will often be more consistent in their work. They should be given the same consideration on the job that you give others. The best way to do this is to have them work side by side with other employees.

16.1 How to Recognize People with Potential

Recognizing people who have potential and who will probably advance in the company is usually a simple matter. Such people perform their work in a positive and enthusiastic manner. The ones who are ready and capable of taking on greater responsibilities show it by the following behavioral characteristics:

- They display good judgment and common sense. They have the ability to see the simplest approach to a problem rather than the more complicated.

- They communicate well. They get unspoken messages quickly and they are at home with the jargon of the various people with whom they associate.

- They are optimistic. They believe the future will be better than the present, and that confidence in themselves leads to success.

- They readily accept change. They are concerned only with what is to be changed and how it is to be accomplished.

- They are goal-oriented. They understand that achieving objectives is what pays off.

Technical knowledge and stamina are desirable but not vital for most supervisory jobs. However, you should hesitate to promote someone who doesn't have most if not all of the above characteristics.

16.2 Ways to Determine Where People Will Do Their Best

If you put a person on a job for which the person is not suited, you do not make the most of the person's skills nor do you enable the person to get satisfaction from the work. Even worse, if you misfit a person to a job, you may disrupt the department organization and cause poor morale as well as low productivity. Effective supervisors know how to match people with jobs and work situations which will turn out best for both individuals and the company.

You can give employees psychological tests to help you discover what type of work best suits their preferences and interests. But you must recognize that tests merely indicate the niches employees should occupy. Furthermore, employees like to feel they have some choice in the matter. Supervisors should draw on human inclinations for insight to proper placement of their people.

Workers do not like to fail on the job. Thus, they prefer work which they feel they can handle and at which they will be a success. They do not want to be embarrassed, which they would be by failure. And they like to feel they are contributing in turning out the company's product or providing its service. If you are sensitive to people's feelings about their work, and fair to them without bias or prejudice, you will have no trouble in finding the best spots for them in the company.

An expert's comment: People who dress oddly and men who wear long hair may be trying to tell you that they want to be recognized as individuals; often they feel they aren't. More serious symptoms often accompanying these actions are lack of commitment, drive, or enthusiasm, and general apathy along with inefficiency. Dr. Norman Sigband, Professor of Marketing and Business Communication, University of Southern California, Los Angeles, says the solution to the problem is relatively simple: effective internal communication by management in defining goals, directions, and values with the worker. The person then becomes somebody.

16.3 Three Keys to Capitalizing on People's Strengths

Supervisors who have strong people to work with should take on the responsibility of inducing them to grow on the job, accept challenging work, and strive to utilize their abilities to the maximum. Exceptional talents should not be wasted anymore than a company would waste its expensive raw material or its highly technological equipment or machines. The keys to effective capitalizing on human strengths lie in the way you treat and work with people. Here are three approaches you should take:

1. Look for and expect the best from people. Supervising with high expectations gives strong people the incentive and drive which they need to see purpose and get direction for doing good work.

2. Build on and promote people's strong points. Ignore and play down their weaknesses. Publicize accomplishments and report progress. Relate achievements to company objectives.

3. Classify strengths and abilities of individuals. Then design and make work assignments accordingly, measuring the individuals by the progress they make. Increase responsibilities as you see that capabilities to handle them are attained.

16.4 How to Maximize the Output of Highly Potential People

One of the attributes of successful leaders is a sensitivity to the potential of their people. The skill enables them to help individuals discover and attain their full potentials and guide individuals to levels of accomplishment which they might not otherwise reach. You can maximize the output and productivity of your highly potential people by dedicating yourself to such efforts.

How-to-Do-It: Study a person's background, interests, and motivations. Line these up with the job positions and opportunities in the company where the person can apply himself or herself and advance to the level where the person's potentials will be reached. Then, show your interest in the person's future by discussing with him or her this long range program as you see it. Provide stimulation and encouragement to persuade the person to pursue this course.

If you can inject some flexibility in your plan and provide adequate time for the person's development, you are more likely to get understanding and acceptance. You should also point out the logic of your proposal. This will help motivate the person to overcome roadblocks which occasionally may appear along the way.

Case-in-Point: An industrial plant manager told me how he brought along one of his people to a high position in the company. "I recognized that Bob Rollins had managerial capabilities the first day I talked to him. But I also saw that I would have to do a real selling job to convince him of it. Thereafter, I took steps to see that he had opportunities to learn all the operations, and I encouraged him to accept temporary supervisor jobs whenever possible. Rollins consistently did a good job as I was convinced he would. He continued to move up in the organization and recently accepted the position of Production Manager."

16.5 Successful Placing and Use of Professional People

Professional people are different from other employees in that they feel they are highly skilled and knowledgeable; therefore, they resent any treatment that suggests they are thought of as ordinary workers. Supervisors should be aware that the key to getting along with them is to treat them as special people.

Professional employees want to be recognized as members of a profession. They are often more career-oriented than company-oriented and dislike regimentation. If professional people work for you, remember that their job titles are important to them and they are jealous of their own ideas and accomplishments.

Scientists and staff people doing research work develop data and information. They are creative and usually have quite a bit of education. They get the advanced degrees at universities; their viewpoint is more theoretical than most people's. Engineers use and apply the information which the scientists develop. Although they may also be creative, they usually don't have the advanced degrees. They are more practical and less theoretical than scientists.

Professional people expect better working conditions than rank-and-file people. They also want fewer personal restrictions. You may not be able to go along with all such desires, but try to do so if you can. They will appreciate it. If you can assign creative work and work that is challenging or complex, you give professional people the chance to show their worth. They like work that is investigative in nature and not routine or repetitive. Be sure to give them recognition for what they are and what they accomplish if you want to get the most from them.

Case-in-Point: Technical ideas conceived by Research and Development employees at the Goodyear Tire and Rubber Company, Akron, Ohio, have been evaluated in the company's Genesis Program. Joe Gingo, Director of Projects and Materials Coordination, and Chairman of the R & D Genesis Program, explains, "The program is designed to create a route through which technical people can originate ideas for new products and processes not necessarily in their line of work. The keynote to the program is recognition—to let the idea generator's colleagues know that he or she went above and beyond the call of duty." Employees who submit ideas are eligible for recognition and rewards not only under the Genesis Program, but they may also receive recognition and cash under the company's suggestion award program, providing the ideas meet the criteria of the suggestion award program committee.

16.6 Sure-Fire Ways to Keep Exceptional People Enthused

Exceptional people, in addition to being skilled, creative, quick, and having other attributes not found in the average person, are often impatient. They may lose interest in their work much faster than other employees. You must be aware of such tendencies and be alert to combat them.

Varying a person's job assignment and rotating the work keeps a job from becoming dull. It also promotes creativity in that the person is exposed to different situations and runs into more problems where the individual's ingenuity and skill may come into play.

Always listen to the suggestions of exceptional people, and avoid being critical in judging their ideas. At times it may pay to let persons further investigate a suggested idea even though it may not seem practical or plausible at the time. You will keep them interested in the work and you will not overlook any bets in searching out solutions to difficult problems.

Above all, avoid misusing the talents of exceptional people. Although you must give them some routine work along with other assignments, try to limit servile jobs as much as possible. Two major reasons for talented people leaving jobs are: their company fails to give them challenging work, and too little is expected of them in the way of performance.

16.7 Tips on Managing Creative People

People who are very creative sometimes present problems for supervisors because they handle their work differently than people who are not creative. Recognizing their traits and characteristics is essential to understanding and getting along with them. Here are some tips on how they think and what you can expect from them:

- Creative people want and expect personal freedom. They are independent in their thoughts and judgments; they should be given latitude to pursue and develop new ideas if you can possibly do so. Although they want challenge and responsibility, they prefer these matters to be in areas of their special interest.

- Such people tend to work on their own ideas, not those of others. Their concentration in this respect may extend to intolerance with disagreement. They may become impatient when they are not understood. They prefer to avoid group activities and thus do not do a good job of cooperating with others.

- The creative urge which they possess is stimulated by challenge and inhibited by routine. They thrive on intricate problems that only their intelligence and talents can handle. Creative people are usually very competent and take pride in their accomplishments.

- Although creative people expect and appreciate recognition for work well done, they are prone to judge what you think of them by the nature of the next assignment you give them. You must try to make it appropriate for their capabilities—the more difficult the better.

- Creative people lose track of time. They may work for long stretches without rest or relief, and then require a longer than average break time to recover. You will find that their productivity over the long run is better than that of people who don't possess creativity.

- Creative people with scientific training often are perfectionists. Their preoccupation with checking and double-checking often makes it difficult for them to meet deadlines.

16.8 How to Handle the Person Who Prefers to Work Alone

It is worthwhile for you to know if an employee is most suitably a "group" worker or a "loner." Such knowledge helps you in motivating the person, making the best work assignments for him or her, and in assessing the capability of your department.

Don't think of lone workers as being people who prefer to be physically separated from other people. Although some people are of this nature, most loners simply prefer not to interact with others or be team members. They want to work *in* groups rather than *with* groups. They prefer to be inconspicuous on the job.

Supervisors should accede to such people's desires as much as company regulations and work situations will allow in order to have such people like their work and be productive. Promotional moves as well as transfers to different environments should be carefully thought out and discussed before being implemented. A loner may leave the company rather than make a change, even though the change may appear to be to his or her best interest.

16.9 Young Employees: Understanding and Motivating Them

Many supervisors have been finding it more and more difficult to motivate their people. The problem is particularly acute with young employees. But it is a mistake to believe that young people do not want to work—they want to work provided they have the proper incentive—the incentive isn't always financial. Several social and economic changes which have taken place in recent years explain why young people now want more out of a job than just the pay.

Young people today are better educated than their parents. Their aspiration levels are also higher. They become bored more rapidly with routine work; thus, they shun such work for that which is different and challenging. Most young people have not experienced a lack of jobs available to them except for the minorities; they don't know the hardship of being without work. So they are more demanding of the type of job they will accept.

The increasing power of unions has made members more militant. Job security is not a motivator to union members. They do not hesitate to express their grievances because they have no fear of retribution. Supervisors must listen to and do something about the complaints of young employees if they expect them to be productive.

As the affluence of today's society increases, the needs of workers have become more difficult to satisfy. With the basic needs of food, shelter, and clothing satisfied, the higher level needs become the main motivators. But these needs are more difficult to satisfy under today's style of management unless supervisors allow employees to participate in making decisions.

16.10 Tips on Supervising Today's Young Employees

Supervisors often find that their young people have different values and aspirations than their older employees. Supervising them may be frustrating until the supervisors discover what makes them tick.

If you are a wise supervisor, you can use your people's values and aspirations to help them do a better job. Here are some tips on how to do this:

● Avoid placing young people in long apprenticeships and training programs. They want to be where the action is and to participate. So move them along fast to get over these hurdles quickly.

● Do not expect most of your young people to place a high value on the security of rigid job descriptions and standards of performance unless they have participated in developing such standards.

● Give them big jobs and assignments. Remember that many of the early job enrichment and job enlargement programs were successful because young people were involved.

● Recognize that young people will not be motivated to go beyond what is expected of them unless the extra work offers them some promise of personal growth.

● Don't be overly concerned if young people occasionally fail on the job—nonproductive effort should be part of their experience. They have to fail sometimes to know what success really means and to learn to succeed next time.

16.11 Proven Advantages to Employing Older Workers

The number of retired and older people who seek jobs has been increasing as the elderly population of the country steadily increases. More and more businesses are using older workers and retirees with great success. Here are seven proven advantages to employing such people and why supervisors like to have them in their departments:

1. They usually are more reliable and steady workers, particularly in jobs where no advancement is possible.

2. They have a high standard of ethics and feel a strong responsibility to do a good job.

3. They are almost always on time and are absent less than other workers.

4. They are exceptionally cooperative. They are not impatient for promotion.

5. They set an excellent example for others and exert a stabilizing influence on younger workers.

6. They are more receptive to odd jobs and will readily substitute for other people. They are invaluable for fill-in work and sometimes may agree to work partial days.

7. They are not usually concerned about pay rates nor varying wages since in most cases they have other income.

16.12 Hostility: Pitfall to Young Supervisor/Old Worker Relations

Young supervisors sometimes encounter hostility from workers who are older than themselves. Since you can contend with hostility better if you know the reasons for it, here is some insight and advice on handling this problem.

The most common reason why an older person may be hostile to a younger supervisor is fear. The person may be afraid that he or she may be looked down upon, discriminated against, even lose the job. The degree of fear depends on the amount of uncertainty which exists within a particular work situation.

Jealousy is another reason why older persons may be hostile to their younger supervisors. Older workers may wish they were supervisors or held positions which carried higher status and received more pay. The older workers may resent their younger supervisors even though the younger persons had nothing to do with their plight.

Hostility is usually shown by antagonism or withdrawal. Then again, lack of motivation and job satisfaction as well as lack of self-confidence may be behind hostile actions. The best way to contend with hostility is to take the person aside and talk to him or her about it. Explain that you sense that the person is uneasy in your presence and that you would like to be on better terms with him or her. Try to learn the reason for the hostility so that you can refute it. Assure a hostile person that you are fair and treat all people equally. Then, be sure that you do so.

16.13 How to Criticize a Top Performer

Most supervisors have a person in their department on whom they depend more than any others. You probably do, too. The person may have many years of experience, be the most efficient one on the staff, and know all the ins and outs of how your department functions. But, since nobody is perfect, the person will occasionally make mistakes. Although you can ignore a minor miscue, perhaps joke about it, you should not pass off lightly a big or serious mistake. You must let the person know that you're aware of it and offer advice on how to correct the mistake as well as avoid a repetition.

Since top performers take pride in their work, the person will probably readily accept your advice. Good workers, those who also have the right attitude, generally regret their lapses and express their regrets. Some top performers, however, may resent your concern and not willingly accept your criticism.

If you must get tough with a top performer, do it. You really have no choice in the matter unless you are willing to give up control and the responsibilities of your job. If the person doesn't accept your criticism or reacts negatively to your comments, maintain your position. The poor performance will probably not reoccur after the person gets back on the job, thinks a bit, and understands why you had to act as you did.

16.14 Positive Ways of Working with Minorities

Supervisors should not consider minorities as problem employees but as people who may require attention to assure that bias and prejudice are not factors in how they are treated. Most of these people are eager to prove how good a job they can do and often are quite capable. All they need is a fair chance. Some of them may require a little extra training because of lack of experience.

Because of limited education as well as lower-than-average cultural advances, many minorities are ignorant of what is expected of them on the job. They may not be aware of the accepted procedures nor of how to conduct themselves in certain situations. They hope you will consider these matters and make allowances for them. Minorities can be just as good workers as other employees. You should not expect them to be exceptional in order to gain your acceptance. Nor should you condemn their group on the basis of poor performance of one or more of their members.

Don't segregate minorities on your work teams. Put them on jobs where they can be most effective and where they'll do the best job. Minorities don't want preferential treatment. They may be embarrassed if you give them very easy work. Doing that might also bring on a discipline problem as well as result in your being accused of showing favoritism. Expect and insist upon the same standards of performance from minorities that you do from other employees.

Case-in-Point: When talking about hiring a black for a job, Whitney M. Young, Jr., Executive Secretary of the National Urban League, said, "A black will usually value the job more than his white counterpart because his opportunities are fewer. Where the white fellow may be taking an ordinary job as a stop-gap until he can find something better, this may be the best job the black ever dreamed he could land." This attitude of the black toward the job means more loyalty to the company and more dedication to succeed. Records of companies who have placed blacks in other than hard-labor jobs are endless with testimonials to this fact.

16.15 Guidelines to Avoiding Charges of Discrimination

It is accepted that business and industry should not discriminate against people because of their color, race, religion, sex, or anything else that does not pertain to the job. Reverse discrimination that favors a minority person over a more able majority person is equally wrong. Supervisors need to take every precaution to avoid charges of discrimination in the treatment of employees.

But, under no circumstances should a supervisor put up with incompetence or rule breaking to avoid discrimination charges. The best way to help people who perform unsatisfactorily is to counsel them and give them a chance to meet acceptable standards. No one benefits if standards are lowered to make it easy to get along with poor performers. Here are some procedures to follow which will help you avoid charges of discrimination as you carry out the responsibilities of your job:

1. Set performance standards for people. Explain the rules and what you expect from people on the job.
2. Warn people when they do below average work. If they cannot improve, try to find jobs for them which they can handle.
3. Offer a second chance after a poor performance. But do not be more lenient with minority persons than with majority persons.
4. Tie salary increases to performance. Treat everyone alike in this respect.
5. Keep records of performance on each person. Also document discussions you have with people about their performance.
6. Discuss serious nonperformance which could result in termination with the personnel department. Make sure your records are complete.

Most people are unhappy on jobs they cannot handle. They will feel better on different jobs, and the people who work with them will also benefit from a change. Although you may risk a charge of discrimination now and then, you must rotate assignments and move people into work where they will do their best. You are responsible for keeping up the efficiency of the people who work for you.

16.16 Effective Techniques for Working with the Handicapped

Supervising handicapped people is really not much different from supervising other people, providing they are properly trained. Many companies feel that the handicapped people in their employ are better in several ways than other employees. Supervisors usually get greater respect, much better attendance, and a low rate of turnover from them. Furthermore, once you train them to do a job a certain way, they won't make variations—they'll do the job the same every time. The techniques for working successfully with handicapped people are simple:

- Show that you care about them. Don't begrudge the extra time required to train them. Adjust jobs to their abilities and arrange the people accordingly.
- Don't ever lose your temper. Patience is very important. Learn what provides the strongest incentive to good performance and try to provide it.
- Treat handicapped people with the same consideration you give other employees. Emphasize cooperation and team effort. Have them work side by side on the same jobs with other people.

Case-in-Point: Eighty percent of the employees at Markade, Inc., Knoxville, Tennessee are mentally or physically handicapped. Most of them are mentally retarded; many were trained at Knoxville's Sunshine Sheltered Workshop. Yet, shift supervisor Bob Simmons says, "I have more problems from other people on my shift than from the handicapped. You can do a profile of work quality of other employees who are not handicapped. If the handicapped employees are trained right, their work will be better nine times out of ten."

16.17 How to Help the Mentally Slow Person

It is up to the supervisor to make the most of a mentally slow person on the job. You cannot afford to neglect this individual for both his or her benefit and the company's. People who are mentally slow often suffer from their own frustrations. They are frequently hurt because fellow-workers abuse them. You can help a handicapped person overcome these problems and make the most of his or her abilities.

Try to build up the person's ego by encouraging and praising good work. Practice patience—don't rush the person with new or strange work. Get the person's confidence so that when something isn't understood, the person will tell you.

Always give orders in slow and simple words, repeating if you sense you are not getting through. Explain in great detail. Then ask if the person understands what you want done and how it should be done. Above all, never imply or suggest that the person is slow to understand or is inferior in any way to other workers. Recognize that you may have to spend more time with the person than with your other people. The person will appreciate your help. Your company will also benefit from your efforts.

17

WORKING OUT
ANSWERS TO YOUR
PROBLEM PEOPLE

SUPERVISORS' work would be much easier if they did not have to contend with problem people. However, supervisors would find their work less interesting and lacking in challenge if they didn't have to make use of their skills in solving human relations problems.

Understanding human nature, being perceptive, knowing what makes people tick, and having empathy are invaluable in coming up with answers to why some people act as they do. Of equal value, if not more, is being able to reason with people and persuade them to change their behavior; this is the skill you need to work out personality conflicts, referee arguments, handle complaints, and cut down bickering. The problem people who talk too much, the know-it-alls, and the prima-donnas may appear minor in comparison to other people problems, but they also must be solved if you are to have a productive, enthusiastic, and efficient work force.

Serious problems facing many supervisors today are those having to do with people's weaknesses. Typical of such problems are absenteeism, alcoholism, and drug abuse. However, companies are successfully dealing with problems in many cases by training supervisors how to handle them. Another way that is working well is substituting positive discipline for punitive discipline.

17.1 Understanding and Getting Along with "Difficult" People

As a supervisor, you should expect that you will occasionally find yourself having to work with someone who is difficult to get along with. The person may be a misfit in your eyes or have a personality that clashes with yours. Regardless of the reason for his or her undesirable behavior, understanding the person may be a real challenge. However, there are some strategies you can use and some procedures you can follow that will help you to better get along with such a person. Consider the following suggestions:

- Avoid getting in trouble by not making assumptions about why someone is behaving a certain way.
- Try not to let it bother you when a "difficult" person behaves toward you by doing something you never would do. Don't judge people in light of your own preferences.
- Be patient with people who seem to be always in a hurry. Treat perfectionists similarly. Realize that both types are being driven.
- Never think you can change someone.
- Ready yourself to be disappointed when you must work with a difficult person. Remember that no one is perfect. Forget bad incidents and be optimistic about future relations.
- Trust people and expect them to treat you fairly. Most people are honest, supportive, and cooperative.
- Recognize that troublemakers exist in every group and society. However, there are very few such people.

17.2 How to Work out Personality Conflicts

When you have a personality conflict between two of your people, you have a serious problem to contend with. If permitted to continue, it may cause hard feelings, affect productivity, and hurt team effort. You must take steps to improve the compatibility of the individuals involved and do it quickly.

Although a transfer of either person to another job would probably handle the matter, this strategy is not always possible or desirable. One or both of the individuals may be highly skilled and not easily replaced. Then, too, no other job may be open in the company. The best way to solve a personality conflict problem is to work out the disagreement with the persons involved.

Bring the two individuals together to discuss the situation. Point out the disorder they are causing by their failure to get along with each other, and how the failure is affecting other people and the company. Say that you want to help them settle their differences.

Tell each person what he or she means to the company and that you do not want to lose either one. Show them how their disagreement has affected their work, and as a result, why you cannot permit the present conflict to continue. Give them the opportunity to have their say, but do not take sides with either person. If the two do not seem to be able to work out a peaceful answer, suggest compromises. Push for commitments from both on how they intend to act in the future, and end your meeting on as friendly a basis as possible.

If you learned that one of the individuals was mainly at fault, approach this person later. Talk to the person privately to save his or her face. Discuss the fault and ask again for a promise to change.

If better relations don't materialize from your talks with both persons, discuss the situation with your boss. You may have to insist that one or both persons must change or leave the company. More people lose their jobs today because of their inability to get along with other people than because of their inability to do the work expected of them.

17.3 Tips on Enforcing Rules and Regulations

Your boss assumes that you will enforce the company's rules and regulations. He or she also believes that you will maintain standards. But if you are practical and knowledgeable with human nature, you should realize that you can't continually enforce *all* the rules to the letter—if you tried, you wouldn't have time to carry out all your other responsibilities.

When it comes to enforcing rules and regulations, there are many factors that must be considered. This means that you have to give people some leeway before you take action on substandard behavior. In addition, you must handle each violation quickly in accordance with what you learn and how you feel when you get all the facts concerning it. Then, adopt the following tips on how supervisors should handle these problems:

- Treat a safety violation differently from a production matter involving quantity or quality.
- Feel that "old-timers" *should know better* when it comes to breaking rules.
- Give a flat-out, deliberate violation your special attention immediately.
- Handle a new employee, unfamiliar with the rules, differently from someone who has been on the job for some time.
- Ignore, now and then, the breaking of a rule for one reason or another, even though you may have observed it.

- Believe that other supervisors occasionally overlook the breaking of rules.
- Agree that the breaking of a well-publicized rule merits different discipline than the breaking of a rule which is not as well-known.
- Know how long the breaking of a rule has been taking place before you act on it.
- Recognize that a violation of a rule for the first time is a factor to be considered.
- Know how many people are involved in a first-time infraction before you take action.

17.4 What to Do When You Must Act as a Referee

No place of business where work is performed always runs smoothly. Inevitably, two or more of your people will have a disagreement either about who is to do a job or how it is to be done. Since you as supervisor are responsible to see that the work gets done, the dispute becomes your concern. Here are the steps to take when you must act as a referee:

1. Don't call a halt to the discussion or dismiss the problem. This doesn't reach the issue or solve it.
2. Keep your cool as you listen to both sides of the story. Don't become emotional or let the problem get out of proportion to its importance.
3. Check the stories and make sure you have all the facts. Keep company rules in mind and confirm company objectives.
4. Try to be fair to everyone concerned. Put aside bias and prejudice, personal likes and dislikes.
5. Make a decision. You are responsible for getting to the bottom of arguments which affect your department and its efficiency. Carry out that responsibility to the best of your ability.

There will be times when you must act as referee on matters other than the job but still related to your department functions. In most cases, you will find that the steps to follow given above will work equally well in those cases.

17.5 How to Tell People Their Work Is Unsatisfactory

Nobody likes to tell someone that their work is unsatisfactory, yet supervisors periodically must do this. The reason why you must criticize people about their unsatisfactory performance on the job is to get better work from them. To get that, you must tell them specifically what is wrong and what you expect of them. Your manner, how you control yourself, and how you treat people determines how your words are received as well as how quickly and completely people make a change for the better.

Case-in-Point: Fred Schmidt, supervisor in a machine shop in Akron, Ohio, told me, "I don't put up with sloppy work in the shop. I feel I'm much better off telling machinists what I really think than what I think they want to hear, and I believe people respect me for it. In fact, a fellow once told me I was very tactful after I let him know what I thought about the waste he created."

If an employee is not doing what is required or expected, the person should be talked to privately about the matter. However, before you talk to a person about failing on the job, plan what you intend to say and what you're going to ask of the person. Realize that the person may not expect this criticism and that the occasion may be a traumatic one.

Be sure you have the facts about the performance of the individual. Have specific cases and situations to talk about so that you don't generalize, such as saying, "Your reports are always late," or "You make too many errors." Go over the performance and history of the person's deeds, making notes which you can refer to during your conversation. Never accept hearsay or rumors about the person's performance. Dig out and document facts.

To lighten the blow to a person's ego from your criticism, you can accept part of the blame for unsatisfactory work. You might say, for example, that you perhaps didn't make yourself clear. Another way to share responsibility is by making statements that contain the word *we,* such as *we* take pride in our work in the department, or *we* seldom if ever get behind in our schedule.

When you talk with people about poor work performance you must, of course, listen to their side of the story. If you don't, you won't be able to help them. Most people will defend their actions and want to explain. When they do, you will usually learn how to help them.

Never ridicule a person or be sarcastic about his or her efforts. When you do this you are finding fault with the person rather than the work. Better to tell the person what's bad about the work. Explain exactly what's needed and follow up later to make sure you are getting what you asked for.

17.6 Tips on Dealing with Rule-Breakers

You must take action when one of your people breaks a company rule. Overlooking the offense and saying nothing about it is equivalent to condoning it. You must do something because the incident can affect the person's future behavior, your department's morale, and even your company's relations with the union, if you have one. Here are some tips on dealing with rule-breakers:

1. Know the company rules, and see that your people also know them. You can't maintain discipline without knowing what is permissible and what is not.

2. Get all the facts when you believe someone has broken a rule. Try to establish exactly what was done or what happened.

3. Give the person who is guilty an opportunity to explain his or her actions. Don't expect the person to volunteer an explanation—take the initiative and ask for it.

4. Decide on the most appropriate disciplinary action. Keep in mind what you hope to achieve—a change in the person's behavior, not punishment or revenge.

5. Administer the discipline, telling the person why you are doing so. Never give a person a penalty without explaining it.

17.7 How to Counsel the Problem Employee

When machines or equipment break down, they can be repaired or replaced. When a process or project fails to work well, either can be changed or revised. But the answer isn't that simple when people don't do their work or they behave abnormally or badly. This is why supervisors should realize that people are much more of a problem than the machines or equipment they operate or projects they try to complete.

It's your job to handle the problem employee and bring his or her performance to an acceptable level in terms of the department's operation. The best way to accomplish this is to meet with and counsel the employee.

Start by first asking the employee to talk about his or her problem in terms of performance. Put the person at ease before you begin asking open-ended questions. By all means, avoid putting the employee on the defensive, and certainly don't be judgmental. Put yourself in the place of the employee to try to understand his or her problem. You will be able to do a much better job of counseling.

After listening intently and getting the facts, state clearly how you expect the employee to perform; make sure he or she understands you. Employees sometimes perform poorly simply because they do not know what their supervisors expect of them.

In addition to communicating your expectations, be consistent in carrying out your own responsibilities. If you expect your people to follow all the company's safety regulations, for example, you must lead the way. It would be poor practice for you to counsel someone for tardiness if you are frequently late for your work yourself.

Once the employee changes his or her behavior for the better, offer positive reinforcement. Tell the employee that you have noticed the change and are pleased with it. Such recognition will be appreciated and also will make the person more likely to continue the better performance.

17.8 Sure-Fire Ways to Overcome Slowness on the Job

Slowness of one or more of their people is a common problem for supervisors of work crews. Too many people are slow to get to work, slow to get started, slow to understand orders, and slow to get the job done. If you want to keep up the productivity of your department, you've got to solve such problems.

One of the several ways you can go about this is to simply talk to the slow person about it. Of course, you must be careful with what you say. Question the person in a soft-spoken manner or you may have an angry employee on your hands instead of a cooperative one. Point out that you feel the person can be more prompt and efficient, and that you would appreciate the effort to do so.

Often a person is slow because he or she has no interest in the job and is simply bored. With this person, you must talk about the work in detail. More variety or responsibility may be an answer—can you enrich the job? Perhaps the person should have a different job. If a change would likely improve matters, go ahead with the move with the understanding that if the person doesn't improve his or her performance, the former job will be the permanent one.

Sometimes a person is slow on the job because of the fear that speed will result in errors. You can solve this problem by giving the person work where the chances of errors being made are few. Both the person and you will be glad of the change.

If you learn that one of your people has always been slow regardless of the job assigned, you may as well give up trying to change him or her. Your best bet is to find work for the person where speed is not a factor. Look for a job where precision, care, or perseverance are required of the worker.

17.9 How to Handle Slowdowns

A slowdown of the work force can be very costly to a company. Not only does the work not get out and jobs are not finished, but also the need for overtime work is created. People working extra hours are paid additional money and are usually more inefficient besides.

You must notice when people are making a job last too long, when their rest and coffee breaks take too much time, and when they're doing more talking than working. If you suspect that one or more of your people are deliberately slowing down, act immediately. Handle slowdowns in one or more of the following ways:

1. Break up bull sessions promptly by joining the group, asking if they have a problem and if there is anything you can do to help. Another way to break up a group is to give one of the people a job, saying that you need it done right away.

2. Point out to inactive workers that a job is urgent, that the department is behind schedule, or that the order must be gotten out today. Express your concern over progress of a job.

3. Mention to a person the time standard for a job. Say you know the person is capable of meeting it.

4. Increase your coverage of a trouble area. Make your presence felt. Do what you can to assure availability of materials, tools, and supplies so that there can be no excuses given relating to those items.

5. Warn guilty persons that disiplinary action will be taken if the inefficiency continues. Take that action if your warning isn't heeded.

17.10 Tips on Effective Handling of Complainers

You're bound, in most work groups, to find someone who has a gripe. All workers are not happy with their jobs or get satisfaction from their work. Unfortunately, the person who frequently complains can be a problem for you because he or she is detrimental to the morale of the entire group. You cannot afford to let such a situation continue. Here's some tips on how to effectively handle complainers.

Learn all you can about a complainer in order to understand his or her attitude. What work did the person do before joining the group? Is the person lazy? A poor performer? Does the person suffer from a psychological or physical handicap? Look into the person's needs since they evidently are not being satisfied. Does the person feel superior to the job or the people he or she is working with? Perhaps there is a feeling that the work is demeaning or degrading. What specifically does the person complain about?

Talk to the person. Say that you noticed that he or she is unhappy. Ask if there is something you can do to help. Explain that you want people to get satisfaction from their work and that you don't want the morale of other people to suffer if one person isn't satisfied.

If there is something you can do to please the complainer, get busy at it. But if ending the complaining is a matter of changing an opinion or viewpoint, mention this. In either case, try to get a promise for no more complaining on the job.

17.11 How to Deal with a Sensitive Person

The more you get to know your people, the sooner you'll learn that some of them are more sensitive than others. Working with sensitive people requires that you be alert to what you say and do—they may take offense at the slightest thing and when you least expect it.

As soon as you learn that a particular person may be overly sensitive, do your best to not offend or irritate him or her. Here are some steps you should take with that objective in mind.

- Note and remember the comments you and others have made that seem to offend the person. You may detect a pattern or approach that will enable you to avoid future incidents.

- Whenever you think you may have said something that offended the person, bring the subject up immediately, even if you have to directly ask what is bothering him or her.

- Watch your tone of voice every time you speak to the person. Make sure your words are not taken as criticism.

- Avoid placing blame when things go wrong. Instead look for answers and solutions to the predicament or problem.

- Be as complimentary as you can if you are asked to judge a performance.

- Take a good look at your own behavior. Do others besides the sensitive person often not laugh at your attempts to be humorous?

17.12 Eight Ways to Attack Absenteeism

Absenteeism costs business and industry in many ways. The man-hours not put into the work result in low productivity and lost profits, the replacement labor is inefficient, and the overtime costs are excessive. Solving the problem of absenteeism of their people requires a strong effort on the part of supervisors. Here are eight ways that you can join other successful supervisors in attacking it:

1. Know your people and show an interest in their personal lives. Encourage discussions of problems that affect attendance.

2. Insist on prior requests to be absent for personal reasons rather than explanations after the fact. Ask for real explanations rather than dubious excuses.

3. Have personal discussions with the people who cause most of your absentee problems. See if someone in the personnel or medical departments can help.

4. Insist on prompt notification always when someone must be absent unexpectedly. Don't treat such incidents lightly.

5. Avoid the serious effects of unexpected absences by having standard procedures to follow when they occur. Designate replacements and who is to do someone else's work.

6. Keep good records of absenteeism. Examine them for Monday and day-after-holiday occurrences to alert you to problem people.

7. Have a group meeting to discuss it if absenteeism becomes serious. Point out the costs to the department and the company to emphasize its seriousness.

8. Set up a progressive discipline system for offenders. Carry out its terms religiously all the way to dismissals, if necessary.

Case-in-Point: "The solution to chronic absenteeism or tardiness can be a simple matter of keeping accurate records or a properly given suggestion," according to Andrew Filicky, Supervisor in the Anodizing and Painting Department of General Extrusions, Inc., Youngstown, Ohio. Producing his attendance record, Filicky told an habitual offender, "This shows a consistent pattern. Are you deliberately avoiding the cleanup detail? If I let you get away with it, pretty soon I won't have anyone left on cleanup."

"The record did it," says Filicky. "He hasn't been off since."

17.13 Company Checkup: An Effective Absence Deterrent

Recent surveys in business and industry have revealed that when employees take sick days by single day absences, actual sickness is the cause only 50 to 60 percent of the time. Employees go shopping, visit relatives, or take care of personal business the remainder of the time.

Among the various ways that employers use to fight such absenteeism, company checkup is rated by personnel experts as the most effective of them all. Simply telephoning the absentee to ask how he or she is feeling and whether he or she plans to come to work the next day can have a powerful effect. And it's embarrassing and incriminating if the person isn't home to receive the phone call.

Where chronic absentees are involved, some companies send the company nurse to the home. Merely knowing that this can happen is enough to make most people think twice before taking that desired day off.

17.14 How to Handle the Know-It-All Person

In most work groups you'll find at least one person who will participate in every argument and has an answer to every problem. The person may be likable as well as competent but still is disruptive because of his or her disturbing interference, egotistical attitude, and superior manner. Your effectiveness in handling your people depends in part on what you do about the know-it-all. Here are some tips on how to handle this type of person.

You must be firm with know-it-alls. They generally try to get away with as much as possible. Let them know where they stand, being sure to make yourself clear. Plug up any loopholes they might find to twist your instructions and orders.

Avoid disagreements and arguments. Know-it-alls are usually clever, enjoy showing off, and even delight in confusing an issue. Such behavior can make your supervising job difficult. Show know-it-alls that you know what you're talking about and they'll usually respect you.

Give them more responsibility. It will tend to make them settle down, especially if you let them know you're sure they can handle it and you are counting on them. Expect more of them in quality and quantity of work but don't make an issue of it if they don't come through—simply let them know that you noticed their failure.

Let know-it-alls try new ideas and procedures, and let them make mistakes. Give them credit if something new is successful, but also explain when something fails. A failure may cause them to realize that they're not always right—they'll be less ready to question your decisions in the future.

17.15 Effective Ways to Cut Down Bickering

Many team efforts have failed to pay off because of one or more argumentative, sarcastic, and backbiting employees who just can't seem to get along with other people. Too often, supervisors may tolerate such behavior with the result that the efficiency of the group is not what it could be. Some supervisors, fortunately, have found ways to handle the problem.

You can, for example, not permit extensive conversations on superheated subjects such as religion and politics, even to the extent that they are banned entirely. For better compatibility, you can pair up people who have similar interests and viewpoints.

Another approach to cutting down bickering among your people is to take aside an offender and talk to him or her about the problem. Surprisingly, the person may not have realized the aggravation that he or she was causing. It's up to you to lay the groundwork for the future by being firm in making the point that such behavior won't be permitted.

Bickering among people or between individuals sometimes occurs because the persons aren't speaking the same language. This happens with people who differ with each other in age, sex, and cultural levels. You can watch for such communication roadblocks and do your best to translate and straighten out word meanings. Learn to listen carefully to your people and help them understand one another.

17.16 How to Control the Person Who Talks Too Much

Similar to the know-it-all, the overly talkative person is often a problem in group discussions or meetings. When the person dominates the discussion, other people experience difficulty joining in. Although you may at times tolerate such a situation because the person is contributing greatly to the topic being discussed, if he or she is simply showing off or exaggerating to appear important, you should take action.

One way is to ignore the person, hoping that he or she will get the message that you prefer to hear from the other members of the group. Another is to challenge the person, forcing him or her to justify a statement or idea, particularly if it is farfetched.

You may decide that the best course to follow is to talk to the individual after the meeting. Tell the person that you recognize that he or she is far ahead of the others in thinking and reasoning. Ask the person to withhold comments in future meetings until all of the others have had a chance to contribute.

Caution: Recognize that an overly talkative person can keep a discussion active and moving. If other people in a meeting are reticent and reluctant to speak up, the talkative person may be the catalyst to draw them out. Thus, you may not wish to suppress this individual completely. Consider the hostess who, when making out her guest list, says, "I'll be sure to invite her because she's a good 'mixer.' "

17.17 Pitfalls to Putting Up with the Prima-Donna

A supervisor sometimes runs into a temperamental worker, one who goes about jobs in an unusual manner or who on occasion displays extreme behavior. The supervisor might be inclined to overlook or not react adversely to it, yet sight should not be lost to the pitfalls of accepting it. Here are three such pitfalls you should be aware of:

1. A supervisor's favored treatment of a prima-donna suggests the wrong performance criteria for doing a good job. Instead of promoting the fact that outstanding work is most important, what is indicated is that the person who puts on the best performance is most accepted.

2. By overlooking the temperamental individual, the supervisor wastes a possible good performer or prevents the person's replacement by a person more steady and productive.

3. Special treatment of the prima-donna by the supervisor arouses resentment in other people. This can result in a letdown on the job as well as a loss of respect for the supervisor.

Temperament on the job may not be a problem if it is backed up by exceptional performance. But, as the person's supervisor, you must be sure that you are not letting the prima-donna get by on only nerve.

17.18 How to Contend with Extreme Emotion

Contending successfully with extreme emotion on the job requires that you be very tactful and discreet. Emotion is particularly difficult to handle when it interferes with the normal routine of getting the job done. Experts in the field of human relations generally agree on the best way to handle it. Here's what you should do:

- Don't take emotional outbursts as personal attacks. The person displaying the extreme emotion is usually venting his or her feeling to anyone who will listen. If you take the words or action personally, you will not be able to do a good job of handling it because your own emotions will be strained.
- Don't try to stop the emotional flow—let the person work it out and get rid of it. The person will feel much better sooner than if you interfere.
- If you are expected to respond, agree with the person's expressed reason for the emotion. Say that you would probably feel and act similarly if you were in the same situation.
- Don't attempt to reason or discuss the work with the person; say that you will return later when the person feels better.
- Return to the person when he or she has unwound. The person will probably be very considerate because of your previous tact. However, don't bring up the incident. If the person wishes to discuss it, he or she will bring it up.

17.19 What to Do About Alcoholism

Many companies have a program for dealing with alcoholism of their employees, and some organizations have instructed their supervisors on procedures to follow in working with their people on this problem. The immediate supervisor is the key to the success of any program of this type. You must act promptly when an employee's performance drops off. If the cause is alcoholism, the situation can only get worse.

Companies which have employee assistance programs want their supervisors to encourage people who are failing on the job without clear cause to discuss the matter with appropriate personnel. The program consists of diagnosis, counseling, and treatment by professionals. Usually the alcoholic must first be talked to personally by his or her supervisor. A good start is to say, "I have noticed that something is affecting the way you handle your job. I think I know what the problem is, but I can't help you until you tell me about it." If the person is honest with you, all to the good. Too often, however, the person will claim ability to handle alcohol and stop drinking anytime if it is necessary. Whether or not the person admits to the problem of drinking, you must tell the person that the company will not continue to accept the particular failures in job performance of which the person is guilty. You must point out that failure to do better will eventually cost the person employment with the company.

An alcoholic values his or her job and will do almost anything to protect it. The problem drinker must believe that you are serious when you say that he or she must give up drinking or suffer such consequences. If the person doesn't believe you, you will probably not get results. Talking with and trying to help the alcoholic isn't easy. While you may feel sorry and want to be protective, covering up for the person doesn't help—you will only delay solving the problem. Encourage the person to get professional help. You cannot depend on promises made by an alcoholic. Although the person may mean well and fully intend to do better, having this disease often makes the person incapable of changing. An alcoholic may also lie as well as offer all sorts of excuses. You should see these for what they are and realize they are of no benefit.

Being patient and not losing your temper may be difficult but you won't get anywhere with lecturing, criticizing, or scolding. Helping the alcoholic requires the best you have in dedication and human relations skill, realizing that the person probably is incapable of handling the problem without your or someone else's help.

17.20 How to Handle Drug-Abusers

A supervisor faced with having a worker suspected of using drugs should be concerned and want to help the person. Whenever the job performance of someone begins to decline because of drug use you should act immediately. Similar to handling alcoholism, a big help in rehabilitation of a person on drugs is getting the person to admit to the problem. The person whose job performance has begun to be affected by drugs should be told that he or she has to decide between holding the job and continuing on drugs.

You must be practical and levelheaded about drugs to not alienate a person who is inclined to use them. Encourage the person to discuss the problem and try to present the arguments against drugs, but be careful in how you do it. Scare techniques usually are ineffective because the person most likely has firsthand knowledge which can contradict them.

As a supervisor, you can demonstrate that people can enjoy life and have fun without resorting to the use of drugs. The person who is enthusiastic and gets satisfaction from his or her work shows the world that happiness and enjoyment can be realized without taking drugs.

The problem of drug abuse cannot be solved easily, but success is possible if several elements of a withdrawal program are adopted. Most important, the drug user must be determined to overcome his or her dependence on them. Professional help, both medical and psychiatric, is usually needed. The drug user must be persuaded to get it.

17.21 Positive Discipline: Why It Pays Off

The use of positive discipline is a relatively new way of dealing with problem workers. Reasoning instead of punishment to correct and prevent behavioral problems has proven to be very effective at several major companies.

These companies have found that the system provides benefits for both management and employees in that there are fewer disciplinary problems to handle and fewer terminations. Also, employees have better morale, and supervisors have more confidence in their ability to handle problem workers.

Positive discipline differs from punitive discipline in two ways:

1. Early discipline steps consist of oral and written reminders instead of warnings.
2. A decision-making leave is the final disciplinary step.

Both of these differences contribute to better relations between management and employees.

The major problem with punitive discipline is the difficulty which many supervisors have in meting out punishment. These supervisors do not act until they have to; meanwhile the problem is getting larger and larger. When they finally do act, they usually overreact. There is also the problem of employees who become experts at circumventing punishment by becoming immune to criticism, avoiding supervisors, losing initiative, and going strictly by the book.

Positive discipline provides the answers to these problems, especially when supervisors receive training as counselors and management provides them with backing and support. Employees should always be told when they do a good job, and supervisors should do as much as they can to make the jobs easier.

How-to-Do-It: Whenever you detect the signs of lax attitude, poor productivity, absenteeism, and failure to follow company rules, take the guilty individual aside and give him or her a friendly but serious talk, explaining the problem. If the individual's behavior doesn't improve, talk with him or her again, and follow up afterward with a letter summarizing the conversation and encouraging the individual to improve. After this, if the individual still does not try to change for the better, take the critical step.

Suspend the individual for one day with pay, and tell the person to take that time to decide whether he or she wants to continue working for the company. Say that pay will be provided to reduce the punishment aspect as much as possible, but the person must understand that the next violation of company policy will result in termination.

Although positive discipline may not be the answer to all human relations problems because some employees simply will never perform up to the expectations of management and must eventually be discharged, it is still a systematic procedure that provides many benefits and advantages to both management and employees.

18

TRIED-AND-PROVEN
WAYS TO HANDLE
SAFETY AND HEALTH

RESPONSIBILITY for the safety and health of workers is one of the most, if not the most, important of all the responsibilities of supervisors. Some people on the job resist safety, requiring that supervisors constantly promote it and insist that safety rules be followed. Supervisors who can get their people to share the responsibility for safety are going to have better safety records in their departments.

There are many ways by which accidents can be prevented. But, in general, you must search out unsafe conditions and unsafe acts of your people—then take steps to eliminate them. By observing people on the job and making accident investigations, you can learn how accidents happen and what you must do to prevent them. You should also see where the adoption of ergonomic principles and practices will make the workplace safer and more healthy for your people.

Federal laws require that companies protect and maintain the health of employees. The task is not an easy one, especially when people are exposed to toxic materials and some employees are reluctant to wear protective clothing or use protective equipment. Companies are doing the job by process changes, material substitutions, isolation, ventilation, providing personal protection, and maintaining sanitation. To participate in and be responsible for these functions, supervisors should be familiar with right-to-know laws and recognize the signs of substance abuse.

18.1 Effective Methods of Promoting Safety

The safety of employees in business and industry places a great responsibility on supervisors. It also presents a challenge for supervisors to show initiative in the prevention of accidents.

Safety can never be taken for granted. No organization attains a good safety record through luck or chance. Behind every fine safety record that a company achieves you will find much planning and a great deal of hard work.

You promote and communicate safety by creating an awareness of it in the minds of your people. You accomplish this by setting up a safety program and carrying it out conscientiously and thoroughly.

Case-in-Point: When the Chemigum Plant of the Goodyear Tire & Rubber Company in Akron, Ohio undertook a major expansion of its chemical reactor area, Bill Lamper, Plant Manager, made sure that safety of the employees was foremost in management's mind. All supervisors, foremen, and managers were asked to attend a meeting to discuss safety before anything was done in the plant.

At that meeting, the plant's safety procedures and rules were reviewed. Machines and equipment which would be involved with the work were scheduled for inspection and plans were made to test all safety devices. The company's safety and fire departments were informed and contractors were given instructions on how construction and welding operations were to be carried out. By being thorough and maintaining tight control, the company was able to complete the expansion work without an accident or a fire.

You and other supervisors play key roles in your company's safety program. Aside from the obvious demand of knowing the company's safety rules and setting a good example for your people, you must actively participate by instructing your people in safe work methods. You should also encourage workers to discuss accident prevention through anticipating unusual risks in the work areas, by providing safety equipment, and by insisting that protective clothing be worn when appropriate. When you see a hazard, you must immediately do something about it. You must also investigate, analyze, and report every accident.

No job is so important or so urgent that time cannot be taken to do it in a safe manner. This means that you must always see that your people are performing their work safely and that they are not taking shortcuts that could lead to an accident or injury. Continuous training in safety is a requisite of an effective safety program.

Case-in-Point: At the Russellville, Arkansas plant of Morton Frozen Foods, hoses on the plant floor were getting run over, stepped on, and worst of all, tripped over. Glen Ray, a supervisor, solved this problem with a hose reel. He put the reel and hose in a box, mounted it on wheels, and designed it with an inlet and coupling on the outside for quick hookup. Now floors are clear, hoses are not damaged, and people don't have tripping accidents.

18.2 Four Positive Ways to Get People Involved with Safety

Efficient production or service has come to mean safe performance. You achieve it by reducing and eliminating accidents. Although there are many ways to do this, four stand out above all others from a supervisor's viewpoint. All of them relate to working with people: planning with them, training them, communicating with them, and motivating them.

Planning involves considering the work factors. You must have the correct tools for a job your people are to do because the right tools not only make the job safer, but they also make workers more efficient. You should plan which people will be asked to do the work, preferring experienced people for safety reasons. However, if more than one person is required, you might assign one inexperienced person to learn the job. When planning, always discuss the work with the people who will be doing it. You will be able to point out hazards that exist as well as talk about safe work procedures.

Training your people to work safely is especially important because many accidents today involve an inexperienced employee. Begin by showing a person the main steps of the job slowly and thoroughly, going only as fast as the person learns or understands. Then, test the person by letting him or her show you how to do the job. If a mistake is made, tactfully correct the person and help him or her to do the job properly and safely.

Talking to your people daily about safety and observing them on the job enables you to learn how they do their work, if they take chances, and if they tend to be careless. By paying attention to them and what they are doing you will be able to spot a weakness or omission which could lead to an accident. When you explain safe practices, be sure that you also follow them to the letter. See that your people abide by no smoking rules and wear the safety clothing required in certain work areas.

Motivating your people to work safely is a never-ending task. An effective way of doing it is to point out to a person what an accident would mean to his or her family, doing this especially when you sense a laxness toward safety or a violation of safe procedures. Another approach is to ask a person "What would you do if ... ?" inserting a specific incident which has a possibility, however slight, of occurring to a person on the job. If you can get people to think about an accident which could happen, they may go just a bit farther in trying to do their work safely. That little bit may be all that is needed to prevent an accident.

18.3 Guidelines to Overcoming Resistance to Safety

When people on the job resist safety they do it subtly and shrewdly, not outwardly or defiantly. Thus, you may misjudge the magnitude of the problem of selling them on the importance of safety.

Some people resist safety because they associate it with work—work which doesn't give them satisfaction. They can see the effects of not following safe practices but they cannot see any reward for doing so.

Most workers like to make their own decisions on how to do a job. They feel they know what is safe for them. Following safety rules sometimes restricts their activities and insults their intelligence, they feel. People naturally resist conformity. They do not always agree on how serious a safety problem is in their area.

Employees may turn a deaf ear to safety if their supervisors don't show interest in it or enforce the rules. Why should they be compelled to wear safety glasses if their supervisors don't? Aggressive supervisors meet the challenge of their people resisting safety by continually stressing the advantages and benefits of it. You've got to do this daily if you want your people to be safety-conscious.

18.4 Getting People to Share Safety Responsibility

You have the responsibility to provide safe working conditions for your people and you must insist on safe work practices on the job. To carry out these responsibilities, you need to make equipment and work area inspections, train people on procedures, and make accident investigations. Yet, since safety should be everyone's business, why shouldn't you ask your people to share these safety burdens? After all, no one is in a better position to spot safety hazards and to make sure the work is done in a safe manner than each and every person on the job. Besides, you can't be in all work areas at the same time. The answer is to get people to share safety responsibility.

How-to-Do-It: Explain to your people that the company intends to meet all federal, state and local regulations on safety. This means that safety devices will be provided and must be used, protective clothing will be provided and must be worn, and safe practices will be established and must be followed at all times. Tell them that you cannot enforce all the rules by yourself, so you are going to share this responsibility with them. Say that you will see that each person is well-informed on safety so that anyone can immediately report to you conditions and practices which are not safe. Show that you are serious about safety—you're bound to get results and have a better safety record in your department.

18.5 Tips on Using a Suggestion System to Improve Safety

Don't overlook your company's suggestion system as a way to promote safety. Here are some tips on how you can use it to give a boost to your safety program:

- Give your safety program lots of publicity. Put up posters in the office or plant calling attention to the campaign and stating the awards which will be given for safety suggestions which are adopted. Use the company newspaper and the bulletin boards. You can even send letters to employee's homes.
- Get the union or employee's committees involved. Suggestion systems are good for promoting cooperation between labor and management on mutual problems.
- See that supervisors, foremen, and managers support the program. Positive attitudes on their part will help put it across. These people can aid employees in clarifying ideas and getting them in writing.
- Announce winners and awards as soon as possible. This adds to the authenticity of the program as well as creates interest in the people who were undecided on participating.

18.6 Five Common Accidents—How to Prevent Them

The ways to prevent accidents are often simple and direct, yet supervisors may overlook them or not enforce the safety rules concerning them. Here are five common accidents which people experience on the job along with what you can do to minimize their happening:

Improper Lifting—Many people suffer painful back injuries because they don't know how to lift properly. You must explain to your people how to do it. The six steps for safe lifting are:

1. Stand close to the object. Have firm footing.
2. Squat down keeping your back straight and bending your knees.
3. Grasp the object firmly making sure your grip won't slip.
4. Breathe deeply to inflate your lungs.
5. Lift with your legs, slowly straightening them.
6. Hold the object close to your body.

Failure to Lock Out—The failure to guard against power being turned on during repair or maintenance operations on equipment has caused many injuries and deaths. You can prevent such accidents by adopting a lockout procedure. Each person who works on a power-operated machine is issued a lock and key.

Locks are put on the start switch using a multiple hasp if more than one person is involved on the job. Keys are retained by the lock owners and locks are not removed by the owners until they have completed their work on the machine. With this procedure, no one can turn the machine on until all locks have been removed and everyone is clear of the machine.

Falling into Pits and Excavations—Often not considered as a serious danger to people is a hole in the ground or an uncovered pit. Yet such things are potential cripplers or killers simply from falls into them. The walls of an earth excavation can also collapse to crush or smother a person. Protection against collapse of the walls is accomplished by shoring them, but a person should also take the precaution to never work alone in a pit or excavation. Although barricades and roping off can warn people of the danger of a pit or excavation, if you also cover the opening with a supportable material you provide additional protection against an accident. And it's a wise move to see that the area is well-lighted at night.

Experiencing Electrical Shock—Electrically operated tools are potential killers, especially if they are used around water. Every tool should either be double-insulated or fitted with a three-wire cord and plug. Many people minimize the danger of 100-volt circuits and are not careful when using extension cords. Temporary wiring is also a shock hazard—you should see that it is eliminated as soon as possible.

Using Tools in Poor Condition—All cutting tools such as knives, chisels, bits, saws, and planes need to be kept sharp. Sharp tools are safer and do the job more efficiently. Dull tools often are the causes of serious wounds in addition to turning out poor quality work. Other tool-related accidents are caused by chisels with mushroomed heads, hammers and axes with cracked handles, and screw drivers with chipped or bent tips. You must get rid of tools that are damaged or in poor condition to protect your people from needless injuries.

18.7 Answers to the Accidents Which Keep Repeating

The accident-repeater, the person who continually has accidents, is usually well-known to supervisors. Most supervisors are concerned, as they should be, about this person and they search diligently for the human factors to explain how and why the person is so accident-prone. Not receiving as much attention from supervisors, however, are the accidents which keep repeating but involve a different person each time. Supervisors should be just as concerned, if not more so, about those, particularly because there are definite steps which can be taken for preventing them. You can get at this problem by analyzing all reported accidents for their causes, picking out the causes which are repeaters, and taking action on them.

A second matter for you to handle is to tell your people you want to hear about near accidents and other accidents, small and large, which don't result in injuries. Correcting unsafe conditions and unsafe practices are sure ways to improve the safety record of your department. By following up on accidents which keep repeating, you will be able to learn of those conditions and practices.

18.8 How to Promote the Wearing of Safety Clothing

Supervisors can accomplish much toward increasing the safety of their people if they can convince them of the importance of safety clothing and persuade them to wear it. When workers understand how safety clothing protects them, and when they've been trained how to use it, they will more willingly wear it. Here are some of the ways you can promote it:

1. Set an example. Wear safety glasses and other appropriate clothing such as a hard hat or safety shoes. Point out to your people that you would not feel safe without these things.

2. Get the backing of the union or the informal leaders. If those people set the pattern for proper clothing on the job, others will follow.

3. Let people participate in decisions relating to the type, style, and model of protective clothing they're going to wear. Discuss with them the hazardous conditions and the kinds of clothing that will provide them the best protection.

4. Be firm and persistent that the safety clothing be worn, going so far that you take disciplinary action if it is not. Point out that some companies make the wearing of safety clothing a requirement for being employed. Remember, you are responsible for the safety of your people.

18.9 Sure-Fire Ways to Prevent Office Accidents

Accidents don't happen only in the plant, at the construction site, or on the road. They occur in many other places where people work such as in offices, stores, and recreational areas. A report from the Federal Occupational Safety and Health Act Agency states that office workers alone suffer more than 40,000 disabling injuries and over 200 deaths every year. If you are a supervisor in an office, here are some of the hazards you may have to contend with along with advice on how to make the place safer for your people.

1. Watch out for loose rugs, carpeting, or other floor coverings which could cause falls. Highly waxed floors are a hazard, too, and even a paper clip or thumb-tack on the floor can cause a slip.

2. Provide adequate lighting and a contrasting color scheme to make furniture, files, and machines stand out. Brightness and color fight boredom, a common cause of accidents.

3. See that desk drawers, file drawers, and desk slides are kept closed. Protruding items can cause serious injuries when a person inadvertently bumps into or stumbles over them.

4. Prohibit running in the aisles or up and down steps. Hurrying results in accidents.

5. Make sure that electrical cords and phone wires and computer leads are either covered or set in floor recesses so that they are not tripping hazards.

6. Advise people to not leave sharp-edged tools loose in table or desk drawers. Also, they should never put broken glass in waste-baskets.

7. Don't permit papers, books, and other material to be stacked on top of filing cabinets or lockers. This practice is not only an example of poor house-keeping but also the cause of injuries when such things are knocked or fall off.

Case-in-Point: Several years ago, Carl Burton, supervisor of the janitors at Plant 5 of The Goodyear Tire and Rubber Co. in Akron, Ohio, approached his manager with an idea. Burton said that his people were unable to keep the locker-room neat and clean because many employees were putting lunch bags, gloves, and workshoes, among other things, on top of their lockers. He suggested that sloping sheet metal be installed on the lockers so that nothing could be put there. His idea was quickly adopted resulting in safer, more healthy conditions in the locker-room.

18.10 Three Keys to Preventing Falls

Falls have always been the cause of many disabling injuries and deaths. You should be continually alert to anything that you might do to eliminate conditions which lead to them. Three key steps you can take are:

1. Study the equipment, material, and work areas. Look particularly for oil and grease spills, waste, damaged floors, poor stacking of material, and obstructions in aisles and walkways. Promptly clean up spills and put absorbents on grease or oil. Provide racks and bins for material.

2. Study people's work clothing and protective equipment. Look for poor fits, frayed or torn material, and floppy trouser cuffs. Check for good repair of rips and tears. Observe if clothing is appropriate for the job. See if protective equipment is being used properly. When you find a variance or exception, speak to the person involved, pointing out how the item should be used properly.

3. Study the accident records. If an injury resulted from a fall, determine how and why it happened. Look for unsafe work habits. Survey areas where falls took place to see if there is a change you could make such as providing additional lighting or relocating equipment.

18.11 Ergonomics: A Supervisory Resonsibility

Unsafe conditions and discomfort in the workplace can hurt productivity, result in poor workmanship, and cause disgruntled and angry employees. However, these perils can often be avoided by the application of ergonomics.

Ergonomics, sometimes called human engineering, is a science concerned with people in workplaces. It covers the elements of design, hygiene, comfort, and safety of people on the job. The principles of ergonomics aim at reducing unnecessary muscular and sensory fatigue.

If you can make jobs safer, correct causes of excessive fatigue, and improve the environment of the people you supervise, you can and should try to do so. Here are some specific areas you can work on with intentions of improving them.

- *Overexertion:* Study jobs where people are very active physically. If a male worker, for example, repeatedly lifts very heavy objects using only his arms and hands instead of distributing the weight by also using his back and legs, the oxygen expended by his arms and hands will exceed the supply, resulting in excessive fatigue. Such physical jobs usually result in the most accidents in addition to causing back problems and sore muscles.

- *Room to Work:* Determine if more room can be provided for your people to move around as they do their work. Confined or congested work areas limit freedom to shift weight and relax muscles. Tight quarters also tend to tense muscles, a condition which leads to cramping and muscle spasms. The relocation of a single machine or the elimination of a fixture may benefit several workers.

- *Comfort and Convenience:* You should consider changing a job if it entails static loading of muscles. Examples of this are jobs requiring fixed postures, sustained reaching, or unbalanced stances. You may have to change the sequence of some of the operations or else relocate some of the facilities to overcome such problems, but your people will be less tired and will have made fewer mistakes at the end of the work day.

- *Tools:* If you can have the tools and accessories your people use modified or designed to make them easier to handle, you will have contributed to the ergonomic cause. Also, look for new tools to do difficult or unusual jobs. When a tool is easy to handle, the user is less likely to have an accident involving it. Proper tools lessen stress and strain on the people using them.

- *Lighting:* Look for poor or inadequate lighting in work areas. Decide if controls and activating devices are readily visible or if they should be relocated to make them more easily seen. Eliminate glare which can irritate as well as temporarily blind a person. Glare can often be prevented by simply relocating a light. Consider paint as an aid to enhance lighting. Note that contrasting colors distinguish one machine or structure from another, and specific colors identify them. A good example of this is the color-coded pipelines common in many industrial plants.

● *Acoustics and Vibration:* Have noise levels determined wherever people work, especially around machines. Excessive noise puts stress on people, often without their knowing it. Such stress can bring about carelessness and result in an accident or poor quality workmanship. Vibration and unsteady work surfaces also cause stress. Dampers and isolation pads, properly installed, will reduce and often completely eliminate vibration.

18.12 How to Make an Accident Investigation

Supervisors rather than safety engineers or directors are expected to make accident investigations in most companies. The reasons for this are that supervisors know the operations better and have the responsibility and authority to take whatever corrective action is necessary. If you make a prompt and thorough investigation of an accident, you gain the trust and confidence of your people because they see that you are looking out for their interest and are concerned with their safety. However, your investigation must be more than simply reporting the explanation of the person who saw or had the accident.

Investigating an accident requires that you be patient and tactful in getting information about it. Talking to the person who was involved is the first thing to do. Try to put the person at ease. Point out that the purpose of the investigation is not to put the blame on anyone, but only to prevent a similar accident from happening again. Say that you need help to do this.

Go to the accident area, if possible, and also do your talking to an individual in private. The person involved in particular will be more at ease if the two of you are alone; also what you report will not be influenced by comments and opinions of others in the person's presence. Let the person describe what happened without interruption. If you don't understand something, ask about it later.

Avoid judging what happened or is said. You don't want to put the person on the defensive. Limit your questions to asking for facts rather than opinions to learn what happened, what was done, and how it was done. "Why" questions may make the person defensive. Ask your questions in a friendly, helpful manner, and ask the type which cannot be answered with only a "yes" or "no."

It's a good idea to repeat the account of the accident to the person after you've heard it and written it down. This will enable the person to correct any errors in your account as well as add something you omitted. Finish the investigation by discussing what should be done to prevent a similar accident. You thus confirm the purpose of your investigation and prove that you want to help.

18.13 Right-to-Know Laws: What They're All About

An important OSHA regulation went into effect on May 25, 1986. If your company manufactures anything, the Hazard Communication Standard (right-to-know regulation) means that the company has some serious additional responsibilities. From that date on, the company must formally train every worker on chemical hazards, plus educate them on how to use warning labels and Material Safety Data Sheets.

The Hazard Communication Standard was needed because there was no guarantee that workers would be told about the chemical hazards they might face on the job. Container labels and warning sheets, even when they were provided, didn't always give enough information on potential hazards, what to do in an emergency, or where to turn for help. While your state or city may have additional regulations, the federal standard sets basic hazard communication requirements that take preference and must be followed.

Three groups are involved with the right-to-know laws:

1. Chemical manufacturers must determine the physical and health hazards of their products. Then they must publicize those hazards by using container labels and Material Safety Data Sheets.

2. Employers must tell employees about the Hazard Communication Standard and explain how it's being put into effect in their companies. They must also provide information and training on the hazardous chemical in use. This includes how to recognize, understand, and use labels and Material Safety Data Sheets, and what safe procedures they should follow when working with hazardous chemicals.

3. Employees must do what is necessary to protect themselves. They must read the container labels and the Material Safety Data Sheets, and, of course, follow those instructions and warnings.

Every container of hazardous chemicals is labeled by the manufacturer. While the format may differ from company to company, the labels must contain similar types of information. The Material Safety Data Sheet gives details on chemical and physical dangers, safety procedures, and emergency response techniques. All facts and data about the chemical are given here. Employers must have one for every chemical in the company.

18.14 What Labels and Material Safety Data Sheets Cover

Workers should always read the labels on chemical containers before they touch or expose themselves to the contents. They need to know the chemical's possible hazards and the steps they can take to protect themselves against those risks. Labels use words or symbols to provide the following information:

- The name of the chemical and the name, address, and emergency phone number of the company that made or supplied the chemical.
- Instructions on handling, opening, and storing the chemical.
- The physical hazards of the chemical such as whether it will catch fire or explode, is reactive or radioactive.
- The health hazards of the chemical such as whether it is an irritant, a poison, or could cause cancer.
- The protective clothing, equipment, and procedures recommended when using the chemical.

The Material Safety Data Sheet contains much more data and information about a chemical than what appears on the container label. This additional information includes:

- The substance's hazardous components and common names. Worker exposure limits to the chemical are also given.
- The physical and chemical characteristics of the substance such as its boiling point, melting point, evaporation rate, water solubility, and appearance and odor under normal conditions.
- How the substance could enter the body; for instance, inhaling, swallowing, and through the skin.
- The signs and symptoms of exposure; such as, nausea, dizziness, headache, skin rashes, and eye irritation.
- First aid procedures if an accident happens.
- Control measures, including what type of body protection should be used.
- Steps to take if the substance spills or leaks and how to dispose of the substance.

18.15 How to Safeguard Your Workers' Health

Federal laws require that the atmosphere of offices, plants, and other work areas be monitored for harmful physical agents and toxic substances, and that these materials be removed if found in quantities hazardous to people's health. Adequate protection for workers must be provided if the substance can't be removed.

An accurate assessment of the hazard is the first step. Supervisors may become involved with this because the procedure requires thorough knowledge of the process, equipment, materials, and byproducts which could possibly create a health hazard to employees. To do a comprehensive job you must take air samples with the proper instruments to test for oxygen content and concentration levels of particulate or gaseous contaminants. These samples must be taken in the working area, in the surrounding area, and at the machine or equipment putting out the toxic gas or dust. Some companies bring in a trained industrial hygienist for professional advice on the evaluation of health hazards which the company suspects or knows exist.

The National Safety Council has listed the main elements to consider when evaluating a health hazard. They are:

1. The amount of the material in contact with a body cell that is required to produce injury.
2. The probability of the material being absorbed by the body resulting in an injury.
3. The rate of generation of airborne contaminant.
4. The total time of contact.
5. The control measures in use.

When you take corrective action, be sure to consider possible emergency conditions which might arise. Assure that the control equipment is handy and that the procedures for using it are understood by the workers.

Case-in-Point: "The best time for my customers to learn all about air masks is before they have to use them," says Bob Cox, field representative for Mines Safety Appliances Company. Cox conducts training programs for the industrial workers in his California territory. You should train your workers in using emergency equipment such as air masks if there is any likelihood that they some day may be exposed to hazardous materials and need to wear masks to survive or save the life of a fellow-worker.

18.16 How Substance Abuse Endangers Safety and Health

Substance abuse is the harmful or dangerous use of alcohol or other drugs. It affects everyone including workers, supervisors, managers, and executives. Anyone can have a problem with substance abuse, and working with substance-abusers can be unpleasant and dangerous. Their work habits can affect other people's safety and efficiency.

Employees often need good judgment and physical skill to avoid accidents. Substance abuse can cause impaired eyesight, slower reflexes, lessened concentration, and poor coordination. As a result, people experience injuries from hazardous materials and from improper use of tools or machinery; they trip and fall more frequently, and they also cause fires.

The health effects of some drugs may be long-lasting and even fatal. Here are the sad facts:

- Cocaine may produce changes in blood pressure, heart, and breathing rates. It may cause coma or even death. Severe weight loss and liver damage also may result from continued use of this drug.
- Marijuana affects coordination, short-term memory, and heart rate. Continual use results in changes in one's reproductive system and lung damage. Also, it may affect the immune system.
- PCP, LSD, heroin, mescaline, and morphine produce a variety of bad health effects resulting in mental confusion, hallucinations, convulsions, and death.
- Stimulants ("uppers"), depressants ("downers"), and narcotics used improperly can cause physical and mental dependence, malnutrition, heart problems, coma, and death.

18.17 Tips on Contending with Substance Abuse

Since substance abuse causes work injuries, lowers productivity, destroys quality of workmanship and hurts motivation, supervisors should consider the problem one of their major responsibilities. You must know how to contend with it. The first step you need to take is to observe abnormal behavior of your people.

Some of the signs that may indicate existence of the problem are:

- Inadequate job performance
- Frequent absenteeism
- Long work and lunch breaks
- Inability to get along with others
- Arriving late and leaving early
- Avoiding supervisors
- Experiencing financial problems
- Changes in personality
- Poor personal hygiene or appearance

When you think one of your people is in trouble, discuss the situation with your superior. Also, talk to the Medical Dept. to get information about assistance offered by your company. Many companies today have programs that are designed to assist employees who need help. Such programs may provide assessment and education; counseling and other direct assistance; and referral to other specialized help programs. Treatment is always private, the same as for any other medical matter.

One of the most effective ways to fight substance abuse is for employees to unite against it. Supervisors can spur such a move by making it clear to their people that alcohol or drug use on the job is absolutely unacceptable.

18.18 Guidelines for Maintaining the Health of Employees

Business and industry today must give continuous attention to the health of employees and not limit their concern to a one-time examination of them when they are hired. Occupational health must be monitored and managed just as any other responsibility of management. An individual's medical condition cannot be used as a criterion for employment under Equal Employment Regulations. Thus, the preliminary medical exam may be used only to decide in what position a prospective employee may be placed. A person can be turned down for employment for medical reasons only if the person's medical capability is insufficient to do the job or if the person's performance in such a capacity would place himself, herself, or other workers in physical jeopardy.

In many industrial plants, periodic medical exams are performed on employees based on time and exposure to the hazards in the environment to which the employees are exposed. If their state of health has significantly changed, the reasons for the change must be determined. But, regardless of the cause, once a negative effect has been noted, thought must be given to reassignment of the employees to a better environment and steps taken to improve their condition.

Case-in-Point: "Change the machine, don't try to change the human body, if you want to protect a worker's health," says Joseph Stelluto, Corporate Manager of Industrial Hygiene for FMC Corp., Philadelphia. "It is much easier and more economical to modify a machine to do the necessary task than to alter the basic anatomical and physiological functions of a human to fit a poorly designed machine. Efforts are best spent in designing processes and machines which enhance the productivity of the operation, prevent unnecessary safety hazards, and reduce physical stress."

Mr. Stelluto gave an example of what he was talking about when he said, "One electronic firm was able to reduce employees' continued wrist tendonitis by redesigning the pliers used in chassis assembly. When the employees' discomfort and complaints were eliminated, increased productivity and enhanced employee morale soon followed."

18.19 Smoking: A Major Health Hazard

Early in 1986, the Surgeon General released a report stating that cigarette smoking represents a greater health threat to most American workers than do workplace exposures. Dr. C. Everett Koop, the Surgeon General, also said that cigarette smoking greatly increased the threat to life already faced by workers in hazardous industries such as asbestos.

The report, *The Health Consequences of Smoking—Cancer and Chronic Lung Disease in the Workplace,* says that disease risks for workers in high-hazard areas can be countered through a combination of smoking control and reduced exposure to hazardous agents. It urged that employers should be required to provide "a work environment that does not promote smoking or interfere with cessation."

Part of the report deals with the multiplying effect of smoking on occupational hazards. Studies have established a connection between asbestos exposure and lung cancer, and the increased risk faced by asbestos workers who smoke. Other industries were also studied for the multiplying effect of cigarettes and workplace hazards, including coal and metals mining, petrochemicals, pesticides, and cotton textiles.

The Medical Society of Virginia claims that smoking accounts for an estimated 350,000 premature deaths each year, 80 percent of chronic lung disease, 83 percent of lung cancer in males, 43 percent of lung cancer in females, and 77 million work loss days per year. Cigarette smoking is also a major cause of heart disease, emphysema, chronic bronchitis, strokes, and circulatory diseases.

What can supervisors do about smoking as a health hazard to themselves and their people? Unfortunately, there is no remedy other than complete abstention. There are now more than 33 million ex-smokers in the U.S.; more than 31 million of them quit smoking on their own.

18.20 Ten Positive Ways to Control Health Hazards

The National Safety Council has suggested ten methods by which business and industry can control health hazards. They are:

1. Substitute a less harmful material for one which is dangerous to health.
2. Change or alter a process to minimize worker contact.
3. Isolate or enclose a process or work operation to reduce the number of persons exposed.
4. Use a wet method to reduce generation of dust in operations such as mining and quarrying.
5. Provide an exhaust at the point of generation and dispersion of contaminants.
6. Ventilate with clean air to provide a safe atmosphere.
7. Provide personal protective devices.
8. Maintain good housekeeping. This includes cleanliness of the workplace, waste disposal, adequate washing, toilet, sanitary eating facilities, healthful drinking water, and control of insects and rodents.

9. Provide special control methods for specific hazards such as reduction of exposure time, film badges, and similar monitoring devices, continuous sampling with present alarms, and medical programs to detect intake of toxic materials.

10. Train and educate people to supplement engineering controls.

Case-in-Point: During an inspection of the B.F. Goodrich plant in Grantsville, West Virginia, an OSHA inspector observed that employees working with toluene solvents weren't wearing hand protection. OSHA cited the firm for an alleged serious violation of section 1910.132, which requires "protective shields and barriers" to be used "wherever it is necessary by reason of hazards of processes or environment . . . " A $280 penalty was proposed.

Goodrich contested the citation, and the case was heard by Review Commission Judge George Taylor. In its testimony, OSHA pointed out that employees who continually dipped their hands in and out of the toluene solvents risked contracting or aggravating dermatitis. Therefore, OSHA concluded, some type of personal protective equipment, be it a barrier cream or rubber gloves, was needed.

Goodrich countered that it recommended both creams and gloves for protection of employees working with toluene solvents; the protection became mandatory if an employee contracted dermatitis. Since employees were urged to take advantage of the hand protection offered them, Goodrich reasoned, plant officials could not be held responsible for the failure of employees to avail themselves of such protection.

Judge Taylor ruled in OSHA's favor, finding that a hand hazard did exist, which Goodrich should have made a concerted effort to alleviate. Merely suggesting that employees wear gloves and leaving the final decision up to them didn't fill the bill, Taylor ruled; a mandatory program backed up with effective enforcement was what was needed.

19

HOW TO PROMOTE
CREATIVITY AND
SELL CHANGE

YOU or your people don't have to be intellectual or highly educated to be creative. Nor do you have to be born that way. Although creative people have certain traits which distinguish them from others, those characteristics can be developed with determination and practice. Being creative results in getting ideas, making improvements on the job, and performing one's job better. Supervisors should try to promote and develop creativity in themselves and their people. There are many ways this can be done.

Ideas come easiest to people when they think and study problems under conditions and at times which are most conducive to generating them. But ideas are of little value unless they are publicized, accepted, and implemented. Knowing how to present your idea and doing it under the most favorable conditions can significantly increase the likelihood of it being accepted.

Change is inevitable yet many people resist it. The supervisor who is adept at selling change will have an easier time on the job and get along better with people. Numerous techniques have been developed to sell change. Communication plays a big part in preparing people for change and in allaying their fears.

When people are kept informed and told why a change is necessary, they will accept it much more readily. Enriching and enlarging jobs enable people to get more satisfaction from their work. Retraining answers many questions on labor supply and productivity.

19.1 How to Recognize Creativity in People

The experts on the subject of creativity say that there are some key characteristics or traits present to a greater than average degree in persons who are creative. If you can detect or observe these behavior modes, you will be able to recognize creative people when you meet them. The key characteristics which the experts refer to are: imagination, sensitivity, curiosity, persistence, motivation, and flexibility.

The ability to envision and picture in the mind the implementation of an idea and to think in terms of the unorthodox is the trait of imagination. Creative people usually have a stronger sense of imagination than those who are not creative. Being sensitive to a problem or situation is demonstrated by being aware that it has more than one possible solution. A sensitive person goes beyond routine thinking in analyzing and studying a situation.

Curiosity is behind a person's challenge of the obvious way of doing something. A curious person wants to know why things are as they are and why they can't be different. A persistent person doesn't give up easily, continues to search for an answer to a problem or for one better than that on hand.

Creative people are usually self-starters. They don't need someone to motivate them. They realize that getting started is more difficult than continuing to work. People who are flexible adjust easily to changing conditions and situations. This trait is also reflected in an ability to think of many approaches to a problem and a willingness to consider all alternative solutions.

19.2 Creativity Leads to Better Work Performance

If you are creative, you probably will be continually improving your department's operation. But you don't have to be creative to make improvements. Any supervisor can do it if he or she can persuade others to be creative and is able to recognize a good idea when it is presented. There are, however, some contingencies to be considered.

First, you must be honest enough to concede that your department is not perfect and that improvements are possible. You must feel that most if not all jobs can be done better than they are now being done.

Second, you must be confident that your people can come up with better ways of getting the work out and with solutions to problems that arise along the way. You must believe in people and their potentials.

Third, you must be bold and aggressive enough to try new ideas. You must be willing to experience an occasional failure and not let it deter you from trying another idea which looks like it might have promise.

The art of being creative is something that supervisors should try to develop in their people. Creative people like their work and get satisfaction from it. As a result, they do better work and their company benefits.

19.3 Ten Sure-Fire Ways to Promote Creativity

Your people don't have to be highly intellectual in order to be creative on the job. It does help, however, if they are aware of the inevitability of change and they know that change is going to occur whether or not they contribute to it. Here are ten ways you can help your people to be imaginative and innovative:

1. Assure them that they will not be laughed at or ridiculed when they make suggestions or offer ideas that don't pan out.

2. Respect their right to disagree and let them know this. "Yes" behavior impedes innovation and the search for a better way. It also leads to mediocrity.

3. Make the rewards for being right greater than the penalties for being wrong.

4. Be sure people are aware of goals and objectives. Give them things to shoot for.

5. Invite communication. Ideas must be transmitted to the right people if they are to be brought to light and evaluated.

6. Teach innovation and ingenuity. Push imagination. Get people to have open minds to problems and ways to solve them.

7. Encourage people to be curious and inquisitive. Make them want to see how other people handle problems similar to their own.

8. Remove blocks in the way of creative effort. Give people leeway. Downplay rules of the game.

9. Furnish tools and assistance. See that conditions are conducive to coming up with ideas.

10. Display a positive and enthusiastic attitude toward creative efforts. Work to change unusable ideas into usable ones.

Case-in-Point: "The one thing most needed for creative ability is improvement of mental habits," says Robert Wells, a Supervisor at General Electric Co., Schenectady, New York. For most people, this means reviving dormant creative skills. Children express themselves freely and are greatly enthused by a discovery largely because they haven't been "burned" by ridicule and social embarrassment.

19.4 Answers to How to Be More Creative

Some people think creativity is something mysterious and to be creative you must be born that way. They are wrong about that. Any person can be creative if the person sets his or her mind to it. Creativity in its simplest form is only problem-solving; everybody solves problems every day. If you feel that you aren't as creative as you'd like to be, adopt the following thinking and procedures:

• Organize your thoughts and ideas. Although only a few of your many thoughts may ever help you solve a problem, if you make an effort to retain those which you think may help, you increase the chances of finding answers to problems. When you have thoughts that may be of value, write them down on a pad or notebook.

• Question what you see and hear. Ask yourself why jobs are done in certain ways, in certain places, and at certain times. By challenging the ways you find things, you may get ideas on how to change them for the better.

• Break up a system or procedure into its elements. Alter the order of steps, rearrange parts, and look at matters from a different angle; most of the ideas that come to you may not be practical, but eventually a good one will come along.

• Relate a problem or situation to one with which you are familiar or have come up against before. Ask yourself what something reminds you of, what you can borrow to use elsewhere.

• Do some "way out" thinking. Don't be afraid to consider some weird ideas. Many things that are done today are because of habit, custom, and tradition, and for no other reason. An answer to a problem doesn't have to be conventional. What really matters is whether it works.

19.5 Roadblocks to Creative Thinking

Although some people, particularly those doing research and development work, may try to be creative, most of the answers to problems they come up with are conventional rather than innovative. Psychologists who have studied creative thinking explain this with the statement that the barriers to creative thinking are inherent with the individuals and with their approach to their job. Many personal characteristics can and do inhibit creative thinking. A lack of curiosity, mental illness, and inadequate motivation are a few. Viewing change as a threat is another. The fear of criticism is a major roadblock with many people, particularly with those who feel they can't afford to make a mistake or appear impractical.

Work habits and degree of familiarity with a subject can also have a negative influence on creative thinking. The person who has little knowledge about a problem area feels unable to be creative in that area. Still, too much knowledge may also be an inhibitor if it leads the experienced individual to "know the answer" even before the problem is fully defined.

Lack of pertinent data and information limits creativity drastically. Yet, lots of it is no better if it is not investigated and organized. You can do a poor job of creative thinking if you overlook the obvious, but you can also fail if you stick with the obvious. Narrow definition of a problem may prevent finding a creative solution. Then again, too broad a definition can block any solution.

A willingness to accept the first solution that appears to be a logical answer puts a damper on further creative thinking. Further, it is foolhardy to conclude that the first solution is the most creative one. The work environment can be a block if management philosophy is to make the rewards for innovation small and the penalties for not playing it safe great.

Case-in-Point: L. W. Langley, Director of Material Handling Systems Management, Rexnord Material Handling Division, said, "The value of creativity to the material handling industry is closely tied to the role the material handling itself plays in business. It is generally acknowledged that material handling is taking an increasing share of the responsibility for profits. It seems safe to say that creativity is thus becoming more important to the material handling industry. It is almost certain that the major material handling companies of tomorrow will not be the suppliers of hardware, but will be the skillful system builders who are able to attract and effectively employ creative people."

19.6 Ten Ways to Generate Ideas

Do you feel that you're not getting your share of good ideas? Do you often say to yourself, "Why didn't I think of that?" You can make a better showing and be more creative if you decide to do so. Here are ten ways to do it:

1. Be alert for a change in your or your people's jobs. Look for an unexpected result, reaction, or problem. Noticing these things can prompt you to come up with a corrective idea.

2. Try to continually expose yourself to new places and strange people. In your spare time read about subjects which are not in your field.

3. Work at solving problems when you are fresh, have a lot of energy, and can think things through. Early in the morning is best for most people.

4. Try to be alone part of the day to think. Go over some of your problems without feeling that you must find answers immediately. Let your subconscious mind go to work for you until you again have time to think.

5. Forget about being logical and practical when you're looking for answers to problems. Most of the ideas you'll get with this approach won't amount to much, but there's bound to be one now and then that will pay off.

6. Don't let ridicule or criticism hold you back when expressing your ideas. Keep trying even when other people say you are on the wrong track.

7. Be ready to take time out from what you're doing to think about a problem. Daydreaming is not a waste of time, nor is relaxing and talking with a friend. You can sometimes induce ideas with a walk, a shower, or by listening to restful music.

8. Always have a pad and pencil with you so that you can make notes of your thoughts and ideas when they come to you. Many valuable ideas are lost because people don't make a note of them.

9. Make a habit of using checklists when you plan. When it comes to carrying out those plans, you'll do a more thorough job. A checklist is worthwhile also because you have to think to make one.

10. Set deadlines for yourself. The need to meet them can spur you to more accomplishment. The fear of failure to meet them can intensify your thinking and dedication.

19.7 How to Spur People to Get Ideas

Getting ideas is not easy, particularly when you're trying hard to do so. Remember this when you talk to your people about being innovative and how they should attack difficult problems.

Nevertheless, it pays to occasionally bring up the subject of being creative and how a person can train himself or herself to get more ideas. Here are some suggestions and advice on what you can say to spur people to think:

- Point out that searching for ideas must be done constantly, and this means with both minor and major problems.
- Mention that people who are highly knowledgeable about a subject are excellent sources of information.
- Recommend that they should also talk to people holding similar jobs to theirs.
- Tell them that they should always listen carefully. Some ideas may be picked up even when what's being said has no direct application to the current problem or situation.

- Warn against being satisfied with the information at hand when they have a tough problem to solve. Keeping an open mind and remaining flexible work best when trying to solve difficult problems.
- Recommend that they refrain from discarding an idea just because it does not seem right when they first think of it.
- Caution against completely giving up on an idea they've developed simply because it won't solve a problem at hand.

19.8 Six Traps to Being Innovative: How to Avoid Them

If you sincerely wish that you could come up with more ideas, think about how you're going about it. You may be handicapping yourself by making it more difficult than it need be. Here are some traps which may be preventing you from being more innovative:

1. Noise and distraction. Are you doing most of your mental work under poor conditions such as near noisy machines or where people's conversations can distract you? Get off by yourself in a quiet area.

2. Thinking in generalities. Zero in on the specific problem which needs to be solved. Break up a big problem—try to solve it in parts or steps.

3. Being satisfied with things as they are. You have to believe that anything and everything can be improved. There is always a better way to do something.

4. Having your senses dulled. Beware of too much food or drink if you have some serious thinking to do. Your mind will not be sharp if you eat or drink to excess.

5. Thinking deeply at the wrong time. You can't do your best when you're fatigued or weary. You need to be fresh to be inspired.

6. Unwilling to express yourself. An idea that you keep to yourself or file away for future use isn't worth much—it hasn't a chance of being adopted now. Don't worry about an idea being rejected. Talking about it may even lead to a still better one.

19.9 Positive Practices to Gain Idea Acceptance

People with ideas can significantly increase their success in selling them if they carefully prepare for and use strategy to put them across. The more positively and enthusiastically they go about it, the more influential such practices become. If you adopt the following techniques and master them, you will be able to significantly increase the number of your ideas which are accepted:

- Know the likes, dislikes, and needs of the people who judge and evaluate your ideas. You can then slant a presentation with those matters in mind. If you also know why and how these people resist change, you can search out ways to reduce their resistance to it.

• Go beyond economic considerations when talking about benefits and advantages of an idea. Talk up, for example, the social, cultural, or educational aspects. Some persons are reluctant to accept a change unless they can see new or different benefits.

• Be sure your idea is fully understood. Clear, well-presented proposals reflect a high competency of the suggestor which helps to overcome any doubt of this nature. Avoid jargon and technical terms, if possible; you may appear to be trying to impress rather than inform.

• Present an honest, complete story. Resist being biased by giving both the positive and negative features of the idea, but be sure to include recommendations on how the negative ones can be overcome. This type of presentation eliminates many questions before they are asked. At the same time, it fosters more confidence in you and what you can do.

• Share the credit for ideas, even though others may have contributed little. You gain doubly: first, by letting it be known that you listen to others, and second, by acquiring the support of the people you credited.

• Tie your idea to another which has already been accepted. Point out similarities and comment on the logic of the comparison. This helps to allay the "newness" of your idea, a matter which some people unconsciously object to.

• Seek cooperation to make people feel they played a part in the promotion or development of the idea. When people think they have contributed, they will more willingly accept and lend you their support. You may have to modify some part or detail a bit, but that's a small price to pay to gain their acceptance.

19.10 How to Protect Your Idea

Ideas to improve operations, make work easier, reduce waste, and cut costs should be discussed and publicized when they are put into practice. People who come up with such ideas want to receive credit for them, supervisors included. This is natural and to be expected. But how can you publicize an idea and be assured of getting credit for it if it is not immediately accepted and adopted? You can protect your idea as well as promote its acceptance very easily.

How-to-Do-It: If you get an idea in a meeting or a discussion with other people, write a follow-up letter to the person or persons who are in a position to act on it. You can also use the letter as a means of adding to or refining the idea beyond your original proposal.

Getting your idea in print enables you to point it out to other people who might be interested. This is a low pressure way to show your involvement and interest without blowing your horn excessively.

Another way to protect as well as promote your idea is to orally present it to a higher level of authority. Avoid letting someone else speak for you, if possible, especially if other people are also talking about it. A good idea is worth fighting for yourself so you don't get lost in the shuffle.

19.11 Guidelines to Handling Change Smoothly

It's natural to fear change. Change is seldom welcomed unless people demand it to relieve themselves of a burden or a discomfort. People fear change mostly because they don't know what to expect. Even minor or insignificant changes disturb habits and routines causing worry and stress. It takes time for new habits and routines to be formed, and some people need more time than others to get accustomed to something new.

Change sometimes is more acceptable if it is managed without a lot of fanfare and publicity. Although it isn't always possible to make a change this way, the less adjustment that is required of people, the less apparent it is that you are making a change. Here are some guidelines on how to make a change smoothly:

1. Announce a change promptly; the word is going to get out anyway. It's much easier to present truths in the beginning than it is to correct untruths and rumors later.

2. Maintain the status of individuals whenever possible. You get into trouble if you build one person's status at the expense of another's.

3. Avoid decrees. People are offended when you dictate. Suggestions are received much better than demands.

4. Show confidence that the change will be a success. If other people sense that you have doubts about it, they will also have doubts, and the road ahead may then be rocky.

5. Recognize and respect resistance. Don't try to have your way at any cost. Discuss an objection and reconsider. You could be wrong in what you're doing.

6. Be patient. Allow time for a change to take effect. People cannot be expected to completely and enthusiastically accept a change immediately after they learn of it.

19.12 Tips on Selling Change

If you acknowledge that there's more than one way to sell change, and you have developed a perceptiveness to people's feelings, you are on your way to perfecting a selling technique. Here are some tips on following through to become an expert in the art.

Play change in a soft key. When you are going to make a proposal, don't give out the whole deal at one time—present only enough so that people can see what you're thinking about, but not enough to put up a strong argument against it.

Proceed slowly by talking to only one person at a time and by giving that person time to think before you bring up the subject again. People need time to adjust to a new idea before they will wholeheartedly accept it.

Watch a person's manner and his or her body language to see if you are getting agreement with what you're saying. Feel your way if you perceive resistance. Tactfully probe for what the person does not agree with or thinks is wrong.

Truly listen to a person's objections and study them. Recognize that you may have to modify your idea, that it may not be perfect. Try to learn how you might improve it so that it is more acceptable.

19.13 Sell Change by Saying the Right Words

When you feel that a change should be made but you don't have the authority to make it without another person's approval, you are faced with selling that person on the worth of the change. You may have to convince your boss, for example, that your idea will improve a work situation or a process operation. Saying the right words will increase your chances of selling your idea.

How-to-Do-It: Start by emphasizing the benefits; show how costs will be lowered, safety improved, production increased, or efficiency raised. Use figures if you can calculate them because they enable you to be specific.

Be careful not to exaggerate or make exorbitant claims. Also, admit to extra costs, drawbacks, and difficulties which might be encountered in the implementation of the change. Yet, ask for the full amount of help or money you believe will be needed to accomplish the change.

Condition yourself to answer questions. This means that you must know the details and steps to get started, the people that will be involved, and the problems that might arise.

Finish your proposal for a change by asking for authority to make it. This action is similar to the one a salesperson must take who, after a sales presentation, should ask for an order. Although you may not get a green light to go ahead at the moment, at least you will have made your point and left the decision up to your superiors.

19.14 Making It Easier: Explain Why

You can sell change much more easily if you explain why it is needed. Too often, the "what" of a change is explained adequately while the "why" is handled poorly if at all.

When you tell people why a change is to be made, you help them to understand it. In addition, explaining strengthens your selling message.

By explaining why a change is necessary, you also overcome part of the natural fear that people have of it. With this knowledge they can be more assured, for example, that their jobs are not going to be lost or that they are not going to have to work harder. The more information you can give people about a change, and the more positive way you can do it, the easier it will be for you to sell it.

19.15 Five Ways to Take the Pain Out of Change

Since employees naturally resist change, supervisors should do what they can to get their people to expect it, understand it, and prepare for it. The more supervisors can do along these lines the less resistance they will encounter when they make a change. Here are five ways you can take the pain out of change:

1. Be sure the change is beneficial and worthwhile. Change for the sake of change alone is only a waste of time, and you may build up resistance to a later worthwhile change besides. If you don't have a lot to gain from a change, it's better to forget the whole thing.

2. Ask for advice. Employees will feel involved and become committed when they have a voice in a decision, especially if they can spot an oversight or a weakness in a plan and are able to point it out.

3. Make the change as simple as possible. Break it up into steps if you can so that it doesn't have to be taken all at once. Change is less disruptive if you can space it out.

4. Give the change time. Resistance won't disappear immediately. All people need time to adjust.

5. Admit it when a change doesn't work. Back off and return to the conditions before the change. If you persist, you show that you are either stubborn or a poor judge of people and situations, both of which will hinder you on the job.

19.16 Steps to Getting Greater Acceptance of Plans

You can get better acceptance of your plans and ideas if you keep the people who will be affected informed about them. This is best done in steps:

- First, inform people that a change is being considered. Tell them that it will result in benefits and advantages to them.

- Second, after you've settled the details, give the reasons for the change and an explanation of it.

- Third, describe the plan's elements as to who, what, where, when, and how much.

- Fourth, periodically report on progress of the change. Mention any deviation from the original plan.

- Fifth, confirm that the change has been made and is now the standard procedure. Ask for comments on difficulties or problems encountered with the new way.

19.17 How to Enrich and Enlarge Jobs

Attitude surveys have shown that today's job seekers, particularly young people, want more than just a job. They want to get satisfaction and a sense of achievement from their work. Security and money are not as important to such people as a challenge, a chance for self-expression, and an opportunity to make a contribution to society. Educators and psychologists say that jobs must be enriched and enlarged if these desires of new employees are to be achieved. They suggest four ways by which it may be done:

- One way is to create the proper environment or climate. Supervisors and workers must do a good job of communicating with each other, identifying common goals, and trusting one another. There should be no pressure on the workers to obey rules and work harder.

- A second way is to design jobs to permit people to make maximum use of their skills while at the same time motivating them to do so. This involves giving workers more responsibility to run their jobs as they see fit and to make decisions on how the work is to be done.

- Another way is to design equipment and systems which promote motivation, create interest, and provide satisfaction with accomplishment. This is done by making the work exciting and challenging, and by providing pleasant, comfortable work conditions.

- The fourth way of enriching jobs is for management to provide the means for learning and growth, and to participate with workers in setting goals and solving problems. In this way performance is rewarded on the basis of goal achievement.

19.18 Retraining: The Answer to the Labor Shortage

Retraining people to do a new job or perform a different task is common procedure today because of the rapid change in technology and the need to increase the productivity of people in general. It is also the answer to where to get people to operate the new machines and equipment which are being installed in offices and plants in all industries.

Retraining is the word used to describe two procedures: one, training in a different line of work, where a person's present job skills are of little or no use;

20

GUARANTEED WAYS
TO MOVE UP THE
MANAGEMENT LADDER

IF you are like most supervisors, you hope to be promoted to a better job and continue to advance in your company. But at this stage of your career, you may not know the extent of your potential nor what it takes to convince management that you have the capabilities to justify their promoting you again and again.

There are many ways you can boost your image, properly assert yourself, and carry out your responsibilities in a manner that will enhance the probability of your continual advancement. Just as important, however, there are many types of behavior you must avoid since any one of them could bring a halt to further promotions. Getting ahead depends a great deal on getting along with people and getting their cooperation.

Your communication skills, both oral and written, probably carry the most weight in how far you go in your career. The better you handle these, the easier you will find the road to a high position in your company.

20.1 Five Ways to Learn the Degree of Your Potential

Most supervisors at one time or another wonder whether they have the potential to get better jobs than the ones they currently hold. Many of them also have no idea about how far they will be able to move up the management ladder. How can those things be determined and what are the factors which decide whether or not a person has potential?

If you are interested in your destiny, here are five ways to learn the degree of your potential. Ask yourself the following questions:

1. *Are you mature and stable?* If you are usually down-to-earth and practical in your viewpoint and how you handle problems, you are mature. A stable person can control his or her emotions and also handle considerable stress.

2. *Do you enjoy your work?* If you get pleasure and satisfaction from your job, you will probably always be self-motivated. Also, you will never be content to do only what is necessary to get by on the job.

3. *Does your boss encourage your ideas?* If your boss tells you that you are doing a good job, he or she is confirming that you have the potential to move up in your line of work and in other similar types of work.

4. *Do you like to solve problems?* If you get a kick out of solving puzzles and problems, you are demonstrating your potential to move up to more responsible positions. People who submit suggestions and gain creative satisfaction from having their ideas adopted are destined to receive awards and recognition throughout their career.

5. *Do you read a lot?* If you read quite a few newspapers, trade magazines, and books, you are keeping up-to-date with current events and of happenings in your line of work. This shows you have interests in many areas, any one of which you have the potential to become active and successful.

20.2 Make Sure Your Career Is on Track

Successful careers mean different things to different people. Some people consider themselves successful if they progress rapidly through a series of promotions, with each step demonstrating their extensive knowledge and broadness of skills. Others equate success with reaching positions of power and authority. Whether you are trying to get into upper management as quickly as possible, or simply want to make sure you continue to move up, you should want to know if your career is on track.

Most successful careers begin with two distinct stages of development: starting and indoctrination followed by independence or specialization. Both stages bring into play a different combination of knowledge and skills.

Supervisors face several challenges when they take their initial supervisory job. First, they must learn how to get along and interact with people. Second, they must determine which parts of their work are critical and which responsibilities will demand most of their attention. Third, they must learn how to get things done through others using both formal and informal channels of communication. During this learning period, they are also expected to show initiative and enthusiasm while being creative and innovative. The better they become in problem-solving, the sooner they can expect to move into the next stage of development and take on more responsibilities.

While the desire to advance in their company is understandable, supervisors who pursue promotion with a vengeance can come up short on important aspects of career development. For example, they may fail to gain valuable experience. In addition, they risk getting a reputation for mediocre performance by taking on responsibilities they are not prepared to handle. Another matter concerns how they adjust to routine tasks. If they lose interest in the job, they may acquire a black mark on their record that compromises their future development.

Most supervisors look forward to being promoted to a position of more independence or specialization. At this point in their career, they are expected to demonstrate skills and abilities within special areas—they become managers in various departments. By focusing their efforts in a single area, they show competency and professionalism.

This accomplishment tends to raise their self-esteem and enhances their visibility within the company. Performing well at this time is very important in career development. However, many managers remain here for the rest of their careers, making substantial contributions to the company and experiencing satisfaction in doing so.

No matter what your aspirations at any point in your career, you should be aware of where you are currently and where you want to go. You may have aspirations to become a tutor and mentor, a position which also offers a degree of satisfaction that many can never attain. Finally, you may want to be a consultant. Be assured, few get to this point without career planning.

20.3 Planning: A Prerequisite for Success

It is generally believed today that to be effective and efficient in your work, you must do a good job of planning. In addition, many experts in various fields insist that you must plan if you want to be successful. Since planning is so important, it should be a part of your life style and a constant activity.

The procedures you follow when you plan usually determine whether you have good plans or just mediocre ones. Good planning takes many things into consideration. It derives from a distinct procedure, one that is orderly and complete.

To plan effectively, you must first define what you want to achieve. The more precise and accurate your definition, the easier it is to come up with a good plan. Put your goal in writing if it is extensive and will take some time to achieve. This will help to make it inclusive and clear. Your notes will aid your reasoning and logic; they also will give you a record for future planning.

When starting to plan, try to see problems or roadblocks that will or might make it hard for you to reach your goal. While it is usually difficult to foresee all your problems, the more you can anticipate them, the smoother the path will be to your goal. Next, determine what information and facts you'll need to complete your plan. No one can reason logically and work out a plan without accurate information.

Study and analyze the facts. Decide how much weight you should give each factor and assess the true meaning of each statistic. Look for cause-and-effect relationships. Also, list the assumptions and all estimates in your plan. Then, decide whether you have enough information to act. If there is a question in your mind, take another look at your contingencies and those matters that are not facts.

Periodically review your various plans. Since people and conditions change, you may decide to alter a plan to meet new contingencies. This is especially true of a plan that is a long-term one. While planning is a prerequisite for success in many endeavors, it is only so when you make good plans.

20.4 Recognize the Importance of Getting More Education

Personnel experts say that the best way to go about getting a promotion, as well as to ensure that you will be promoted again and again, is to acquire more education. Of course, how you gain knowledge and a better education is up to you. People learn basically in two ways—from their own experiences and from others. While learning from personal experiences is automatic, learning from others is another matter. It takes effort and dedication on your part, yet the opportunities are almost unlimited.

One of the easiest ways to learn is to do a lot of reading. With so many newspapers, magazines, and books available, all you need do is read with the intention of picking up information as well as ideas. Don't overlook radio and television as excellent sources of information. Public broadcast stations, in particular, present many in-depth studies on technical subjects.

If you believe you need the kind of education you can get only by attending classes or seminars, investigate where such training is available. See if you can register for some evening courses or if you can attend a two-or-three day seminar that isn't too far away. Determine how much time the sessions will take and decide whether you have the time to invest in gaining that particular knowledge. Be sure to ask your boss if the company will pay for part or all of your expenses.

Many educational opportunities are available today through a variety of sources. A number of community colleges, colleges, and universities offer continuing education programs, both credit and noncredit courses. If you want a technical education, look into the courses offered by the trade, professional, and commerce organizations. High school adult education courses range from completion of high school credits to writing and public speaking. There are also university extension programs and correspondence courses available through the mail.

Whatever you decide to do to gain more knowledge, put as much effort as you can into your program. You'll never regret it. When you look back later at what you learned, you'll realize that education was the major stepping-stone to furthering your career.

20.5 How to Master the Art of Being Noticed

If you want to get ahead today, you've got to go beyond doing an excellent job or becoming an expert in some field. Your work must be recognized and your accomplishments must be publicized. Since there are few people who will do this for you, the job falls upon your shoulders.

Fortunately, it's usually not difficult to become adept at calling attention to yourself because there are many ways to go about it. Here are four of the most common:

1. *Participate in various activities.* Get into company, industry, and community projects. Be active in trade shows, publicity campaigns, and drives of all types. Volunteer to help various charitable organizations. By being a joiner, you can very quickly become known in those areas where you have accomplished something.

2. *Get yourself talked about.* If you have recently done something that is noteworthy, let the editors of your company newsletter and your hometown newspaper know about it. Many readers will see your name in print, and many of them will mention to their friends that you made the news. Also, let your relatives and friends know about your deeds; you can depend on them to tell others.

3. *Write for publication.* A good way to toot your own horn is to do some freelance writing in the nonfiction field. Many trade magazines want articles on the type of work you do and on solving problems in your industry or business. Not only will your byline appear with the article, but you may also receive an honorarium or payment for it.

4. *Speak at every opportunity to do so.* Since you probably talk to many people during the day, they are likely to pass along part of what you say, especially if it is interesting or unusual. So make as many contacts as possible

when you have an idea or thought that you'd like to circulate. Your opportunities for doing that occur at coffee breaks, lunch, and while on the job.

20.6 Tips on How to Boost Your Image

How well qualified *you* think you are for the next step up the ladder in your company is not as important as how well qualified *other people* perceive you to be. The more effectively you can sell yourself and your capabilities, the better chance you have to be given more responsibilities. Here are some tips on how you can boost your image:

- Act like a professional and look the part. Dress appropriately, smile often and readily, and tactfully make your skills and accomplishments known.
- Let your superiors know that you are ambitious and want to get ahead. At the same time, however, avoid giving any impression that you would take advantage of others to gain your ends.
- Jump at every opportunity to prove that you are a good team player. Don't be afraid to ask for help when you need it. Doing so shows you are eager to learn. It also shows you are willing to work with others.
- Prove that you are a company person. Act and be proud of your department and the company. Make sure that management is aware that you are continually learning more about your organization and how it operates.
- Be willing to say you don't know something when that is the case. This is much better than seeming to be a know-it-all. Besides, if you never admit what you don't know, people may wonder what you do know.
- Indicate that you are human and sympathetic to the needs and problems of others. Prove that you have a good sense of humor and show people that you are able to laugh at yourself.
- Admit your mistakes honestly and openly. Offer ways to make amends and rectify situations. Nothing is worse in the eyes of your boss than trying to cover up errors or place the blame elsewhere.
- Make sure your name is always associated with honest and ethical behavior. Having a good reputation is a valuable asset.

20.7 How to Properly Assert Yourself

It's always difficult to say no to your boss or to an influential person in the company. But if you work for somebody who consistently asks you to participate in functions you do not enjoy, or to do something you weren't hired to do, you have every right to refuse.

Most important, however, you must try to do it without being abrupt or rude. Also, avoid speaking loudly—a soft "no" isn't nearly as harsh. It's easy to say something like, "I'm sorry. I've already made plans for tonight," or "Gosh, I just can't make that." You don't need to offer any further explanations, but you should stick to your guns no matter how persistent the requester of your attendance or participation becomes.

Never be tempted to remark about someone else's behavior under similar circumstances. Make it clear that you're saying no because that's the way *you* feel about it. What other people do, or how they react to what you do, is their business, not yours.

Be assured that it's normal to feel apologetic about saying no. Many of us think we owe others some explanation when we assert ourselves. You can offer a reason or an excuse if you want to, but it's often better that you don't. Why? Because if the other person counters your explanation or dismisses it, you're left with nothing to fall back on. However, if it makes you feel better to offer an explanation, at least don't elaborate on it.

You'll know when you are or have become an assertive person. For one thing, you'll not be swayed by someone's anger, bullying, or ridicule. You'll know also how to react the next time you must manage others without aggression. The best test will come when you must hold your ground and repeat something as often as it takes to make it sink in. If you ever feel that you're beginning to weaken, remind yourself: you don't have to do what other people want or expect. The easiest way not to do it is to say no and mean it.

20.8 Asserting Yourself: Getting Ahead May Depend on It

Success on the job often depends upon the ability to relate and interact effectively with people at all levels of the company you work for. Learning to replace nonassertive aggressiveness with assertive behavior can be one of the best ways for you to achieve interpersonal effectiveness.

A supervisor who is properly assertive can get ideas across, make things happen, and calmly handle crisis situations. Assertive behavior is expressed most simply and clearly by adopting the principle that a person doesn't have to do what other people want or expect. The primary way of carrying out the theme is to learn how to say no.

For some people, this can be a difficult thing to do, especially if it is their boss they are saying no to. That's because they have been raised all their life to defer to people in authority. Saying no to people who work for you is sometimes much easier, but saying no to a boss can be very difficult. Yet, sometimes it's necessary, especially if your boss is an aggressive or assertive person.

Although you may think at times that you are not being controlled by others, that's exactly what is happening when you go along with something you don't want to do simply because other people expect it. If you've been in this position recently, you probably were irritated as well as disturbed. You realized that you were pushed into saying yes, ashamed of yourself for saying it, and worst of all, stymied because you didn't see how you could possibly say no.

Only a strong leader can say no when he or she would like to say yes and people expect it. Persons who are weak in this capability would be better off if they knew how to assert themselves.

20.9 Why You Don't Want to Be Indispensable

Has anyone, including your boss, ever told you that you are indispensable in your job? You should hope that you never hear those words. Being labeled indispensable is not a compliment, and you shouldn't feel it is one.

What's bad about being indispensable is that you are probably stuck in your present job. You won't be considered when the boss is looking for someone who can or should be promoted. The company can't afford to take you off your job if no one is available to replace you.

Also, if you know you are thought of as indispensable, your ego may inflate to the point where you begin to think you're better than you really are. Such thinking could lead to carelessness and, in extreme cases, sloppy work, even though you might deny being guilty of those things.

Furthermore, you should be part of a team in your company. No matter what your specific responsibilities consist of, you must interact with people. If you are labeled indispensable, you are probably not mixing or cooperating with fellow-supervisors as you should.

Nobody is indispensable today, although a few people think they are. Some people seem to be proud of being classified as such and, as a result, are content to remain that way. They don't see themselves as trapped and therefore do not look for ways to move up to better jobs in their companies.

20.10 How to Avoid Being Identified as Indispensable

Here are some steps you can take to escape the fix of being considered indispensable in your organization:

1. Keep alert to what's going on in your department and the company. Determine what goals the company is working toward, and set some goals for yourself.

2. Learn what training and education you will need to reach your goals. Investigate the courses and classes you might take at local universities and trade schools to enable you to become knowledgeable and skilled in those disciplines. Follow through by enrolling and participating in those programs.

3. Start communicating with your boss and others who could be influential in getting you a better job in the company. Ask them for suggestions on what you should do. Be objective with their advice and carefully consider their ideas.

4. Ask the successful people in your company to tell you the paths they took in getting to their positions. You can learn a lot about what your company is looking for by talking to and watching people who are moving up.

5. See that your boss is up-to-date on your goals and your activities. Always mention it when you accomplish something worthwhile or pass a milestone. Keep studying, learning, and gaining experience. Never pass up an opportunity to better yourself in one way or another.

By taking these steps, you'll remain a key individual in your company while continuing to do a better job. You won't be indispensable, but you'll be valued.

20.11 Tips on How to Get Along Better with Your Boss

Having your boss pleased with you raises your enthusiasm for the job and makes it more interesting. In addition, you feel more secure and your goal of an even better job seems more attainable. But to be in this position, you must know what it takes to please your boss. You should also know what bosses look for, expect, and sometimes demand in the way of action and performance from the people who work for them.

A few things the boss may ask of you may seem unreasonable, but most, you must agree, are only what should be expected of you on your job. If you wish to move up the management ladder, you'll constantly do your best and continually make an effort to please him or her. Here are some tips on steps you can take to encourage a good relationship:

• *Support your boss whenever you can.* Support means more than just doing your job. It means offering to help your boss with his or her work. You support him or her when you make sure the boss is kept fully informed and when you anticipate problems that may arise in the department.

• *Examine your behavior, not your boss's.* It is very easy to attribute your faults to a boss whom you see as threatening or opposing you. Don't make the mistake of believing that your boss is hostile and that you therefore have every right to be hostile in return.

• *Save the boss's time.* Avoid running to your boss for many decisions— decisions that you should be making yourself. Do this by thinking things out a bit more before consulting with him or her. Get more facts to solve your problems, but get them without bothering your boss.

• *Don't be a "yes" person.* Although people will find it easy to get along with you if you are always agreeable, they may also find it difficult to trust you. Your boss knows that things do not always run smoothly and that he or she isn't always right.

• *Avoid thinking you know more than your boss does*. This may be difficult if you are more up-to-date on new technology or have more education than your boss. But experience should not be overlooked. If you are tempted to question your boss's decisions, remember that you may not be aware of all the facts or the circumstances.

20.12 Impulsiveness: Curbing It Pays Off

People who tend to be impulsive may find it difficult to get along with others. That can be a disadvantage in today's working environment where group efforts are often the norm. In addition, impulsiveness shown by responding too quickly to stimuli suggests a lack of experience and an ability to control one's emotions, both of which are deterrents to moving up in management.

Since your job as a supervisor involves working with others, you can't afford to be impulsive. When you act impulsively, it's likely that you've only considered your own point of view. Think about how this looks to others, particularly those for whom you look to for help and cooperation.

Probably the best way to curb impulsiveness is to deliberately pause when you feel impelled to say or do something quickly. Realize that few situations require an immediate response. Ask yourself, "Is this an emergency? Is this really my problem? What can I gain by acting now?" Difficult as it may be, by being patient you can avoid saying or doing something you may later regret.

Practice being patient by avoiding quick decisions and snap judgments. It's always better to ask for time to think something over before you give your opinion, especially if it's one that your listener may not like. Patience often is a matter of waiting, listening, and standing by silently until an individual comes up with the answer to his or her own problem.

You can minimize being impulsive by anticipating situations and thinking about how you should react to them. Also, delay a reaction or decision whenever you can. After a few hours or a day, take another look at all of your alternatives. If you can resist being impulsive, you'll make much better decisions.

20.13 Tips on How to Handle Pressure

If you are determined to move up the management ladder, you must be able to handle pressure. Of course, as a supervisor, pressure probably isn't anything new to you. By the very nature of your work and your responsibilities, you've been oriented to face challenges, objections, and turndowns from the first day you were on the job.

Nevertheless, some supervisors become discouraged when put under pressure. They're inclined to give up easily. Since they don't fight back, they fail to experience the satisfaction of overcoming adversity. Others react differently. They welcome challenges because they see them as ways to get ahead. Here are some tips on how to handle four kinds of pressure you're bound to experience on the job sooner or later:

● *Pressure when someone opposes one of your decisions.* The way to handle this is to ask the person some questions such as, "Why should I hold up on this? How do the disadvantages of this outweigh the advantages? What's the worse that can happen if this decision is made?"

● *Pressure because you find yourself disagreeing with someone.* Don't rush to answer a question or defend your position. Instead, pause to make sure you have all the information about the other person's view. Sometimes your silence will lead your opponent to expand on his or her opinion and thus clarify the issue.

● *Pressure from learning that someone else's idea has been accepted instead of yours.* Realize that invariably there is competition within an organization, and that you can't always be the best. Don't expect yourself to out-think and out-produce everyone all of the time. As long as you are doing your very best and getting your share of the glory, competition should not cause you to be tense or frustrated.

● *Pressure on your leadership.* You may notice that someone opposes your promoting a project not because he or she disagrees with your ideas, but because the person objects to your leadership in presenting the idea. When you find yourself faced with such a challenge, see if you can switch the discussion to a different area.

20.14 Your Behavior: Seven Types to Avoid

While it's important to know all the things you should do in order to be successful and get ahead, it's just as important, if not more so, to be aware of the behaviors you should avoid. Getting ahead depends on getting along with people. Good relationships are more easily achieved and maintained by avoiding certain behaviors. Here are seven behaviors, any one of which can slow or impede you from moving up the management ladder:

1. *Being unwilling to accept blame.* Recognize that you are human and will make mistakes and errors now and then. The problem lies in not admitting them. You can do even better by saying you were wrong, clearing the air, and trying to make amends.

2. *Criticizing and finding fault.* Nobody likes to be criticized. Finding fault with others simply antagonizes them. You can always find something good to say about a person if you try.

3. *Showing distrust.* When you question people's motives or quiz them about details of an undertaking or project, you suggest that you don't completely

trust them. You give the same impresssion when you check on something rather than accepting someone's word for it.

4. *Acting selfish.* Saying and doing things that benefit only you rather than another person or group indicates you have little regard for other people. If you want to have good relationships with others, you must not be concerned exclusively with yourself.

5. *Being egotistic.* Overuse of the word "I" and talking about oneself too much never sets well with other people. Nobody is perfect. We all have our weaknesses and strengths.

6. *Having a closed mind.* Blocking out information, facts, and viewpoints that you don't agree with shuts you off from considering new data and thoughts. A closed mind makes you weak in evaluating others' ideas.

7. *Going on the defensive.* Even though you may feel defensive when an error of yours is pointed out, realize that the feedback you receive is generally to your advantage. You will know better the next time. Making excuses and trying to justify what you've done doesn't help.

20.15 How to Learn from Your Mistakes

Some people make a lot more mistakes than others, and too many people never seem to learn from their mistakes. Instead of dismissing a mistake as something you can't do anything about, why not take a few minutes to find out why it happened? By doing so, you may make fewer and/or less serious mistakes in the future. In addition, you could become noted as one who seldom makes a mistake.

To learn from a mistake, you must know what caused it. Review what you were doing at the time and why you were doing it. Look into the existing situation and conditions. Consider the factors and people that were involved. Then analyze the mistake to see which of the following situations or conditions applied:

- The mistake was due to the undertaking itself rather than how you went about handling it. You should see that you must be more careful in the future when you are involved in a questionable issue.
- Inattention was the reason for the mistake. You may not have assigned enough importance to the activity. You must be more careful and keep your mind on the job at hand.
- Poor timing accounted for the mistake. Proper timing often determines the success or failure of a venture. If this was the cause of your mistake, resolve to consider timing in the future.
- Misinformation or a lack of data caused you to make the mistake. Maybe you made a decision too quickly or didn't wait to get confirming information.

Perhaps your source of information was poor. Maybe you made an error of deduction or logic.

● The mistake was not solely yours. If another person was involved, you have been alerted to be cautious in the future when working with that individual. You also should have learned to rely more on your own judgment and ability to make good decisions.

● Trying to do too much at once or handle two things at the same time was the reason for your mistake. You may have been under stress or pressed for time when you made the mistake. If so, you've confirmed that it's better to do one thing at a time.

● Insufficient follow-up resulted in the mistake. If something was not done because you failed to follow up on your orders, you have learned the importance of checking back later. Some jobs require much closer supervision than others.

Learning from mistakes is part of learning by experience. It pays to look into every mistake in order to gain that experience.

20.16 The Pros and Cons of Volunteering

Success in business and industry today often goes to those who frequently volunteer to do something, provided, of course, that they are sincere and conscientious in their effort to help. A good way to give your career a boost, therefore, is to identify a problem that bothers your boss and volunteer to help him or her solve it.

Yet, it doesn't make sense to always volunteer. Sometimes you are better off staying uninvolved. Volunteering pays off when:

● Your efforts will benefit your department and help your boss.

● You have an opportunity to help someone, especially one who may return the favor.

● You are confident you can do the job you are volunteering for effectively.

● You will gain a personal advantage from your effort.

When none of these conditions or situations apply, you are probably better off not volunteering.

As for who you should offer to help, the most important person is your boss. You will either advance or stay where you are depending on your boss's evaluation of your work, character, attitude, and personality. If he or she likes you and rates you favorably, you will be considered for advancement when an opportunity arises. Thus, by volunteering to help your boss, you will help your career.

20.17 Guidelines to Working with a Mentor

There are quite a few rewards and benefits you can gain from finding someone to act as your mentor. Many successful people are proud to share their knowledge and experience; they get a great deal of satisfaction from inspiring people, especially if those people work for the same company.

Mentors perform several functions. They serve as trusted counselors or guides, and they act as advisors, coaches, and teachers. But a mentor is not someone who can substitute for you when you are required to participate in some activity.

To stay on good terms with a mentor, you must respect his or her time. Talk to a mentor only when you have something of significance to discuss. One of the quickest ways to turn off a mentor is to constantly phone or visit his or her office to get information and unimportant details on some matter.

If you ask a mentor for advice, by all means follow it. Arguing the point as a way of showing enthusiasm would be inconsistent with your role. Besides, the mentor would certainly wonder why you asked for advice if you didn't intend to accept it. Your taking an opposite stand could appear as a tactic to show your knowledge of the subject.

To show that you appreciate the advice and suggestions you receive from a mentor, always give the person feedback on the action you took and the results of that action. The mentor probably will be curious as to how you fared and whether you were pleased with what happened. There is also a possibility that you should make a slight adjustment or correction in the course you are following. If you are proceeding according to plan and all is well, you need to know that also.

Mentors are pleased and gain satisfaction from learning that they have been helpful. Be sure to communicate that message to yours.

20.18 How to Remember People's Names

Of the many skills that lead to success and advancement, one of the most coveted is being able to remember people's names. Although you may believe you have a poor memory of names and that not much can be done about it, this is simply not true—you *can* learn this skill.

You should want to be able to recall people's names for two principal reasons:

1. When you remember a person's name, you pay him or her a compliment. On the other hand, if you fail to address a person by name, you imply that you don't consider the person important enough to go to the trouble of remembering his or her name.

2. Addressing people by their name is far more likely to get their help and cooperation than if you said, "Hey you," or "Say, kid." Such words are blunt

and crude; they fail to show respect. You can't expect people to willingly respond if you show that you haven't bothered to learn or remember their names.

Learning how to remember names is not as difficult as it might seem. Here's how to go about it:

● When you meet someone, make sure you hear the person's name. The main reason why some people have trouble remembering a name is that they don't catch it when they are introduced. If you fail to hear a person's name, ask for it to be repeated, even spelled, if that will help you. There's a side benefit here in that this interest on your part impresses people.

● Look at the person's face. Most people remember what they see better than what they hear. When you look at a person's face, search for a feature that is easy to remember such as wrinkles, dimples, freckles, or a scar. While you may find it hard to observe people's faces for details because you don't like to stare, remember that it's good manners to look at a person while listening to him or her.

● Connect the name to the face. Since faces are easier to remember than names, use the face to remind you of the name. Then whenever you see a familiar face, it will remind you of the name.

● Repeat the name at every opportunity. Do this when conversing with the person and whenever you talk about the person to someone else. You don't need to preface every sentence with the name, but do try to use it at least two or three times. Also, always use the name when saying goodbye to the person. This serves as a final reminder and enables you to confirm that you have the name right.

20.19 Answers to Why Asking Pays Off

You've probably noticed that some people in your company seem to be natural leaders. Others readily follow them and willingly do things for them. If you look into the secret of their success, you'll find that these people have a knack of getting along well with almost everyone and of being well-liked.

You may also notice that when they need help they ask for it—they never order or demand it. In addition, their asking is done in such a manner that it's difficult if not impossible to refuse. Therein lies one, if not the major, reason for their success.

The best leaders in business and industry aren't afraid to ask. They are aware of the benefits they reap and the advantages they gain from it. Here are some answers to why asking pays off:

● Asking someone to do something rather than telling the person to do it seemingly gives the person asked a choice. Therefore, it makes the request easier to accept. It has another point in its favor: since a question deserves an answer, the other fellow has a chance to respond, and a comment may come of it. At least, willingness to comply can be expressed. A person won't hesitate to speak up as much as when ordered to do something outright.

● People appreciate being asked rather than being told. Asking softens the difference in authority and responsibility; it promotes cooperation, and it puts people on the same level. When people feel equal they feel more reasonable and willing to go along.

● Asking someone to do something for you can also be an ego-booster and a compliment. The asking implies that the person asked has the ability, skill, or knowledge that is needed to do what is asked.

If your managing style seems to be telling rather than asking, you may be making your job more difficult than it need be. You also may be delaying your advancement in the company. Your relations with people both on and off the job could be more pleasant as well as productive if you change your approach to people and begin asking them rather than telling them.

20.20 How to Write Better Letters, Memos, and Reports

Advancement in your company will be easier and faster if the quality of your written communications is high and lacking in faults. Remember that your words and their presentation should promote your company, build goodwill, and persuade your readers. You can accomplish these objectives only if your writing is void of obvious mistakes and easy to understand. Here is how you should handle your written communications:

● Limit the number of words you use. Although the average business letter today contains about 180 words, you should be able to get a shorter message across by being concise. Do it by eliminating superfluous and redundant words and not repeating yourself.

● Be concrete. You sacrifice specificity and impact if your reader can't understand exactly what you would like to have her or him do or what action you will be taking. Figures can be helpful in this respect and they leave no doubt in your reader's mind.

● Avoid jargon. Since every business and profession has words and phrases uniquely its own, it is very easy to permit these to get into your written communications. However, you may be creating a problem of understanding for some recipients of your correspondence, especially those outside the profession who are unfamiliar with the expressions.

● Use short, simple words. One of the best ways to assure clarity and understanding of your communications is to avoid big words. Usually, short, simple words put across the message better. They also enable you to keep your message brief and crisp. You'll never be accused of trying to impress rather than just inform.

● Write the way you talk. Avoid hackneyed words and clichés as introductory clauses in your sentences. Trite expressions suggest that you're behind the times and taking the easy way out in composing your letter or report.

● Explain abbreviations. Many readers are irritated when they see acronyms and abbreviations that they can't figure out. If you must use abbreviations to save space or repetition, spell them out when you first introduce them.

● Express your thoughts and ideas positively. Write positively to avoid any possibility of discouraging or turning off readers. Even letters that report bad news can say that matters could be worse; mention the bright side of a dark picture. The best way to sell an idea is to be optimistic about it and to stress its benefits and advantages. Positive writing will do this.

● Address properly. Always use the last name and the title of the individual you're addressing. Recognize, too, that some readers may be offended by references to the executive as "he." The best course for you to follow is to avoid the use of gender-oriented salutations.

● Refer to the reader. Many business letters contain too many "I's" and "We's" overlooking the fact that "You's" are better attention-getters. Your letters and memos will be better received if you get your readers involved through more reference to them than to yourself or your company.

● Pay attention to detail. Omission of the date, use of a wrong title, or failure to sign a letter brand a writer as careless and irresponsible. Never permit a letter to go out with misspelled words or typographical errors. This degrades you and hurts your company's image.

20.21 Tips on How to Be Computer Literate

Today's executives and managers generally feel that members of management should be computer literate if only to keep their companies and themselves competitive. If you expect to be a top executive or manager some day, you should start doing something about it now.

What is meant by being computer literate? To be literate, you should know what can be accomplished with a computer so you can take advantage of its capabilities not only for your job, but for other endeavors as well. However, you don't have to know a lot about hardware and software.

Many managers have accepted the challenge, particularly those in large companies. Their desire to be computer literate means that they see the need for more efficient ways of handling business's growing information requirements. Decreasing costs and increasing friendliness of computers have contributed to the increased use of the systems. In addition, many executives dislike being dependent on their company's data processing departments for information. With a knowledge of what the database contains and how they can retrieve information themselves, they feel more secure and self-reliant.

Starting with only a little knowledge about computers, you need to take only three simple steps to become computer literate.

1. Overcome any fear of the computer you might have.

2. Know what it can do.

3. Learn how to use it.

Most of today's executives are already at the third step. Recent surveys have revealed that only 3 percent of managers admit they fear the computer and only 16 percent say that computers are difficult to adjust to. Sixty-seven percent of the executives surveyed say that they already know how to operate a personal computer.

If you decide you want to increase your knowledge of computers, consider the advantages of having experts and instructors train you. You might spend as much as 80 hours figuring out the computer on your own while you can achieve the same literacy in about 20 hours in a workshop with other trainees and one or two instructors.

Recognize that computer literacy includes both knowing what the computer can do and knowing how to tell the computer to do it. Education programs stress concepts and potential applications, while training programs focus on actually operating the computer. What this means is that to say that you're computer literate, you must be both educated and trained in its use.

INDEX